6-27-70

Never Strike
a
Happy Medium

Louise Huebner

Never Strike a Happy Medium

NASH PUBLISHING
Los Angeles

*This book is dedicated to the two most
inspirational forces of my life:
        Isis, the Moon Goddess
                and
Ernest E. Debs, the County Supervisor*

ILLUSTRATIONS

PHOTOGRAPHS

LOUISE HUEBNER AND MAYOR ZOLL OF SALEM

SHE'S BEWITCHING — IN MORE WAYS THAN ONE

(UPI) SALEM, Mass. — Politicians swiveled to stare as Louise Huebner went striding through City Hall, dressed in black to match her mane of hair, a silver lame scarf floating behind her. Mrs. Huebner is definitely not the image of your average witch.

The official witch of Los Angeles County had come in a long limousine to forgive the city "for what they did to those people who were not witches" in Colonial times. Mayor Samuel E. Zoll received her "like a national dignitary," presented her with a broom inscribed "May your ride be long and enjoyable," and pronounced her "charming."

"She certainly had the male members of my staff in a trance, I'll say that," he said.

Route 2 Box 618

Harvest, Alaska

35749

June 30, 1970

Dear Mrs. Huebner,

Would you please place a love spell on Warren Entner for me? I would always be grateful.

Thank you.

Ginny Scotter

1
The Call

Eventually parents will be forced to guide nursery school children into the proper study categories, for by the time the children reach the advanced courses, the information they will need in order to specialize in certain fields will long ago have outdistanced them, and they will be sadly far behind and totally unable to complete or compete.

How then will one of the future ever delight in feeling "the call?" What choice will remain with the individual? What would have become of Shakespeare if his parents had enrolled him in a kindergarten of biologists? Or Judith Anderson if she had been entered into a nursery school for home economists? Or Richard Nixon, if he had been sent to a special grade school for small appliance repairmen? What waste!

I contemplate this sort of thing quite seriously, as I personally had a narrow escape.

At five years of age my mother knew I was—"different,"

but she didn't know just *how* different. By the time I was ten, she had become adjusted to the thought that, by society's standards, I was lazy. By the time I was fifteen all she hoped for was that I might marry into wealth.

None of the things I delighted in seemed suitable for a proper path of study, or for any one particular profession. Enrollment in the correct school for my life's work would have been impossible.

I dreamily stared out of the window a great deal. Sometimes I tapped my fingers in varying rates of speed to mimic galloping horses, drums in a parade, trains at a distance, or sluggish car engines. Sometimes I did the same with my unique fancy-lip-vibrations; but usually those were reserved for my airplanes-spiraling-through-space-just-before-the-crash impressions!

Very occasionally I was energetic. Once I made an airplane out of an old ironing board and a small wooden corner table. But, by and large though, nothing too great took place that could have been interpreted as a "direction," or as a "calling," or that could have in any way helped my mother plan my future.

For a while I had even held the milk bubble-blowing championship. I was the best milk bubble-blower in the first grade. I could get the bubbles up higher than anyone else in the class . . . and not have a drop spill over.

Once I won a silver cup in a Coney Island beauty contest, just by walking around in a Little Bo Peep costume.

All this has made my own motherhood a heavy burden. My having started out with such uncertainty preys on my peace of mind. How am I to guide my own children into lifetime professions from present indications? My oldest son, Mentor, started out by wearing costume hats everywhere—to dinner and even to bed. He built a robot in kindergarten out of a hodgepodge of electrical junk. Later he raised pumpkins.

Then he advanced to astronomy, paleontology, zoology, and finally entomology. And, except for the part of Hamlet that he wears continually like a glove, there has been no consistent behaviour.

Eight-year-old Jessica says she wants to do everything. And she does! She paints. She writes. She dances. She sings. She plays the guitar. She is Mount Washington's answer to Shirley Temple.

Gregory, her twin brother, is easy. Since he was one year old he could stand straight up . . . on his head. He writes and he has E.S.P. So I guess he is going to be an acrobat.

I shudder to think of what would have happened to me if it hadn't been for my grandmother.

When my parents listed my disabilities: She cries when you talk to her. Sits and stares out the window. Isn't athletic. She's lazy. Scribbles. Giggles. Can't walk straight. Always makes funny noises. What's going to happen to her?

Grandma said, "Leave her alone. . . . She's going to be a *witch!*"

FIGURE I *THE OFFICIAL WITCH OF LOS ANGELES COUNTY*

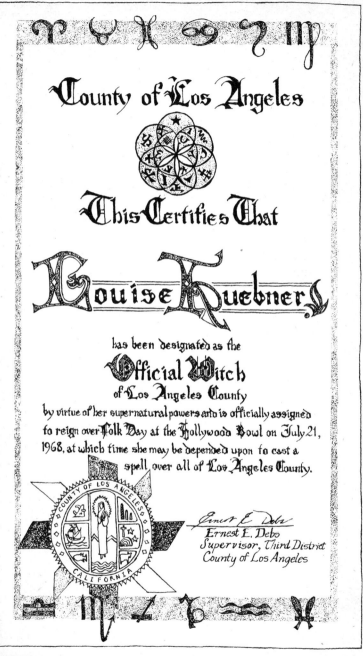

County of Los Angeles

This Certifies That

Louise Huebner

has been designated as the

Official Witch

of Los Angeles County

by virtue of her supernatural powers and is officially assigned
to reign over Folk Day at the Hollywood Bowl on July 21,
1968, at which time she may be depended upon to cast a
spell over all of Los Angeles County.

Ernest E. Debs
Ernest E. Debs
Supervisor, Third District
County of Los Angeles

FIGURE II   *THE OFFICIAL SCROLL*

2

After the Bowl Was Over

THE FIRST ANNUAL
LOS ANGELES COUNTY SPELLCAST
JULY 21, 1968
HOLLYWOOD BOWL
LOS ANGELES, CALIFORNIA
2:00 P.M. - 6:00 P.M.

LOUISE HUEBNER, the appointed Official Sorceress for Los Angeles County, along with a coven of witches, will involve everyone present in the casting of a spell. This is the first time in the history of witchcraft that a spell of so great a magnitude will be cast involving so many of the general public.

The purpose of this gathering is to unite spiritual energies —forcefully; to alter a moment in time, and to thereby create a vibration in this environment that will ultimately lead to raising levels of romantic and emotional vitality throughout Los Angeles County.

Necessary Incantation

"LIGHT THE FLAME
BRIGHT THE FIRE
RED IS THE COLOR OF DESIRE"

Since Witchcraft attempts to deceive, cajole and otherwise disturb natural inclination and occurrance, so then, too, with bits of color, attitudes, and words do children, politicians, actors, and women in love—weave spells; the success of which many times is dependent entirely upon the magic of their confidence.

COUNTY OF LOS ANGELES
OFFICE OF THE COUNTY COUNSEL

**648 HALL OF ADMINISTRATION
LOS ANGELES, CALIFORNIA 90012
MADISON 5-3611**

December 29, 1969

Dear Miss Huebner:

This is to notify you that there is no authority for your use of the title: "Official Witch of Los Angeles County", which has appeared on the jacket of a record album and in other promotional material concerning your activities.

As you must know, the scroll you received at the Hollywood Bowl, July 21, 1968, was purely cere-monial and intended only to publicize the Sunday Afternoon "Happenings" at the Bowl, presented by the County Department of Parks and Recreation as a public service.

We must ask that you immediately discontinue use of the title: "Official Witch of Los Angeles County" or any similar designation creating the erroneous impression that you are affiliated with Los Angeles County government.

Sincerely,
John D. Maharg
County Counsel

JDM/mf

Mr. John D. Maharg
County Counsel
Hall of Administration
Los Angeles, California 90012

January 6, 1970

Dear Mr. Maharg,

Happy New Year!

I would like to clarify my position with the County. It should be understood that the County came to me and asked if they could take advantage of my promotional abilities. They asked that I lend my image and reputation to their activities, rather than as is now being assumed that their activities created my image. It was the Witch who had constant and ample exposure and not the County Department of Parks and Recreation.

Your New Year's Eve greeting to me says I have no authority to use my title: "Official Witch for Los Angeles County". But, I have a signed certificate from Supervisor Debs that certifies that I have been designated as the Official Witch.

You say that something other than what was stated on the certificate had been intended, but I only know what the language on the certificate states and not what Supervisor Debs claims its intention to be. You say I should know that the certificate was meant only to publicize. I do know this and I have publicized it.

The concern expressed about the erroneous impression I may be creating is unfounded. I have never pretended to be employed by the County Government. I have always clearly communicated that my time has been freely donated! <u>EXAMPLE:</u> October 31, 1969, Arcadia Park Party for retarded children . . . which I attended . . . and performed at . . . and publicized . . . before . . . and after . . . by special COUNTY INVITATION, despite the fact that Halloween has always been my busiest and most lucrative season . . . and also despite the fact that from my past experience with County involvements . . . I was fully aware that I would receive no pay and no thanks!

Over the past four years my efforts to broadcast to the public all cultural events available within the community . . . has brought the Los Angeles County Department of Parks and Recreation international attention . . . via radio, television, movies, newspapers and magazines . . . through my own programs and syndicated columns and features and those of my friends. And, up to this date, the certificate of Official Witchery has been my only "reward".

I see no real logical reason why I should discontinue the use of my title for my books, records, syndicated columns and appearances. To my knowledge an award, honorary degree, medal or certificate of thanks has never been revoked! My actions have only added to the much needed sophisticated image of this County. I am hurt and offended by certain political actions. If the small amount of humor created for Supervisor Debs by his press agents has now failed him, then will he please return the gift I gave him of the Magical Golden Horn that was meant to insure his Romantic Vitality. Certainly he must know that it can not work now that he has professed a disbelief in goblins, pumpkins, the good tooth fairy and all things that go bump.

Sincerely,
Louise Huebner
Official Witch of Los Angeles County

cc: Supervisor Debs   Members of the Press

FOR IMMEDIATE RELEASE:

LADIES AND GENTLEMEN OF THE PRESS: You are invited to attend a press conference to be held on JANUARY 9, 1970, at 10:00 a.m., Friday Morning. Location will be the GREATER LOS ANGELES PRESS CLUB located on Vermont Avenue in Los Angeles.

THE PURPOSE: To inform you of the potential "De-Spelling" of the entire County of Los Angeles. As you know, on July 21, 1968, WITCH HUEBNER, by invitation of the Los Angeles County Department of Parks and Recreation and the Hollywood Bowl Association, led the first public spell cast in the world to insure the increased sexual vitality of the County of Los Angeles.

At that time she was awarded a certificate that states: "THIS IS TO CERTIFY THAT LOUISE HUEBNER HAS BEEN DESIGNATED AS THE OFFICIAL WITCH OF LOS ANGELES COUNTY BY VIRTUE OF HER SUPERNATURAL POWERS, AND IS OFFICIALLY ASSIGNED TO REIGN OVER FOLK DAY AT THE HOLLYWOOD BOWL ON JULY 21, 1968, AT WHICH TIME SHE MAY BE DEPENDED UPON TO CAST A SPELL OVER ALL OF LOS ANGELES COUNTY . . . "

It is signed, "SUPERVISOR ERNEST DEBS".

What is not stated is that Louise Huebner helped to publicize the entire 12 weeks at the Bowl series . . . along with continuous publicizing of other events . . . along with producing shows in public parks for senior citizens, retarded children, fund raising, etc. Without payment . . . or, for that matter, *thanks*. The certificate was the only effort made, to in any way, compensate the Witch for efforts that sometimes extended into many months of free service.

The County first approached Louise Huebner and asked her to lend her talents and reputation to their activities and not the other way around as Debs now assumes.

Mrs. Huebner stated today, "If Supervisor Debs persists in asking the Department of Parks and Recreation to unload me . . . or Mr. Maharg to intimidate me . . . that will only create bad feeling and I will be forced through an act of pride to take back the Los Angeles County spell for increased

Sexual Vitality. What with smog and freeways being what they are, I shudder to think of what the De-Spelling could do to devastate the County.

"Surely in these critical times, there are other areas that should capture the attention of both Supervisor Debs and our Mr. Maharg. To think that good and valuable County time and effort could go into getting rid of free publicity and good clean fun in the County parks fascinates me.

"I want to state clearly that I do not belong in any way to the paid aspects of the County Government . . . nor, heaven forbid, if I may use the phrase . . . would I ever want to!"

NEWS ITEM JANUARY 10, 1970

POOR SUPERVISOR AND PRETTY WITCH:
TALE OF POLITICAL MISHAP
—by PETE SEARLS

Tribune County Bureau
San Gabriel Valley Tribune

County Supervisor Ernest Debs once issued a scroll to Louise Huebner at a Hollywood Bowl "happening" designating her as the official Los Angeles County witch. Now a move is afoot by Supervisor Debs and Counsel John Maharg to stop her from using the title to promote books and records. Miss Huebner has retaliated by threatening to invoke her magical powers. Tribune County Bureau Chief Pete Searls, an apparent early casualty of the strange spirits unleashed on the Hall of Administration, filed the following report.

Once upon a long time ago, a county supervisor wanted to give a present to a witch. But, he was only a poor county supervisor. He didn't have a bag of gold or a fine coat of unicorn hide or even a glass slipper.

But, he did so want to find a gift for the witch, who was a good witch and very pretty, too, with flowing, raven hair and a great figure, that he finally went to his adviser, who was a poor woodcutter, and said, "What can we give the good witch who has been so nice to all the boys and girls of our county?"

And, the woodcutter (whose axe made the sound "flack!" when it bit deep into the wood, and so he was known as a flack) said, "You are only a poor county supervisor, so you cannot give her a bag of gold or a unicorn coat. How about a tip on where we're going to change the zoning?"

But, the poor supervisor said he didn't think that would be a fine enough present for such a good witch so finally the flack said, "What about a nice hand-lettered scroll making her the official witch of the whole county?"

And that was such a splendid idea that the poor supervisor, whose name was Debs, and who was so sincere he was called "Debs the Earnest," forthwith returned to his office and prepared the scroll and called all the people of the county together for a great festival.

When the witch came in, he gave her the scroll and the people cheered and the witch, whose name was Louise Huebner, said it was the finest present she could have gotten (although she wondered if the supervisor was so poor he couldn't afford just a tiny little bag of gold).

In return, she gave Debs the Earnest a magical golden horn and on this horn she cast a spell giving Debs great romantic vitality. And, because all of the good people of the county cheered her so mightily, she cast a good spell on them, increasing their sexual vitality. And, so the festival ended with great merrymaking.

Witch Louise returned to her home in the forest and began more good things for the people of the county.

She made some records and wrote some books telling them how they, too, could do good things— but never bad or evil things unless it was really necessary. And, she gave the books and the records to the boys and girls and their mothers and fathers, too, and all she asked was just a teeny, tiny, little bag of gold in return.

But, then, one day, as the Good Witch Louise was stacking all the teeny, tiny, little bags of gold in her corner, there came a messenger from a man who was named John Maharg, who had wormed his way into the confidence of the good, but poor, supervisors and had become their counselor.

The message from Maharg to Witch Huebner was that she must stop calling herself "the Official Witch of Los Angeles County" even though Debs' scroll said she was, and especially must stop this when raking in the teeny, tiny, little bags of gold.

Witch Huebner was furious. She stamped her foot. She threatened all manner of evil spells. And, then she called for her poor woodcutter—also known as flack—and said, "Oh, whatever shall we do?"

And, the flack said, "Why don't we give all the good boys and girls of the county one last chance?"

And, so the flack called all of the scribes and the criers together Friday at a place called the Los Angeles Press Club and Witch Huebner told them she would not give back the wonderful scroll and that she would still be the official witch.

And, she said if the poor—but now wicked—supervisor didn't lay off, she would take away her spell of increased vitality from all of the county.

But, she promised the poor scribes and criers that she would keep her spell on them and, thus cheered, the scribes and criers went to the poor county supervisor and asked Debs what he meant.

Debs—who was not wicked but just harassed by evil spirits and constituents—said: "If only you could know the trouble I've had. Now that witch Louise has a scroll from me, all the warlocks and elves and angels and fertility goddesses — not to mention the fairies—in Los Angeles County want scrolls from me and it is just too damned much!"

And, so he went off to Maharg, and Maharg, muttered something about a magical thing called an injunction, which was so terrible a spell that even the strongest witch or industrialist might be afraid.

And, now all the people of the county tremble at the thought of Witch Louise and Maharg casting spell and counterspell, and some think the moral of the story is that sometimes a cheap scroll costs you more than a teeny, tiny, little bag of gold.

```
157P PST JAN 8 70 LC392 CTB282          DLR BY MSGR
157P PST JAN 8 70 LC 392 CTB282              dlr
CT CHA302 LA PDB CHATTANOGA TENN 8 414P EST
```

MISS LOUISE HUEBNER   D34

        OFFICIAL WITCH OF LOS ANGELES COUNTY

LOSA
DEAR LOUISE I UNDERSTAND THAT YOU PLAN TO DE SPELL
THE ENTIRE COUNTY OF LOS ANGELES. AS OFFICIAL LEG-
END IN MY OWN TIME I WOULD LIKE TO INVITE YOU TO BE
THE OFFICIAL WITCH OF CHATTANOOGA, TENNESSEE. WE
BELIEVE IN YOU AND WE ALSO BELIEVE IN GOBLINS, PUMP-
KINS AND THE GOOD TOOTH FAIRY. YOUR PREVIOUS SPELLS
HAVE MADE US ALL VERY VIVACIOUS. OUR SOUTHERN HOS-
PITALITY GOES OUT TO YOU. PLEASE BECOME OUR OFFI-
CIAL WITCH OF CHATTANOOGA, TENNESSEE. WE ARE BE-
LIEVERS.

   LARRY, THE LEGEND JOHNSON

WDXE RADIO CHATTANOOGA TENNESSEE

Motto, "To the farthermost parts of the rich East"

Presented to _Louise Huebner_

By _Samuel E Zoll_

SAMUEL E. ZOLL, MAYOR, MARCH 24, 1970

FIGURE III   *THE SALEM SCROLL*

3

A View from a Third Eye

Officer Petreivich

Los Angeles Police Department:

"There are things I have known that I had no business
knowing. Many of my hunches have paid off. But who knows
where they come from. And who is to say what they are.
There have been times I have even dreamed of something
that later happened. But I believe many people do this. It's
normal. Within my own family—we will frequently "know"
things about each other—and have telepathic contact. I will
be sitting with my wife—and suddenly—out of the blue say
something to her—and she will say it's just what she was
thinking. Everybody does that—it's human nature. I think
it's a quality that stayed with us from primitive times. No

A lawyer I know who had polio and had been left partially paralyzed said that later he felt it had made him more introspective. He said since the illness his psychic flashes have increased, and he has experienced a great deal more intuition. But his added insight is usually about nothing of value. He suddenly imagines he is driving along, on a particular road in another city, and he clearly sees a building with a red door, and out in front there are three green trash cans. A small boy is bouncing a ball on the corner, and a German Shepherd puppy is barking at a red cat. He sees it all in a vision. Then he may be driving along one day, and sure enough, that scene that he had imagined . . . appears. Only this time for real. He says in the beginning, when these things happened, he would think, since he had imagined them beforehand, maybe they were a warning that something important was about to happen to him at that moment. But nothing ever happened! Nothing! So now he just accepts the phenomenon. There seems to be no reason for the precognition. Many times of course he is accurately "aware" of some hidden facts in connection with a case in court, but most times the occurrances have no real value.

Once he imagined a baseball—coming right at his head. He saw it and he ducked. Then later he was in a situation at a park or somewhere, and then it happened in reality. But it meant nothing! It was of no great importance. He says he would have ducked anyway—with or without the insight. The precognition, he tells me, seems to be wasted on trivia. He wonders why he tunes into it at all.

doubt there are some people who have a great
this ability. Just as everyone can sing. Mankind
how? We are not all opera singers. If there isn't a g
I don't care how much training and study goes
either you are born with a good voice or you are n
it certainly can't be called supernatural, can it? It's
It's the same with this extra sense. My extra sense if y
to call it that—has helped me in my police work. A
the years it has developed more and more. The olde
the greater my intuition or insight increases. It was
when I was younger, but now after twenty years on the
it's become stronger! If I get a hunch—I pay a lot of atte
to it. My extra sensitivity has helped me through life,
ticularly in my work.

You know though—sometimes things happen—that ca
be explained. Like once my mother dreamed of a close frien
of mine. She dreamed he was in his car and was hit by a train
Well the next day it happened. This wasn't something she
could have known by experience—. It wasn't something anyone was thinking and that she "picked up". She dreamed it
before it happened.

In most cases though I think that maybe awareness is based
on something else.

Kids are bombarded with "impressions", but tend to ignore
them. But as you get older you attempt to listen to yourself
much more. It's connected with survival. Age makes you
cautious. Eventually you use all the warnings, all the clues,
all the hunches. It's a matter of self-preservation.

It may be that people with a stronger sense of survival have
greater E.S.P., if you want to call it that. I just call it being
sharp!"

It seems to be much the same as when a psychic "senses" that someone in the audience has a scar on his left kneecap. And many times the audience has paid five dollars to see this demonstrated. Really now! Who cares? The lawyer says he has been more or less intuitive since childhood; only since the polio his intuition has become stronger, more intense. This is much the same as when a well-known psychic fell off a ladder and said he became more psychic! The lawyer says, though, that the extra awareness helps him in his work; however he doesn't believe the ability taken alone without his legal training would be of any benefit to anyone. And he says he certainly couldn't imagine ever expecting anyone to pay to see him do it!

When your mother and father both come from families that have always happily responded to "funny feelings," as mine do, then you tend to grow up a little unconcerned about extra sensory perception and your natural ability to "know things" in advance. And if your maternal grandmother happens to be a delightful witch who talks to insects, raises plants on love, breaks wine glasses with *thought vibrations,* teaches you astrology, palmistry, card-reading, and how to use your ability to tune in, then it becomes impossible for you to glory in the frequently illiterate mouthings of any old dingy, sandal-footed, quasi-gypsy fortune-teller, or any emotionally disturbed power seeking clairvoyant.

As a child the peculiar processes of my thinking, that for want of a more apt term must be called "psychic," created no real problems. I drifted about playing jacks, skipping rope, roller-skating myself into physical frenzy, never dreaming that the day would arrive when I would recognize that any difference existed.

Then somewhere around puberty, when most social cover-ups begin, I found myself to be totally unprepared, and unwilling, either to act out or to accept the proper attitudes. My

FIGURE IV   *THE FEELER*

companions were aghast as I met their remarks with impolite, "But you said's." They would scream, "No we didn't say that!" And I would screech back at them, "But you were going to say! You meant!" They would scream louder, "No!" and I would continue in a hysterical vein, "But you felt!" It would then, most times, end with a final, "She's a pest!" as they raged away.

As long as I can remember I have been aware of those around me through very physical body sensations. I accepted the phenomenon. I never bothered to question it. This *feeling* ability I had, was catalogued by me in the same way that I recognized I breathed, ate, cried, laughed, loved, and everything else everybody does in support of their being alive.

Long hours were spent in keeping myself entertained by walking about the house with my eyes shut, attempting to feel doors, windows, furniture, and people—through my pores. I was giddy from the start with the sort of freedom offered by my lack of need for the usual methods of awareness. I soared about, roaming through fantasies of sensation, completely ignorant of the fact that this was considered an abnormal condition being based upon what was most probably an extra sensory perception.

There never was a time in my life when I didn't believe I could sense correctly how another individual might be feeling. Their emotional climate was no secret to me. It never seemed to be a deliberate effort. I just always knew. And the knowing would sweep over me with an intensity to match that of the emotion they were at the moment experiencing. I trusted my feelings as through the years my expressed impressions were met with affirmitive responses.

If someone was agitated, I would become breathless and restless. If they were overcome with sorrow, I would cry. If they were on the brink of joy, I would leap up to meet them. It was an undisciplined method of responding. Eventually imprisoned by my own freedom to feel so readily, my true self existed seemingly as a mere reflection of those about me. Thus, as a young woman I had to become dynamically involved in the effort of separating the influences. It was a serious matter to know clearly what was really me and what was certainly not. Emotional relationships are complicated enough, but when you react to—everything—they can become even more delicately balanced.

Imagine that back in the dim dawn of life, when one energy form, or perhaps when multi-energy forms, made the first subtle transition from a non-seeing existence to the more exciting one offered by a sighted response, it could have, depending of course upon the complexity of the intellectual awareness (if any), created quite a problem.

What a mess we would be in now if a gastropod with eyes had impressed another gastropod without eyes of its eternal infallibility; or if some well-meaning cephalopod with vision had convinced a sightless cephalopod that having vision meant he had a direct open hot line to God.

Let's face it, a fly with a multi-splendored optical propensity, is nevertheless nothing more than a fly. And, an idiot, intuitive or not, is still an idiot!

Why should one person's set of funny feelings be more valuable than someone else's? The value of one's senses should be determined by the quality of the interpretations of those feelings. And the quality of the interpretations would be most dependent upon the mentality of the individual attempting this magnificent clarification!

Grandma supported my confidence by allowing me to impress her friends with my knack for understanding them. She gave me plenty of opportunity to read their cards, palms, or whatnots. And she explained to me that in order to develop into a really terrific "reader" I would have to learn to let myself go. The trick, if it could be called a trick, was to wildly

FIGURE V   *GRANDMA: THE FORTUNE TELLER*

create a story from out of the emotions one felt. Strangely enough the more imaginative the story I created, the closed I would come to interpreting someone's subconscious projections. The idea was to have fun.

I did!

Evidently I inherited Grandma's ability to do this. But for years I believed my success was not due to being psychic, but rather to my extremely clever method of handling people. I was convinced my insight existed because I was intelligent and they were not. This concept had a very peculiar effect upon my personality and moulded my ego into an unbreakable substance. I am certain I am not the only psychic to develop an ego problem. The very uniqueness of the talent predestines ultimate ruination.

At ten I began by reading palms. My first public appearance was in a children's carnival at Ethical Culture School on Central Park West in New York City. There, without any show of compassion, and without any later show of remorse, I told the boy's coach he would have "a very short life!" — and, "Oh, my God — it's awful!" He then replied it was a very strange thing for me to tell him, as he had always "believed" just that!

I never should have been encouraged!

Later, with much the same joie de vivre, I opened an office. It was on Melrose and Fairfax in Los Angeles. There I offered "Astrological Guidance" for my hapless clients.

I shared the office with six fellows, ages twenty-six to fifty. They were writers. They wrote mostly for television, commercials, etc. We were quite a troup. I used the front of the office and they lived in the back. Lived, is the only way I can put it, as they were always facing deadlines and could never go home. Never!

Eventually we weren't able to open the door to the back room without causing a dangerous avalanche. The Campbell

Soup cans they heaped in a corner would come crashing down around our feet. Finally, I chipped in, out of embarrassment, and we called in a rubbish company to haul them all away — the cans, not the writers.

One customer was especially thrilled by my insight. She had telephoned me ordering three horoscopes, and when she came in for the "readings," I was able to tell her which chart belonged to her husband, and which to her lover.

My clients were very impressed with what I could come up with, as I seemed to know if they had just lost a relative through death, or if they were divorced, or contemplating divorce, or were about to change jobs, or were having an affair. And I would tell them — matter-of-factly — with about as much tact as I had exhibited with the boy's coach.

The office venture was the end result of a young lifetime of responding to psychic reactions. I was very able to read palms, cards, tea leaves, horoscopes and people. It was only natural I should consider fortune telling as an inevitable direction.

When the impact of my actions found me, my conscience forced me to stop. I closed the office.

Though I had through clubs, women's luncheons, political fund-raising dinners, shopping center promotions, parties, and private consultations, indiscriminently established intimate emotional rapport with more strangers than a traffic cop has pass him in a week, I never was trained specifically to deal with mankind's problems. My audacity shocks me.

I had been brainwashed into believing that as a psychic I belonged to an elite group. And that I was predestined to be a fortune teller. My witchy Grandmother and my background are not alone to blame. The public helped.

I never go anywhere that I am not bombarded with requests for readings —markets, beauty salons, banks, post offices, business meetings! Still, to be able to feel an unusual, unexplained link with a stranger, and to be able to interpret their feelings and emotions, through this connection, has always been exciting for me.

It could be that the act of psychic sensitivity stems from an origin similar to that of love. I am convinced they both spring from the same motivations. There is a distinct difference between knowing something because you have learned it through experience — and you know it has to follow a logical conclusion from existing facts — and knowing something through E.S.P. The difference is all in the way you feel about what you know. It can be described, but perhaps it's much the same difference that exists between liking someone — and because of that reacting politely to contacts with them — or being so turned on to someone — you can't stand it — and manners are not important.

A psychic contact offers an undiluted sensation. It's full and real.

The feeling is a kick!

One New Year's Eve Party, when I was still exploring my potential sensitivity, I read the palms of seventy-three people, enjoying every minute of it. The feeling one gets from a psychic contact is very much the same as in emotional arousal (not sexual — emotional!). There is no mistaking it for anything else. And, as with emotional arousals, it's best to have an outlet or you can get pretty uncomfortable.

A psychic has to psych!

If you are female, and young and full of empathy, those you tune into frequently mistake the "sensational exchange" for a sex attraction. And maybe it is — sort of. But once you have felt this same thing repeatedly, you begin to recognize that although we are not certain of what this thing we call E.S.P. is, one thing is sure: at the rate of one psychic reading per customer each five minutes for four hours in a shopping center promotion, and four hours of phone calls on radio clocked by the phone company at 1800 an hour — one thing is real sure — this can't be *love!*

At present (and until my mood reverses I will not do fortune-telling for the public) I much prefer to continue in astrological research with politician's horoscopes, and to get my psychic kicks on radio, where there can be no complicated, misunderstood emotional involvements. I enjoy demonstrating and fooling around with my telepathic tendencies. But, I don't feel dedicated; I don't believe I was born to sacrifice my time and energy to the solution of another's problems.

People write to me and ask for help. Some of them I really wish I could assist because they sound like nice people. But a letter that says "Nah, Nah, Nah — if you don't help me you're not a real witch" is usually ignored.

It's ridiculous. I said I was a witch — not Mary Poppins. I don't *have* to help anybody. Being able to feel what you feel doesn't guarantee I will care about it, or for that matter, care to do anything at all about it one way or the other. Just because someone exists is no reason I must like them. However if I ever did choose to help mankind, I would not attempt to cure the world's ailments with the use of any casual insight. My very dedication would inspire me toward perfection, and study, and the utilization of all organized knowledge man has gathered throughout history.

To dare to deal with human emotions and complicated behavioral problems by the mere use of one's "funny feelings" I believe to be an insult to creativity and life.

Certainly, the work of a trained medical man, or a legal counselor, or a police officer, or a writer, or an artist, or an actor, or a dress designer, or a hair stylist, or a politician, or a teacher, is all that much better for their having a little E.S.P. There is no question that sensitivity increases one's chance for success in any area.

But alone — as a thing in itself — by itself — never!

We are still exploring its fuller meanings. Just because phychic fortune tellers have devised various methods for exploiting their extra sensory perception does not increase its validity potential. But if you are psychic more than anything else, it's difficult to break away from the usually prescribed activities. As an intensely psychic individual, it's a lot easier to slip into fortune-telling than it is to gravitate towards any other profession or calling.

And if you are overly psychic and have all your life had peculiar feelings and reactions, let's face it, you are not going to be all that normal anyway, so your decisions at times may appear to be a bit unethical. It's easy to see how one can get caught up in the fortune-telling business, like a wild passionate relationship that once established becomes impossible to sever. You know it isn't sensible, and leads nowhere, but you keep on, hoping that no one will notice. Unfortunately though, if it's really a wild affair, somebody usually does — notice.

As a psychic, the popularity comes easily, and for awhile it creates a wild exilaration. The constant compulsion to establish psychic rapports overwhelms. The reward for this freaky, quirky ability is attention, and soon, an addiction to smiling demanding faces develops. The social years for a psychic offer whirlpools of interesting environments all ready for exploration. No barriers exist. No distinctions. And certainly there are no lack of willing, fertile pulsations for the psychic mentality to mentalate Presidents of companies and countries, all the way to the guard at the KTTV Television gate, want readings. They plead, "Tune in to me! Tell me what you think! What do you feel?" The psychic, warmed by their need, invariably grows cocky and tells them, tunes in, and tells it like it is (at least like it *is* to the psychic). It's a game. There is a certain extra something, an awareness. It begins in childhood with fantastic successes in small games like "button, button, who's got the button?" Later it develops into an instantaneous detection of small white lies. Eventually it leads to insight into another energy form's next move. Whatever the source (some prefer the gift from God theory, while others stress chemical imbalance and electricity), whatever the method used (sight, sound, smell, touch, or *chutzpah*), whatever the original motivation (self-aggrandizement, love of fellow earthlings, a sense of joy or a longing for a buckaroo) psychics do have one thing in common — they are all expected to endlessly do their stuff. Psychics, as is true of piano players, are always a welcome addition to any social gatherings. Also, as in the case of the piano players, the psychics had better soon learn to keep to their places! Sitting on a bench in a corner. Eyes rolling. Busily empathizing! Woe be to the psychic who decides to play metaphysical *Chopsticks* or an Occult version of *Love in Bloom* while hiding beneath the dignity of their creative forces, and who then refuses to relate inter-psychologically! Rejection of the vulnerable and lush psyches leads to danger. To dare to express boredom with the comings and goings of everyone else's unfaithful husband or wife, or financial predicaments, or tricky gall bladder, or bleeding ulcers or menopausal symptoms is to risk revenge! To imply that intimately feeling everyone may leave the psychic cold, is to secure quiet evenings by the fireplace.

Stiffen your aura!

The first sign of a psychic's slip into the blissful caverns of anonymity will soon follow after a demanding and harsh call of "Feel me!" is met by a softly whispered, "Sorry, I don't care to. I'm not in the mood."

"PHONEY!" they bellow.

And next week, if a psychic is lucky, a Zen Buddhist will hold the seat of honor.

4

The Psych-ees and the Psych-ors

"And who are you?" cried One Agape shuddering in the gloaming light. "I know not," said the Second Shape. "I only died last night."
— Thomas Bailey Aldridge

After just one more night passes, One Agape is going to be very impressed. For not only will Second Shape figure out who *it* was, but it will also have been caught up in the after-world's spiritual game of come-back-man-ship, and not only will Second Shape then decide who it may have been, but it will also have decided that it must have been someone who had been pretty special! Maybe it's difficult to believe that it is possible for a return performance. Maybe *Nobody* ever comes back. But one thing is certain, *Somebody* always does!

In the United States today, judging from the evidence that exists, there may be well over two million psychic fortune tellers. Now that's a hell of a lot of people who know what's **up**, racing around telling everybody else what's up, during a

time when most of the people who really do know what's up —
don't! Never before in history, except for the time of the
Ides of March have there been so many soothsayers telling
it like it is to a populace so grudgingly on its way to being
knifed. Between the amateur genies, the astrologers, palmists,
card-readers, tea leaf gazers, across-the-line spiritual Indian
guides, and crystal ballers, the threats to personal survival
stemming from overpopulation, drought, bombs, pollution,
and racial issues shouldn't get anyone down. Chemical uppers
and downers have been replaced by tuner-inners and outers.
The drug problem is fast being eclipsed by Planetary Patterns
as a deadly need for being "read" is rapidly accelerating into
a major international psychoses of astronomical proportions.
Campuses throughout the United States are actively support-
ing witch covens, astrology lectures, and mind-blowing psych-
ins. Students exploring the phenomena are encouraged by
faculties suggesting guest speakers from the Occult world
Reputable businessmen are basing important transactions
on what they have rising on the eastern horizon. Politicians
long familiar with pragmatism and its merits to the "win," do
not suppress tendencies toward magical alliances and some
even have been known to own *lucky pieces*. Dramatists long
accustomed to close association with fantasy and who have
never had any qualms about identifying with the eerie media
are in fact now the technical authorities of the subject.
Anchormen on national news programs seek out spiritualists
to bring back the dead on camera — "And, please don't
wear black or white!" Radio and television technicians protect
the psychic interests by attesting to the needs fulfilled and the
spiritual help offered, stating that somebody after all, *has* to
care. It's not unusual, anymore, to discover that your certified
public accountant, your investment lawyer, or your personal
brain surgeon, support the theory for reincarnation, and freely
admit that there is definitely *something* to astrology. And

many elected government officials unashamedly practice projectile magnetic vibratory communication.

Mediums who ply their trade along the occult circuit in and around Los Angeles proper are frequently not so proper themselves, and though seemingly sensitive, they are often not too. They have not shown themselves to be adverse to being pulled into a heavenly ectoplasmic race in order to speed their grisly climb toward fame and fortune. In fact, several have friends among the well known Hollywood columnists, who are accomplices and participate in bringing back Marilyn Monroe, Janye Mansfield, Errol Flynn, Gary Cooper, Fatty Arbuckle, but what is more important, even many, many more sympathetic well paying customers. It is interesting to note Mozart and Bach run second only to J.F.K., with the repenitent Adolf trailing far behind and a philosophical W. C. Fields far, far, far in the lead!

Sometimes if someone doesn't see a ghost then they prefer to be one.

If Jayne Mansfield were alive today and ten years older than she could ever have been — minus her talent, sex appeal, brains, and professionally bleached hair, and with a brusque coarse approach and an unpleasant demanding ego — we would have a well-known syndicated Hollywood columnist who has the same initials as Marilyn Monroe, but who doesn't seem to notice the existence of any other difference.

M.M., since Jayne's death has been *haunted*. She believes Jayne has been attempting to possess her body — oy vey — in order to utilize M.M.'s writing ability (in order to come out with a best seller, and 75 percent of the movie rights version for the real inside story of Mansfield's life).

M.M. feels her startling similarity to Mansfield may have triggered the visitations. Mediums have been called into M.M.'s apartment with the hope of facilitating the possession. All agree . . . Jayne is there!

Even M.M.'s cats seem to know it. And they act peculiarly at times that seem to coincide with their mistress's increased sensitivity and psychological moments.

So far the only spectacular happenings are the cross-country articles featuring the mediums, written by M.M. in lieu of giving them any more satisfactory substantial appeasement. Perhaps lack of enthusiasm has contributed to failure, for as yet no one has been able to trigger entry. And if the amalgamation doesn't happen soon, it won't be necessary! M.M. may very soon find herself in position to possess Glen Campbell.

Any medium who seeks recognition as a purist cannot afford to risk a lifetime career by putting out the energy and effort that is needed, merely to pull in your father's younger sister's second husband who died of gout, and who no one in the family cared much about, anyway. The spirit knows no bounds and the mediums are free to soar high.

Your Uncle Charlie might be permitted to make a brief appearance, but not for more than just second or two. He may even be allowed to mumble a few unintelligible words about having an Indian guide who doesn't want him (Charlie) to waste any psychic energy just yet, at least not until after he (Charlie) has learned all the truths there are to learn from the other side. Charlie suggests you content yourself with a visit from his dear, dear friend, Betsy Ross who has been gone long enough, obviously, to have learned about all the truths, and who is now able to dare the expenditure of the precious energy that is needed in order to establish verbal contact with you. Of course, you wouldn't know Betsy Ross from One Agape, Second Shape, Mozart, or W. C. Fields, and certainly you wouldn't be able to notice if the pitch of her voice is up to her usual metaphysical excellence, or not. You paid your money in advance, anywhere from five bucks to five hundred — so you may as well lean back, smile and enjoy it! Listen to what old Betsy has to say. After she tediously clues you in on the government's foreign policy, or your future potential (provided you decide to take up ballet) you probably will sadly decide that she should have stuck to her sewing. Universal truths she hasn't. But she is a comfort. And that's what it's all about.

Betsy Ross tells you not to worry about Uncle Charlie. He is busy and happy gathering up energy. He'll make out OK. His Indian guide is one of the best around. In fact, would you believe it, this is the same Indian guide who helped Abe Lincoln and FDR over some rough spots when they first entered the twilight zone. Betsy informs you that the Indian guide is called CHICAHAWDHAG-OF-SILVER GLEN. He is a tall, bronzed, strong brute of a man, filled to over-flowing with truth and brotherly love. You don't have to be a fortune teller to pick up on the fact that either Betsy or friend Medium has got a thing about Indians.

Not wanting to knock the worthwhile efforts of a small minority, you control yourself and remain silent, but you may be led to wonder if the Indians are all so damned smart . . . HOW COME?

Americans by their very nature and philosophy often try to see the good side of everyone and everything. We're not stupid but we do let slide over some sore spots and because of this tolerant attitude are frequently . . . taken. The United States offers a glorious haven for not only your tired and your poor but your activated and richly blessed besides. Where in all the world is there another country that supports psychic happenings within such a big business structure? We accept as normal and good, any and all attempts by the mystics to see clearly things previously relegated to the domain of the enlightened theologians, dedicated philosophers, or students of this tolerant attitude are frequently . . . taken. The United cases we go to sensible and established lawyers for counseling.

For surgical treatments, we seek out licensed and certified members of the medical profession. We hire plumbers, carpenters, painters and tutors with equal care, but when it comes to things of the emotion and the soul . . . where do we go? Usually down the pier boardwalk or back shop or a side street run-up to a friend's old grandmother or maiden aunt. Or to that nice boy in the supermarket who gets funny feelings. There is a poem that says "a starving tramp can't eat a silver shoe or some beggar slightly alcoholic enjoy with Donne a metaphysical frolic." But it looks as if the Donnes not only encourage the frolicking, but in fact hold hands with the mystics and skip along with them, through the sensitive and eerie regions of the psychic whirlpools of emotional chaos, all the time gleefully hiccupping through the tragedies. How curious that the spirit world should choose to manifest and make itself known through a fifty-cent-a-question meeting in a dingy parlor, every other Tuesday, environment. The concept of a dynamic personality exploding into pallid surroundings stupifies me. I canot conceive of so dramatic a miracle taking place under such mediocre conditions. But perhaps I am engulfed in spiritual darkness.

Imagination allowing for the possibility, logic does not support presented facts. The force needed to establish contact must surely have originated during life. Does *style* alter with death? It is not reasonable to believe virile spirits frequent such dreary locations merely to comment upon a salegirl's next salary increase, a wife's suspicious nature, a husband's indiscretions, an aunt's lost will, and one's greedy gall bladder, but comment they do and loudly!

HOW? Usually through a medium who is devoid of any magnetic attraction. Pale-eyed, anemic, wispy-haired, unsophisticated and evidently by the trade's necessity . . . dull! And always, the grand experience must take place in a parlor vintage 1928. Worn pattern linoleum adding insult to the already injured painted wooden floor. Faded gray lace curtains adorn the narrow, smudged windows barely covered by an indecently green tinted shade. A lamp flickering attempts to cast a reflection on all too dark subject through a beige plastic shade that lights a small podium, which in turn has been pathetically decorated with artificial flowers backed up by nondenominational religious prints. The spiritual rapport takes place only after the third hymn is sung off-key and all the envelopes with the donations . . . have been collected.

Whatever is the attraction that would pull one through the veil and lead them into such a sad performance? If there is a force, if there is a way, and my name is called, I will only make the effort if the medium is Richard Burton and the parlor is at Caesar's Palace.

That psychic phenomena exist is unquestionable.

That psychics suffer from the prophet complex is obvious.

Do you remember the uneducated psychic, well meaning but sound asleep, who predicted a time-slot that extended over a period of fifty years from 1928 to 1980? And then the other psychic, a menopausal female, who trembled, as her hand shakily flew over a map of the U.S., stopping only when her hand convulsively pointed to a spot — Fresno, California! A sensation-seeking psychotic later cautioned against April. And a few would-be prophets noted that an eclipse of the moon was due on the second day of April, 1969. Publicity motivated fortune-tellers denied any part in the chaos. Their denials managed somehow to reach an even larger audience than did the original predications. If there ever had been an *original* prediction. The denials created even more unrest. Mix it all up with a willing populace and you get *EARTHQUAKE!*

Much the same sort of situation occurred in February of 1962 with the END OF THE WORLD hysteria. At that time the astrologers in the U.S. who had no part in the lunacy

were criticized and blamed for the prediction. The astrologers
for some unexplained reason had controlled themselves and
managed to predict that there would be *no* earthquake in California. At least not one that would devastate it during April
of 1969. The astrologers in the United States cleverly predicted that the world would not end in February, 1962. However negative appears this approach, the astrologers have at
other times acted more aggressively. According to published
reports the U.S. astrologers did predict that the President who
took office in 1961 would die in office (though thousands of
reports noted the impending tragedy, only one woman, in
Washington, takes credit for the prediction). They did predict
wide-spread rioting in the U.S. They did predict Nixon's
victory. They did predict Onassis. They also came in strong
with space predictions, timing, etc., and they knew well in
advance that Johnson would retire, and why, and when. (I too
made the prediction one year in advance of the date — stating emotional difficulties as the prominent reason). So only
the psychics and East Indian astrologers can take credit for
the California earthquake predictions. When the shock waves
coincidentally did rock many parts of the world on April 4,
1969, the lunatic fringe gleefully squealed, "It's coming . . .
it's coming . . . it's coming . . .," and would, I am certain,
have been willing to forfeit a year of healthy sexual expression if indeed it only had!

But it didn't!

It's a big world as worlds go, and everyday, somewhere, the
earth does throw her weight about a bit, and someday a big
earthquake might just happen in California. But it didn't happen on April 4, 1969. The poor psychics were left with the
same feeling one gets after they find out they're a little pregnant — or a little dead.

The New Testament wonders if the prophets live on forever. Well not only do they live on forever, but they turn

into scientists, too. At least one of them has — a Genie who lives east of the Mason-Dixon line. According to a news item out of Ohio that appeared in the *Los Angeles Times.* September 28, 1969, a famous seer (who, while promoting a new book, had given readings, and was fined for fortune-telling), has now switched over to predictions based upon, to quote her sacred words, "ASTROLOGY." "Winston Churchill," she says, "used it. It's a science, you know."

OH YEAH!

This then by virtue of celestial rights granted to all mystics makes our little Genie a scientist, no?

For the past thirty years or so would-be prophets have sought the help of God whenever seeking social acceptance. Psychics with ambition have even gone so far as to establish small churches where fortune-telling covered itself with angel wings and let loose with regular nightly flutters called spiritual guidance meetings anywhere from a dollar a feather and up.

Very rarely, unless caught overstepping their call, did the psychic ministers ever have a run-in with any practical heretics from the bunko squad. It has always been a bit tricky to interfere with one's personal interpretation of maternal reputations, the rearing of children, and one's concept of God. If God's desire is to tell your fortune via a self-ordained psychic minister, there isn't too much our brave men in blue can do about it. Unless, of course donations of fantastic and specific amounts are demanded by God's spokesmen in return for your cosmic blessings. So for about the last few years on television and radio other less group-oriented, and slightly more power-motivated psychics have demonstrated their abilities and communicated with God quite openly and unashamedly all the while rolling their eyes as psychics are want to do, sighing and occasionally gasping, whenever and if ever the rapport became too emotionally charged for them to handle.

Body chemistry was never considered a legitimate source of wisdom, and psychics who thought of themselves as only possessors of a different form of mental energy, or as a small link in the ever-expanding chain of evolution, were said to be expressing only personal opinions, and therefore not worthy of trust or public notice. A direct line from the Almighty was a must, especially if one ever hoped to appear on the Joe Pyne television show. And a direct line from the Almighty seemed to be responsible for many of the psychic world's "Goldwater will win," "Brown will beat Reagan," "Yorty won't make it," "The war in Vietnam will end inside of 57 days . . . ." Very wrong predictions!

But even though the Supreme Being sometimes slipped, the psychics never did. The past always was predicted with great ease and always while "having lunch with a friend" (eight years ago); or while at a "Republican cocktail party" (usually after the fourth drink); and frequently "in a personal diary" that is kept next to the bed in the top drawer of the bedstand . . . "saved" for publication until after everyone concerned . . . PASSES ON.

Usually exciting headlines hit the press — always a few days *after* an event — with the startling announcement THE PSYCHIC KNEW SIX MONTHS IN ADVANCE IT WOULD HAPPEN! That the psychic failed to establish that point *before* the fact is ignored.

Times have changed!

Religion no longer offers the protective cloak of respectability some psychics have indicated they need, and if the quote out of Ohio is accurate some psychics are now looking toward science for the easy ride. Besides believing astrology to be a science, Genie has made other errors in judgment. We shall never know for sure if the genie's prediction of "Jackie will not marry for a very long time to come," was based wholly upon a quick communique from above, or from the feverish and frenzied study of the "science" of the stars. But wherever it came from, it was wrong! Very elegantly wrong! Genie made a boo-boo because the week of her prediction was *exactly* when Jackie did it.

Maybe God made the mistake!

Everybody makes mistakes — even, I suppose, God. And everybody gets carried away at times when the Joy of Illumination hits. But really now, no one should get so carried away that they call astrology a science. It isn't.

If you have ever had an opportunity to meet with the happy group of psychic astrologers who float about, you would know at first glance that not only is astrology not a science, but the psychic astrologers are not *scientists,* either.

There is a dearth of research.

There is an absolute abhorrance for strict and rigid controls or in-depth examinations of supposed learnèd knowledge. There are astrology clubs that only cater to the social-minded thrill seekers who perpetuate beliefs stemming backwards into the thousands of years and who delight in discovering no new interpretations or techniques.

The few attempts made by the rational to establish study groups with controlled methods have been met with violent and almost psychotic rebellion. The inquiring mind has had a thick door of stupidity shut in its face. The sane refuse to associate with existing groups of occult students for fear of being thought nutty, and rightly so. Not all the psychics are fortune-tellers, but all the nonfortune-telling variety are quiet about their abilities. Many prominent, seemingly rational, sensible, interesting, and intelligent people are psychic, and have experienced beyond doubt the existence of psychic phenomena, but prefer to remain silent. Many are also convinced that there is something to astrology, but under the circumstances would prefer to remain in the shadows. There is unfortunately a low level of intelligence exhibited and a frightening and very high level of emotional disturbances shown among the astro-scientists. They suffer from high percentages of infidelities. Exhibit lack of control in personal relationships, and erratic behavior. There is a predominance of homosexuality and lesbianism. There is much immoral and offensive behavior found within the ranks of those who have set themselves up apart from the general population and who have imagined themselves to be the world saviors.

Astrology is the study of the possible coincidence between planetary patterns and human events. It is philosophical in nature. The methods used may be considered orderly and scientific, as the hour and location of the date of birth are needed in order to calculate the position of the planets for any one latitude and longitude. But then what? There is a planetary pattern, and a map is drawn up depicting it. SO! What do the astrologers then do with the exact map of the planetary pattern. A thirteen-year-old can do the mathematical calculations necessary. But what does it all mean, if anything? The astro-scientist who, while autographing her books in a store promotion was fined for fortune-telling, is silly. I suggest that she pay the hundred-dollar-fine for fortune-telling, leave old Winston Churchill out of it, and pack up her crystal ball in mothflakes.

A psychic is someone who is able to, for unexplained reasons, sometimes know what you know, think what you think, and feel what you feel, without ever having to experience in reality what you experience. Since there are many times when a psychic can know what you know, they frequently use this ability to hold the balance of power in a relationship. Especially when, with noticeable odds against them, the things they know in advance manage remarkably to come about!

One of the world's most honest psychics is without a doubt Peter Hurkos, who says it like he sees it (right or wrong!). Peter does not make his predictions based upon friendly connections in Washington. He bases them entirely upon his own real emotional reactions — whatever they may be. Another honest predictor, however un-psychic he may be, is Criswell. His predictions are made as he sees fit. Without a thought to political advantage. An admirable trait for anyone who holds the eye of the public, and especially an admirable trait if one is involved in peering into the future.

A psychic impression is a reaction to unseen stimuli that can be interpreted by the psychic to indicate a variety of information. The psychic's previous real experience, education, environmental level, emotional relationships, curiosity, intellectual capacity, and current social status all combine as a filter through which pass sensations that later emerge as fantastic insight into whatever situation, problem, or individual hapless enough to have attracted the passionate probe.

A two-year-old pounding his fists with enthusiastic delight and relentless ambition along the 88 keys of the grand piano does not forfeit his future potential to rank with Mozart, Bach, or Brahms, and it certainly should not alter our belief in the possibility of music. However, should we, the recipients of the sound, reward the precocious one with endless and tireless praise along wtih chocolate cookies and red lollipops? Surely once in a while, when occasion demands, the noise may be met with a "Shut up," or a smack on the knuckles, without fear of severing permanently a sensitive relationship.

When the aggressive clairvoyants have first explored the inner secrets of their own psyches, and have solved successfully the problems of their own often self-confessed perversion, sexual and otherwise, and when they have at least attempted to deal with their own blind and not too forcefully suppressed inner desire; and when once they have obtained legitimate certifications from various educational agencies that will warrant their offering psychological guidance or other exquisite advice, then, if they feel they are able to curb their overly-expressed desires to impress others at all cost, then and only then should they feel free to concern themselvs with the fates of the Kennedys, the United State's position in Vietnam and Cambodia, the tragedy of Bishop Pike and the question of whether or not Johnny Carson will ever leave NBC.

Meanwhile, with due and proper respect to everyone's unique hormonal and chemical makeup (though they are, admittedly, nature's novel and exciting playthings), and until further scientific research indicates evolution victorious and demands universal celebrations, the psychic fortune-tellers really should calm themselves, remain tranquil, and stick to calling the cards and playing the shell games.

FIGURE VI

A THIRD EYE

5

The saviors

"Great thoughts, great feelings, come to them, life instincts unawares."
— *Richard Monckton Milness*

Since the "readers" of the future have always managed to ignore the Municipal Codes, the "readers" of this book may do so also!

"LOS ANGELES MUNICIPAL CODE"

SEC. 43.30. FORTUNE TELLING
"No person shall advertise by sign, circular, handbill or in any newspaper, periodical or magazine, or other publication or publications, or by any

47

other means, to tell fortunes, to find or restore lost or stolen property, to locate oil wells, gold or silver or other ore or metal or natural product; to restore lost love or friendship or affection, to unite or procure lovers, husbands, wives, lost relatives, or friends for or without pay, by means of occult or psychic powers, faculties or forces, clairvoyance, psychology, psychometry, spirits, mediumship, seership, prophecy, astrology, palmistry, necromancy, or other craft, science, cards, talismans, charms, potions, magnetism or magnetized articles or substances, oriental mysteries or magic of any kind or nature, or numerology, or to engage in or carry on any business the advertisement of which is prohibited by this section.

Where the appellant maintained a sign in her window: "Spiritual Science Readings"; offered to tell a witness "everything he wanted to know," for $2.00; she told witness his wife would return within three days, he was going to receive letters with money in them, he would take a trip, and would back to sea, such facts constituted a violation of Section 43.30 of the Los Angeles Municipal Code, and a conviction was affirmed, even though the appellant defended on the ground that she was a duly ordained minister and that the $2.00 was a donation to the American Church.

People v. Merino, CR A 1921.

Even though the appellant received a salary from the church in return for her collections, she was not exempt under the provisions of Section 43.31.

<u>People v. Merino, Supra.</u>

Where the appellant told the witness that she would be married twice, would marry an attorney, would go to a new job, that the unhappy part of her life would end July 15, that she was in danger of having an accident, but would live to be 70 or 80 years old and appellant charged the witness $1.00, the conviction was sustained even though appellant was an ordained minister of a bona fide church.

<u>People v. Norvell, CR A 1956.</u>

See also: <u>People v. Whitemore, CR A 2031</u>

"It is not a violation of Section 43.30 of the Los Angeles Municipal Code to tell fortunes unless the person so doing is engaged in or is carrying on any business of fortune telling, or one or more of the other activities therein prohibited . . . a single act does not constitute a business." (In this case the court affirmed a conviction of 43.30 and vagrancy, holding that "a reading of the reporter's transcript convinces us that the proof of defendant's guilt was overwhelming"; (Bishop dissenting).

<u>People v. Abdullah et
Ahmed Saud. CR A 2008.</u>

"Fortune telling . . . is the practice of foretelling events, or prophesying the future, also the practice or art of professing to reveal future events in the life of another . . . Tested by this definition many of the acts proved to have been done by defendant, such as narrating the past history of his visitors and characterizing the personalities of the visitors and advising them as to their present and future conduct, do not constitute fortune telling. But other acts shown, such as stating that one visitor would receive a letter from her brother . . . do come within the above definition . . . But Section 43.30 of the Los Angeles Municipal Code does not contain a general prohibition of fortune telling. . . . In addition to the words quoted after the phrase 'by means of,' there is an enumeration of other arts and practices. . . . But we are satisfied that one who advertised merely to tell fortunes, without specifying any of the enumerated means of doing so, and likewise one who does tell fortunes without professing or exemplifying any of those means, does not violate this ordinance."

People v. Miracles A. Smith, CR A 2034

A minister who tells fortunes as a business otherwise than in the performance of his pastoral duties acts in violation of Section 43.30.

People v. Bradford, CR A 2076.

Section 43.30 is constitutional, and does not offend Section 11 and 21 of Article I of the State Constitution, and even though it were conceded that astrology is a science such a fact of itself would not warrant a person in conducting a business of telling fortunes.

People v. Griffen, CR 9 2190.

SEC. 43.31. FORTUNE TELLING—EXEMPTIONS

The provisions of the preceding section shall not be construed to include, prohibit or interfere with the exercise of any religious or spiritual function of any priest, minister, rector or any accredited representative holds a certificate of credit, commission or ordination under the ecclesiastical laws of a religious corporation incorporated under the laws of any state or territory of the United States of America or any voluntary religious association, and who fully conforms to the rites and practices prescribed by the supreme conference, convocation, convention, assembly, association or synod of the system or faith with which they are affiliated. Provided, however, that any church or religious organization which is organized for the primary purpose of conferring certificates of commission, credit or ordination for a price and not primarily for the purpose of teaching and practicing a religious doctrine or belief, shall not be deemed to be a bona fide church or religious organization."

"Sometimes I will be thinking of someone — and they will telephone — or come by for a visit — or later I will run into them on the street; and I maybe haven't seen them for a long time — but just as soon as I think of them — there they are — but I don't think that's anything — it's just normal. I'm sure that there are psychic people who can predict the future — but I don't know any. I'm sure that's possible — I just have never met one!"

—*Los Angeles City Hall Garage Attendant*

Have you ever been to a fortune teller to have yourself read? Well, if you're no better informed about yourself or your future after the visit, the experience will at least offer you some interesting conversational material. Most times it is a lot of fun. My teen years were spent racing about visiting fortune-teller after fortune-teller. My girl friend and I would get together every Saturday afternoon and would go to New York City, on the Long Island railroad, with a pocketfull of dollar bills. We visited every gypsy tea room in the area. They were called the "Gypsy Tea Kettles" and for a dollar you could have your cards, palm, or tea leaves read, with a choice of a cream cheese or peanut butter and jelly sandwich, dark or white, toast or plain. I had been very impressed, when I was fifteen years old, by one particularly delightful fortune-teller. She was probably in her mid-forties, and had red hair. I remember she had gorgeous green eyes — they were very clear and shiny. She was glamorously dressed and never without some exotic fur draped over her chair, even in August. She lived in Miami during the winter months and worked at the Gypsy Tea Kettles during the summer. At the time I met her she was no longer married, but she said she had been . . . many times. When she read my cards, she made the prediction that I would marry a man who had a beard (when I met my husband Mentor he did not have a beard, but when we traced back in his life to the time that she had given me the reading, he *did indeed* have a rather full one). She said that his initials would be M or W, and considering there are twenty-six letters in the alphabet she was after all pretty close. She predicted that I would live over 1,000 miles away from N.Y.C. where there were palm trees. My friends and I imagined it was to be somewhere in Florida. But later, as it turned out, the reading could have applied to California. All in all it was a pretty clever exhibition of "something."

When I was a little girl my Grandmother had a friend, a

Cuban woman, Margo, who was a psychic. She read cards. And they would exchange readings. Our family would get readings from Margo and then they in turn would give her readings. She once predicted that my face would be seen and recognized everywhere. On posters. In newspapers. Everywhere. Large photos of my face. When I married my husband, Mentor, who is a painter, we believed that the reading and the prediction had come to pass, because he did paint very many portraits of me. However, later, Warner Brothers Recording sent out thousands of publicity pictures. And since then, my photos have appeared in many newspapers and magazines around the world. Her prediction appears to have come true. Yet at the time she knew me, no one suspected my promotional nature, my vanity, or my nerve. No one was certain that her reading would come true; though perhaps she drew it from a desire buried deep within my subconscious mind.

My Grandmother was a real old-fashioned fortune-teller, and she gave people readings for a small fee. It was a lucrative business for her. And while I was a child, I absorbed the system, the method or whatever it was that was being done. Grandma was known to be psychic — at least she existed and operated within the state or mental condition that most people call the act of being psychic. She was extremely intuitive. And knew things long before they occurred. Whenever she met someone, in an instant she could figure out their birth sign, the approximate month of their birth and where they had been born. The discovery of the birth location of course could have been based upon her clever and immediate analysis of their accents. But I rather doubt it. I think it was rather an instinctive response, and based entirely on a psychic contact and emotional rapport, that she may have felt for them. I don't think that grandma as a native of Europe, could have, during her early years here, readily determined whether someone was born in the Northeast, the Southwest, the Midwest, or Canada, by accent alone. And besides, many times people are born in one place and raised in another. I think something else took place that communicated those facts to her. At any rate she was able to rapidly suggest where they were born, whether they were divorced, married, widowed, happy, emotionally dissatisfied, or whatever — which did make for some amusing reactions. It was certainly a remarkable demonstration of *something,* even though we don't know what! And it could always be counted upon to change the pace of any social gathering!

Grandma didn't let it drop there. She was an auburn, curly haired, green-eyed, chunky mass of energy, with an hour-glass figure a little past midnight. She had thirteen pregnancies, eight live births (including a set of twins), and was left with five living children. At a time when everyone whom she knew spoke Italian, washed sheets white without Tide, and grew fatter on American largesse, her husband was forcibly unemployed. During the first world war he had naively announced loyalty to Austria-Hungary, his native land. And she, to pass the time between bawling babies, making chicken soup, dodging the landlord, wrote poetry, music, short stories, and sculpted. Grandma came from a long line of psychics. Grandma's great-grandmother in Yugoslavia was also a psychic. And grandma's father had been a ship's captain who studied astronomy and . . . dabbled in astrology. Grandma, sensitive and untrained and with a strong creative force that needed venting, discovered the release possible through psychic demonstration, and began a career of "tuning in" that would eventually occupy more than three-fifths of her life. At some times, she could clearly sense accurately the needs of her client, and at other times I believe she no doubt just utilized a shrewd old-country insight coupled with her wild imagination in order to conquer her charges' spiritual and irrational fears.

As I grew up I watched the parade through Grandma's living room with an alert eye and eager heart. Through the Babylon of tongues (Grandma spoke Italian, Yugoslavian, Spanish and Greek fluently and English so-so) could be heard the soft murmur from the hypnotized. "Yes Marie, you're right, Marie, Yes, yes, you're right! You're right! You're right!" and I would think, "God, that must make you feel powerful!" There was no doubt that she had a sixth sense and a third eye, an empathy, and was sensitive, but there was also no doubt that she was a smart cookie.

It was only natural that grandma should become an influence in my life and the filter through which I viewed the psychic world. Everyone in it I saw in relationship to her. She became the yardstick by which I measured the value of other efforts. Including my own. The entire family was involved with psychic phenomena, but only Grandma had put up a sign.

Grandma was brave — a characteristic many good psychics hold in common, and bravery is an essential for psychic behavior that guarantees manifestation of the ability . . . upon demand!

Take a freaky, chancey, mutative bit of natural extra sensory perception, and add it to an innate cleverness, and you just have to come up with a pretty formidable combine. Add a touch of compulsive bravery, and season it with a few years of adventuresome creative experiences and you produce unshakable confidence. Mix everything together with an "I don't give a damn" attitude and you come up with Fortune-Teller's stew.

Another prerequisite that aids the development of the telepathic potential is a psychotic faith in the invincibility of one's insight.

A psychic never doubts! A good psychic cannot ever afford to believe he or she has made an error in judgment.

If ever an impulse, vague thought, or stray emotion *is* misunderstood, a psychic prefers to believe that the *client* is covering!" Most dedicated fortune-tellers are a reckless lot who cover egocentric motivation with a sweet smile and a slightly crooked, off-dead-center, straight-from-God-look . . . out of their *third* eye.

VIRGINIA PELHAM

She is a high-school graduate. Buxom. Flirtatious. Frustrated. Loud. And most of all, she is an astrologer! But luckily, so far as I know, she isn't anybody's mother. Suffering through puberty from an unsympathetic environment and surrounded by rigid puritanical parents and an uncontrollably high-level sexual appetite, she sought solace in a quasi-religious affiliation. There she found a mother image in an older woman — the minister's wife — a "psychic" and an almost lesbian, who herself had no answers, but who managed to suppress all of the questions by dominating her elderly senile husband. Virginia found solace, also, in a much older Latin lover with six children who was married to an uneducated, unsuspecting wife, who cleaned other people's houses to help support his occult interests (including Virginia). Our girl astrologer had a dauntless spirit that would have done well if it had been attached to some intelligence, a bit more education, and a trifle of self-control. She pursued metaphysics with a vengeance that can only be acquired when one is emotionally tied to a lover who is available only every other Wednesday between six and eight. Devouring the spirit world and Astrology I through Advanced, along with a multitude of mimeographed specialized courses, she graduated as a Certified Hermatician, and was able then to teach three nights each week after work, free, as a contribution to the cause, which later invariably turned out to be the pocket of the *turned-on* wife of the *tuned-out* minister. After years of Saturdays and Sundays spent tirelessly typing up courses to be mimeographed for the neophytes, and Monday, Tuesday, and

Friday nights spent lecturing on Mars and Venus squares and Saturn returns, with Wednesdays hardly used up enough, she found her Thursdays getting to her. She began dating, utilizing a variety of near-miss males, so that Latin lover, who doubles as a professor for Personal Magnetism Class Number Two, Saturdays at ten, wouldn't get jealous! To use Virginia's own words, "Planetary Pattern will out," and the heavy load carried with all those conjunctions she had elatedly calculated in her House of Sex, finally forced our spiritually-inclined lass into making a drastic break! Maybe it was her Uranus rising, but she left Personal Magnetism Class Number Two, and the Latin lover. Quit typing. Stopped lecturing on Mondays, Tuesdays, and Fridays. Put up a shingle, and now busies herself with the world's woes, and any Psychological-Personal- Emotional-Sexual-Problems who happily come her way. Twenty-five dollars and up!

MARY JONES

Her mouth is easily held in the tight line of faded dreams. Her hair stylishly tossed a la the forties. And her drip-dry catalogue fashions suit her Middle American look and her broad non-identified twang. Vague, uncomfortable urges had triggered her joining an astrology club. She immediately noted the president of the club seemed to have a good thing going. What with the social rewards of leading the festivities during every fourth Tuesday dinners, and lectures on *The Sun Sign Similies,* and probably picking up an occasional order for a horoscope that would help to catch up on the gas bill or buy extra perfume, it was not too difficult for Mary to see how with a little concentrated effort she, too, could do pretty well. And concentrate her effort she did. And with the ferocious style of an aging lioness in the last throes of a summer's heat, she hit the astrology world with a snarl. Lacking in any natural empathy, a philosophical view, tender compassion, or even a faint trace of extra sensory perception, she embarked upon an astrology career cloaked in the cool, dry logic of a mountaintop. Edging into all the vulnerable circles she took over the dinners, sabatoged years of quiet, meaningless, harmless efforts, and opened up a new school. Loud banners streaming. Neon lights flashing. The first moment of her first lecture on the first night of her first class in her first school, library, and fortune-telling den in Orange County, she was promptly arrested by the bunko squad which had been alerted by old members of the astrology club, the "dedicated to good and truth" sensitives. Paying her five-hundred-dollar fine, she retreated into more lady-like endeavors, and now offers "in-depth analyses" by personal recommendation *only* . . . fifteen dollars an hour. Her specialty? Business charts!

RALPH

His eyes are very bright and piercing. He's a nice sort of fellow and sincere. Years ago he left a steady secure life as an investment broker to establish himself in the never-never world of magic, astrology, and intimate though not always rewarding Karmic relationships. Not very turned-on to making a fast buck from the stars, he manages to live on dividend checks from out of his past and an odd job pulling a fellow companion out of a business-management snarl, via his "mysterious powers." And on the side he writes an occasional feature article for national magazines dealing with occult phenomena. Lighting candles for spiritual help, he is sensitive longing, and mostly unfulfilled, and seeks solutions in the comfort of planetary patterns and their constancy. If pressured he will accept demands to calculate a chart for a friend of the friend of a friend. Exuding a quiet acceptance of destiny's will, he is an ideal astrologer to contact for comfort over the rough spots. After one "reading" you soon see you could have easily saved him the effort and yourself the twenty-five dollars if only you had prepared your own cup of tea, taken two Bufferin, and lighted your own candles!

VAUGHN VAN DERSCHMIDT

He is not terribly literate and has an uncontrollable inner lust that is difficult for him to placate. A crude empathy based upon sexual, emotional cravings support his brutal attempts to break through. There is a never-ending desire to communicate on an emotional level and a never-reached interest in improving whatever raw materials may have existed at the start of things. When he misses badly, it is an imagined weakness attributed to language bariers. If he hits, the strike is dramatized by wild whoops of joy and rewarded with a deluge of self-incriminating compliments. Overwhelmed by the motivation to win, he probes the inner recesses of a subject's subconscious with brute force. With imagination unfortunately blocked by pressing creditors, masculine menopause, too many pills, never enough booze, and a bitchy, bleached, unkempt, youngish, plumpish, shack-job, he staggers into unknown regions with multi-boring perceptions: "You had an operation! Your knee, your knee. What's the key that you have placed on the top of your jewelry box? Your knee, your knee. Did your mother have a gall bladder operation? No I didn't say mother, I mean aunt, no, no, your cousin, your sister, no, no not gall bladder, *affair!* You just had an *affair,* that's it! Come on tell the audience!"

SANDRA THE SPIRITUALLY AWAKENED

Sandra is an attractive, slim, dynamic, and apparently intelligent thirty-year-old. Sandra told me that she has been practicing witchcraft for a good number of years. She studied various facets of occultism and was indeed very well informed. She could quote verbosely from every book and article that has been written in the past fifteen or twenty years. She has an acquaintanceship with many of the well-known psychics in the United States, and is in fact a psychic name dropper. She confided in me that she was reaching a point of great power with her witchcraft. And then, feeling an unwarranted mutual rapport with me, she related her methods for spell casting. They were extraordinary. Sandra told me that in order to reach the high level of spiritual and emotional magnetism that she felt was necessary to cast spells, she would utilize her sexual and emotional capacities. Evidently she felt no real affection for anyone. She had never experienced normal outlets for her drive. She was unable to participate in any usual form of sexual expression. Sandra relied wholly upon herself — entirely — in order to achieve the proper, as she called it, the "proper sexual tension" necessary for effective spell casting. I have heard of witches using their sex drives for selfish ends, but always with a love object. However, Sandra told me that she aroused herself sexually and allowed herself to reach a state of "electrifying tension" prior to casting a spell. Sandra said she was attempting to vamp the psychic energy of a particular male psychic. She was teaching him witchcraft, and allowed him to cast spells with her. He did not know this was being done so that she could divert his energy to her ends. She said that they had practiced self-stimulation, in unison, whenever casting the spells and rituals that they performed together. Neither one of course ever touching the other! I cannot believe that this is the witchcraft of the ages. But I do believe that this is the witchcraft that has invited the sexual perverts from around the world. I believe that this is the form of witchcraft that is being pursued today in many suburban areas of the United States.

ROGER THE MOON GODDESS

Roger has been studying the occult most of his adult life. He is now forty. He has never exhibited any psychic ability, but he is quite known for his psychic work. In other words, although he has never had a telepathic thought or established an emotional rapport with anyone (at least not to the extent of being able to tell them anything of their foreseeable future), he is nevertheless sought after by very many women in the Beverly Hills area, and is considered to be a great psychic. I don't know what it is that they base their belief upon. Roger has never at any time made a prediction. He has never foreseen any incident in anyone's life, ever! But Roger is very actively involved in the field of fortune-telling. I have known Roger for a good number of years. Roger says that he is the reincarnation of a moon goddess. When Roger gets down in the dumps emotionally he casts a spell. Now this spell is meant to bring into his life a happier emotional relationship. Roger first strips nude. Then he rubs himself from head to toe with cod liver oil. On the living room floor he then makes a circle with smooth white pebbles. At the head of the circle, he places a black candle. And at the base of the circle, a purple candle. Roger then lights the candles and lies down in the center of the circle of white pebbles, sexually arousing himself until the candles burn out. Roger considers this as an offering to the god Pluto! Although Roger has for the sake of clarity on the subject been kind enough to confess to me his intimate spell castings, he has not as yet informed me as to the size of the candles used.

CAROLINE: A TRACK HOUSE WITCH!

Caroline is thirty-five years old. She says she's a "Capricorn!" She has three children under the age of twelve. Caroline's husband is a printer. His hours are irregular. His complexion sallow. His temperament dull. Caroline has been studying the occult for ten years. She goes to astrology dinners once a month. She goes to astrology classes once a week. She studies all levels of mysticism once every other week, and has daily contacts with other women and men who are interested in the same subject. Caroline uses pot. Not everyone who uses pot professes to be a psychic and not every psychic uses pot. Caroline feels that in her case the pot helps her to "psych-in".

FIGURE VII

THE OFFERING

Caroline and her friends frequently meet in the afternoons and smoke marihuana in order to reach a higher state of spiritual awareness. At times, Caroline has, just for kicks, put some marihuana into the brownies that she has served to her babysitters when she leaves to go to her mind-expanding meetings. Caroline feels that she has great potential for witch-craft. She says that she is in fact a female who is a witch but perhaps was not aware of it early in life. Caroline has had one love affair after another. All of her personal relationships, all of her love affairs have ended in an uncomfortable, embarrassing manner. One relationship was with an older gentleman who was the head of a television company that was attempting to buy out one of the smaller local television stations. Caroline believed that by having a sexual relationship with this gentleman, she could utilize the energy that was generated to cast a spell to capture a starring role in a movie. The trick of spell casting here, she said, was never to achieve sexual satisfaction for one's self — but only to arouse and satisfy the other individual. Caroline told me that she would visit this gentleman in his hotel each time he arrived in the Los Angeles area from New York City. She did not like him. She was not attracted to him. And in fact she was repelled by him. She felt that by having a physical contact with a male whom she found to be repulsive but whom she considered powerful, the proper energy could be generated that could be later transferred into witchcraft purposes. She performed all sorts of sexual deviations with him. She courageously never allowed him to sexually satisfy her, if she ever once drifted toward such a repugnant need! The relationship lasted one year. The gentleman did not manage to buy out the television station. The trips from New York to Los Angeles stopped. Caroline did not get the part in the movie. Caroline, though, is dauntless. One of Caroline's other witchcraft experiments was with an art director who had just recently divorced and who was in the midst of overwhelming financial disorder. She was very much attracted to him, and felt that she could, by having a sexually meaningful relationship with him, divert the energy that would be generated from the union into spells cast for opportunities, and thereby contribute, in some small way, to his financial success. A noble thought! This was a very dynamic affair. There was normal attraction. Caroline really dug him. However, during this relatonship Caroline decided that for the good of the cause, for Witchcraft, she could never enjoy a sexual union with her lover which did not take place in his office . . . standing up in the closet! This is the only way that Caroline and her lover made love. For three years!

VINCENTE EL BRUJO

There is a man sixty-three years old from Columbia — who says he is a Brujo. A Brujo is a Latin male witch. He claims to be psychic, and has in fact impressed many of his clients with his psychic ability. However, his main forte is curing females of all sorts of emotional problems. His methods for attacking the demons that lie within are very interesting. The female is invited for a consultation in his home in a hill community on the East side of Los Angeles. After an interview of an hour or sometimes an hour and a half, and when El Brujo is impressed with the female's great need and belief in his curative powers, she is invited into the "House of Magic" in his garden. The House of Magic was built by El Brujo himself. It's a little ten by twelve bunkhouse. When you enter there is a heavy sickening sweet aroma of incense. The client is told to strip nude, and is then bathed gently with holy water that El Brujo, himself, has blessed. The client then lies on the floor which has been sprinkled with some very finely-ground flower petals. El Brujo then attempts to pull from the client any of the static magnetic energies that may have accumulated. He gently massages the client from head to toe for at least on hour. At the end of this time the client is massaged quickly with a very fine white ash that is said to be ground dinosaur bones. The ash is rubbed well into the client's body. The tiny pots of incense are placed around the client's body to form a circle, and El Brujo fans the fumes from the incense into the client's body. Sometimes the cure takes several days and the client must leave for dinner and then return to spend . . . the night. El Brujo does not offer food or drink to any of his suffering clientel because he does not have a food or liquor license. El Brujo is very high priced. He has steady customers through the years. He is very well thought of by his clientele. No one has ever suggested that El Brujo had conned them or taken them or that he was a phoney. And he has to his credit . . . a very high percentage of successful cures!

GEORGE AND SYMPATHY

George is a comparatively young psychic who has a reputation of value within his community. Usually a psychic kicks around for ten to fifteen years before becoming established. George is recommended very readily and is only in his early twenties. He has a strange, glassy-eyed look, and for a young man in his twenties, his complexion is still quite uncontrolled. Very slightly built, George is a bit seedily attired, and his physical upkeep has not been excessively energetic. Most of the clientele that visit George are women between twenty-five and forty-five years of age. George is a palmist and a card reader. At times he is extremely clairvoyant. People who have visited him swear to his accuracy. He is said to have fantastic insight into the future. He can be specific — detailed. And is consistently accurate. George is not a homosexual. But neither is George a very potent male. He lies somewhere in a limbo state. Women visit him and are given a fifteen minute reading, at which time George tells them that the key to their unhappiness, the pivot upon which swirls their emotional and financial difficulties, is their unfortunate lack of a proper sexual union with their mates. If sexual difficulty is not the root of the problem that has precipitated a contact with George, then the woman seeking a psychic source of enlightenment leaves, never goes back, and doesn't recommend George. But, if the sexual difficulty is prominent in the lives of these women, they are terribly impressed with George's insight, recommend him highly, and visit him every couple of weeks for other readings. It is interesting to note that George has a very successful business. He charges fifteen dollars for a visit and then gives each client exactly the same reading: that they are not able to achieve sexual fulfillment with their current established partner! His accuracy has so amazed his clientel that some of the women have been visiting George since he was seventeen. There is no end to their sexual problem. There is no end of their need to visit George, and to hear that they have a sexual problem. It would appear that only the women who have a sexual problem, who visit George, are inclined to discuss it. Women who don't have a sexual problem, who visit George, are never heard from again. Therefore the statistics available as to the value of his perceptiveness are of course a bit one-sided.

FAT MARGARET

Margaret is an astrologer who lives out in the valley. She's been divorced for several years. She has one child. Through the years, due to emotional unhappiness and an inability to cope with her problems in any realistic sense, Margaret's put on considerable weight. She has been studying astrology and working as a professional astrologer for many years. Most of her clients are men, and most of her predictions connected with their business opportunities have been fairly accurate. However, Margaret has a personal problem in dealing with these people. Each time Margaret calculates a horoscope for a male client, she immediately calls all the astrologers who live within a radius of fifty miles (her friends), and proceeds to give them a breakdown as to the male's sexual abilities, capabilities, capacities, potentials, and whatever. Invariably, Margaret finds some sort of connection between her horoscope and the male's horoscope that would indicate that they would have a tremendous sexual rapport. Margaret points out to all of her friends that the client would have Mars in good relationship to her Venus, the Moon in good relationship to her Sun, his Jupiter in good relationship to her Saturn. This goes on endlessly. At the termination of the consultation Margaret is left in a dejected state, when it becomes obvious that the male client has come to Margaret for *only* an astrological reading, and *only* an interpretation of his future business potentials. When the client leaves never to return, Margaret goes into an awkward and disturbed state and reverts back to eating. She's a good astrologer but she's getting awfully fat.

THE PSYCHIC EXPLORER

While writing a series of articles for the United Western newspapers and for the American in Asia newspapers, I was brought into contact with a male psychic of some note. I was supposed to interview this psychic and then write a little personality feature about him. I was very much impressed with the man's ability to awe his environment. He is a very dynamic individual — very large, very forceful, and very much believes himself to be capable of all forms of nonverbal nonphysical communication. Honestly *believing* himself to be psychic, he consequently was at times extremely psychic. There seems to be a very definite correlation between a psychic knowledge — a spiritual insight — into another human being, and the sexual response. I interviewed him for forty-five minutes. At the end of the time he offered to give me one of his very expensive readings. He charges and gets $150 and up — ten times more than George. In order to pick up my vibes, he asked if he could hold my wedding rings. Taking my wedding rings tight into his hand, closing his fist about them, he stared at the center of the table, and proceeded to tell me some very interesting things about my married life. The fact that my husband was creative, artistic, and painted. The fact that I had two boys and a girl, and that I lived in a big rambling ranch house on top of a hill. Then suddenly, he stopped, jerked his head up, and said, "I want something from your husband. I want something of his to hold so I can tune in to him. There's something that I must know about him." I had nothing of his with me, but after I searched in my purse, I realized I had been carrying a paycheck my husband just received from MGM, Metro-Goldwyn-Mayer motion picture studios. I had not yet deposited it in the bank. The interesting thing about this check was that my husband had once worked at MGM studios for a long time, but he'd worked there over twelve years ago, and he just recently had gone back to do a small job. This was the first check then, that he had received from MGM in over twelve years. The pyschic could not see the check in my purse. I folded the check up many times until it was no longer recognizable as a check. It just seemed to be a little square piece of paper. I handed this square piece of paper to the psychic, who then clutched at it very tightly, stared off into space, and began to tell me in great detail personal situations that concerned my husband. The exciting part of this reading was that *all* of the situations that he described were true, but they had taken place twelve years before! At the time when my husband had *last* worked at MGM. He told me these things as though they were about to happen in our lives. Soon. Sometime in the near future. Clearly he had indeed "tuned in!" He was a good psychic. No phoney.

It was obvious that this psychic communication was taking place on a subconscious level. Evidently, I carried with me in my subconscious all of the information of all the things that have ever occurred to my husband, that I had heard about while he was at MGM twelve years ago. And in the transferrence of this little piece of paper, this check from MGM, the first one in twelve years, my subconscious had been triggered and had lifted the lid off this information. And a psychic male had tuned into it. It was remarkable that this should happen at all. It was absolutely fascinating. At the end of this reading the psychic relaxed, sighed deeply, and wiped the perspiration from his forehead. I could see that whatever it was he did to tune into my subconscoious had taken a lot out of him. He was good. There was no question of that. But the rest of what took place was disappointing. The psychic told me that he could see that I did not have a strong, healthy, emotional relationship with my husband. Now, had I been the average suburban housewife, unaccustomed to psychic explorations, and had I myself not been a psychic familiar with this type of thing, I may have been more impressed with the delivery. When a psychic tells you something that is true in one moment and then tells you something else in another moment, the inclination is to believe the validity of the *something else* also. The fact that this psychic was capable of tuning in to my subconscious and going back into time, pulling up information that had occurred twelve years before, was very impressive. But this does not allow for the element of human weakness. There is the possibility of a psychic being tremendously impressive with one bit of psychic action and then, later, just operating under the momentum of his own stimulation. The psychic told me that I did not have good, healthy, emotional relationship with my husband. That he (the psychic) liked me very much. That he wanted and needed to know me better, and that he alone, because of his great psychic power and tremendous psychic ability, could form a union with me that would be absolutely out of this world! He outlined how we could feel about each other and mentioned the fact that at present he was breaking up with his current amour. He said that he was a lonely man, like an explorer in the antarctic, seeking the answers to imponderable mysteries. Not everyone could understand. It was difficult having reactions, emotional reactions, not everyone could share — a tragedy in his life. He said his psychic insight into my nature allowed him to recognize that we could have a burning passionate relationship for many, many years. It would be beneficial to me, and of course to him *too*. Not feeling for the moment like the antarctica, I thanked him for the offer, folded up my notepad, put my pencils back into my purse, put on my wedding rings, nodded, smiled brightly, and took off! Shades of George?

6

No Business Like Show Business

I live in a world of make believe
Of fantasy and moon beams
Where all of life consists of dreams
And reality is false.
Bright stars and limpid eyes
Butterflys and lovers' sighs.
A spirit floating through all time;
And all the universe is mine.
Would you that I more earthbound be?
And know of pain and suffering
Of hurt and deaths and nothingness
To earn your sweet caress.
How much better it could be
If you . . . to earn the same from me
Took wing.

And we
In ecstasy of flight
Would touch wings and fly into the night.

—Louise Huebner

It was easy enough to impress a long-haired king and some knights when all the worry one had was an occasional draft coming up from the east wing of the castle or a threat of deliberate drowning in the moat when and if your prediction did not quite make it. But today's jazzed-up, slightly wittier, just as witless, in-tu-i-tits are faced with problems that would defy the cosmic conscoiusness of a pantheon god.

The sensitive psychic of today has to be gutsy. There is a whole new approach to dealing with psychic phenomena that would have given Merlin the shakes.

With the advent of the talk shows, the mystics have become stagestruck and have aggressively invaded the fringes of show biz.

They have been bitten by the bug. Producers of T.V. shows have long lists of stand-by guests — singers, comics, and psychics — who may be depended upon to fill time. The act, if one can call it an act, is frequently limited and unimaginative.

Coast to coast the hosts have fallen into grooves of non-communication with their psychic guests, which is just as well. For, except for the exaggerated quirk, the clairvoyant visitor has nothing much to offer anyway. So it's just as well nobody asks them for it.

The fan mail response to the spot appearances is always

high. The producer tells the host that the guest was a hit, and the guest is invited back again for more of nothing. If Gargantua was billed as a performing psychic on the Johnny Carson show, the in-coming mail would be terrific! The public would love it. Even if the host only nods and smiles occasionally during the gorilla/psychic's grunting and hairy-chest-beating demonstration, there will always be audience response!

Without a doubt, much of what has been presented in this area has been pretty icky-sticky. There isn't a psychic in the country who has not been credited with a long list of predictions that have supposedly come true. No one bothers to ever document the list. But if anyone ever does, they will be forced to report that the majority of statements were made — after the fact. Or in most cases, if they were made at all, they surely were never made in the very precise form that is *now* being presented.

A mid-afternoon, CBS television talk show hostess, who was interviewing me, once gave me quite a start when, during a commercial, she informed me of the "guide" who was seated on her right side.

He was, of course, an Indian, invisible, and from the Other Side. I couldn't believe it.

She said all of her inspiration came through him. With him, she was safe. On the show she was quite articulate and apparently sane. Anyone watching the show would have been forced by my title to categorize me as being way out and she as being sensible — and ultraconservative.

After all, she hosts a daily talk show and I'm the Los Angeles County Witch! I, however, have never attributed what I do to any unnatural origin. I believe everything "magical," may one day be explained and fully understood as coming out of man's very normal potentials. She secretly admitted to having many "friends" among the spirit world, and said she felt "different," "chosen," and dedicated."

I am afraid of "dedicated" people who are motivated by "powers" *greater* than themselves. They are uninhibited, usually, in their dealings with others as they need take no responsibility for any act, and attribute their every move to God. Unfortunately, as a witch, I have no one to blame but myself for any false step.

And as a witch I can be a lot meaner than I could have been if I were Jean Dixon. It's really sort of lucky for me that I'm not.

An example of my meanness was once directed towards a naive newspaper-syndicated astrologer. I'll have to call him Sylvester Mardo because sometimes he knows who he is — and it might just be that his *knowing* and his *reading* my book *happen* to coincide. Anyway, Sylvester invited me to lunch. He was in ecstasy over his good fortune. He told me he was soon to take a big step forward for astrology — a giant step. He couldn't tell me what, but soon he would reveal all, and I would be thrilled. *That* took up the first half of the lunch. The second half of the lunch was devoted to an attempted hypnotic seduction. It didn't work.

I'm pretty husky, healthy, and wise. A guy has to come on with a bit more than crossed eyes, pale face, limp wrists, and flashing rings. And besides I'm married. He and I were never too close anyway. Except as bragging boards. Really, there is nothing worse than a couple of professional, hammy psychics.

As soon as lunch was over, I rushed to KLAC Radio and giggled out all of Sylvester's "hint" to Program Director, Willus Duff. (I always giggle when I'm excited. It's part of being a witch). Willus decided that we should be prepared. Obviously Sylvester was about to go on radio. Willus wanted to scoop the other stations. I wrote forty-eight scripts. We taped them. And we sat tight.

One week later, on a Tuesday, Sylvester called me. Now it could be told! He was to begin on radio on the next Monday, five days a week. I called Willus! On Thursday — four days before Sylvester's show aired — Willus and I began "Radioscope Your Daily Horoscope" on KLAC. I was on twelve times a day, seven days a week. I beat Sylvester, and became the first astrologer-psychic to be hired by a radio station for a large metropolitan market in the U.S. It was an astrology first. "A big step forward," as Syl would say.

Not only did I beat him by four days, but I lasted four years to his four months, which proves once again the "power of witchcraft" over booze.

Most people, after I have been mean — usually agree that it only hurt them when I laughed.

Syl was very hurt.

Despite my easy availability (I once worked on KRLA radio — and wrote and taped thirty-six one-minute features a day seven days each week), rigid, formalized formats don't appeal to me, and I much prefer live, spontaneous programs that offer audience participation — the radio talk shows.

I worked on a KLAC radio talk show in Los Angeles for four years (1965-1969), with Gil Henry. We had a very good thing going. First we bantered just about anything, then we discussed all aspects of the occult field, and then we opened the lines to callers. We explained to the listeners that I would, if I *felt* something, give them a capsule reading. The reading usually consisted of my telling the caller what I believed their immediate and most pressing problems were. If I did not feel anything, I would tell them nothing.

With some types I am able to establish an instant rapport. With others, I would block it. Through the years I found that my ability to tune into them was not dependent upon their belief, my affection or lack of affection for them, my compatibility with them in any area, fatigue or hunger on my part, my recent successes or failures, or my current rela-

FIGURE VIII

LOUISE HUEBNER

tionship with my husband and children. If I felt them . . . I felt them. But *if* I preferred to block them, it was always because of my current relationship with Gil.

The show was usually scheduled between ten at night and two in the morning. Except for a couple of engineers, Gil and I were alone in the building. We worked in the glass-enclosed broadcasting booth, always in the dark, with just a candle flame and a small night light, in order to see the callboard and read the commercials.

It was intimate. However, intimacy is not always an essential for the manifestation of intuitive phenomena. Many times during the past ten years. I have been highly intuitive with audiences of up to several thousand people. My only need is to establish an intimate rapport with one at a time, even though thousands may be involved.

What I did for four years is considered impossible. And that is, I was psychic upon demand. Not public demand; my demand! It is believed to be difficult to scientifically test for the existence of E.S.P. in a clinical structure because those with extra sensory perception (E.S.P.) telepathy, who experience psychic phenomena, are never in control of the phenomena. It just happens to them. Well, I happen to my E.S.P.!

From my mountaintop to KLAC Radio on Wilshire Boulevard is about a forty-five minute drive. About eight-thirty at night I would leave my home for the ten o'clock show. The minute I left the house, I would "snap on." The entire drive to the station was a time of preparation. It's difficult to explain, but I would begin to pull into myself. A quiet control existed "inside." It had nothing to do with my outer appearance or obvious temperament. I would be ready.

But, if I for any extraneous reason, was annoyed with Gil, my psychic potential would be handicapped. It seemed to me that the *kind* of annoyance was very important. If I was turned-on angry, my intuition would be O.K. But if I was "hurt," I would block the audience. Also, if I could flirt with Gil on a sexy level I became more intuitive.

However, the readings were not all that took place, so if anything happened to short-circuit the intuition we would then exploit the other facets.

I always told the audience that since *I* knew I was psychic, and since there were enough listeners who also knew I was psychic, that there was no need for me to "prove" it. In fact, if I was forced into a position of proving it, I would detest it and get so bugged, I couldn't do anything.

For me, always, there has to be no contest, no competition. It has to be fun! On a fun level I operate more effectively.

At any rate, during the four years, not one listener told me that I was not absolutely correct in my "feelings" about them.

Strange things happened. In order to trigger my subconscious and give me a crutch, the listeners calling in would give me their birthdates. They had to give me the day, month, year, time, and place. My responses were never based on astrology, only intuition. My answers were instantaneous. Because of this ability, I have experimented with another psychic, Teresa O'Brien. She gives me initials and I "tune" in. But I am unable to do so with first names. Evidently a birthdate or initial is not as personal. My most effective readings come about when I am removed emotionally from the subject. And even a first name adds too much warmth.

Another discovery was that I, easily irritated by slowness, could not, or would not tune in to anyone who stuttered while giving me their birth data. I had to receive the information crisp, clean, and fast!

During a "tuning in," if Gil pushed the button to begin to fade out the caller, I would lose contact, sometimes even in the middle of a word. Yet the caller was still connected; all that was done was to cut their mike. There is no reason why this should short-circuit me, but in fact it did. So Gil and I learned to leave the mikes open — I had to *feel* them there.

My sympathy goes out to psychics who put themselves in awkward positions. I recall a tragic example of an aging frustrated psychic performing in a theater in Hollywood. Every possible method of thwarting his ability was employed. And, the ghastly part was that he was totally responsible for what was happening.

A performing psychic has a definite personality. And perhaps it is not always obvious on a superficial level — but beneath the exterior — there is a basic similarity between them all.

Proving one's ability or worth is hardly in keeping with one's strong need for immediate acceptance and praise. And psychics need acceptance. If you are born different and feel different, it leaves a mark. And psychics are different.

Unfortunately much of the public's contacts with the phenomena of extra sensory perception have been only through the desperate graspings of insecure mediums who at best are medicore ones too. A faltering psychic who is faced with the dynamic tensions involved in performing on stage or on television, is not the end answer to what psychics are all about.

If I had been psychic last year, last month, last week, or yesterday, and for whatever reasons, I am not psychic today, that doesn't mean I won't again be psychic tomorrow, next week, next month or next year. Not at all.

In fact, if I was psychic once in my life, I very definitely have the capacity to be psychic again. If I am not wanting (subconsciously) to establish psychic rapport with someone at this time, later I may want very much (subconsciously) to establish psychic rapport with someone else.

The psychic in Hollywood, tried to *force* himself into intimate contacts that he obviously fought (inside). Naturally he failed. If someone bugs me (inside) I don't allow him near me while I work.

The Hollywood psychic was not getting along with his girl friend, his secretary, or his manager; yet he had them closely crowded about him.

The psychic leap and the leap toward love have much in common. Both demand total involvement and commitment if they are to survive. And both are acts of bravery. When we look at love we see an excellent example of communication that takes place through some mysterious means. The proximity of so many disturbing personal emotions threw the Hollywood psychic.

Also a performing psychic has to be fast. Quick thoughts and quicker emotions. The pace must move! If there is any drag contact is invariably lost.

He allowed too much insignificant and boring chatter, Though the people had come to see him do his stuff, he offered them what an ill-informed manager believed meant "show biz." He offered them bad rock, and a worse sound system. It cut off his vibes. He offered them jokes. He could have used Jack Burns of Burns and Schriber, who writes for all the top comedy shows. Maybe he could have saved the performance.

When I want to become psychic I first ask myself, "Could I make love under these conditions?" If the answer is yes, then I know everything is correct — for me.

The audience is ignored, mood is all!

I could never make love on the stage of the Huntington Hartford with a novice rock group who played with inadequate mikes. But I could make love in the Hollywood Bowl with Bert Bacharach!

The Federal Communications Commission has a ruling that states in effect, that astrology, witchcraft, hypnotism, etc., are not to be programmed in any way that "fosters belief." Consequently, the subjects must be handled in a humorous way. Jean Dixon, Maurice Woodruff, and most of the other performing psychics are inadvertently able to do this.

I often wonder why in the grand scheme of things a great and powerful creative force (if such exists), would want to contact us (if it does want to contact us) through insipid mediums. It is a bit much to comprehend. Many of the wild-eyed prophets with their continuous predictions and overpredictions, who usually slant their revelations toward their friends in power, or who exhibit extremist views, don't invite belief on my part. The illumination coming to them seems to come from no higher or greater a source than the White House! But surely these poor souls are not the only examples there are to demonstrate the powers that the mind may achieve with it's exciting and multiple potential. These people should not be looked upon as the total statement of psychic phenomena. It can be seen and understood that a psychic who's cornered cannot offer overwhelming testimony to support extra sensory perception. A psychic who at one time started out free and easy, who turned-on quickly, and tuned-in deeply, may now begin to feel the responsibility of fame closing in rapidly, and might be a little uptight about slipping. The staunchest, most fanatical support of the occult has come from the actors. And the worst sort of irrational conclusions by supposedly well informed, "normal" personalities, have been presented with F.C.C. acceptance and approval.

The Prediction Psychosis is not my bag.

If I were to ever develop a need for indiscriminate predicting, it would make me nauseous. My main research interests are political horoscopes, and I prefer to restrict myself to that area. Predictions are after all interpretations of existing factors, and the estimated effect they will have on the future. In the case of psychic predictions, the factors may be just an analysis of "funny feelings."

I have been criticized for what is said to be a calloused attitude toward my "gift." It is because I have never made a big thing about being psychic. It is something I do — along with many other things. It's just one of the ways I am. There is also an erroneous belief that if you are psychic you must not be paid or you will lose your "gift."

Some people, when offered money for their services, when handed a paycheck to perform, become a bit inhibited. And it may be that psychics are not exceptions. Particularly if what they do comes to them easily. Then there are those who feel a money exchange cheapens an act. It's certainly not a discredit to a fabulous oil painting done by Rembrandt to sell for over two million dollars. After all, it doesn't mean that the painting has no artistic value. The value doesn't lessen just because someone who wants it, buys it, and pays for it. That wouldn't be logical. The fact that it exists and has value is not based on whether or not money has been received for it. In fact, many talents may have even improved from the advent of well-paying jobs. It doesn't mean that a talent is commercial because it makes money. An opera star who performs at the Metropolitan *for money* has no less a precious gift because he is paid to exhibit it. How about the men of the cloth, many of whom live in comparative luxury, who sincerely are "called," and do much good for humanity? It is a bit disconcerting to have psychics racing about mouthing trite expressions of brotherly love, spiritual awareness, and unity, insisting that they cannot be paid for their acts or demonstrations of psychic phenomena, because in that way they would not be pure vessels to offer this as a gift to humanity. I think that attitude is for the birds! What takes place has no direct connection with either commercial or non-commercial aspects. Either you sing with a beautiful voice or you don't. Whether you're paid for it or not does not affect the quality of the voice. If you paint well you paint well because that is your gift. It has nothing to do with whether or not someone buys the painting. And if you are a man of the church, you are dedicated with or without financial rewards. And if you're a psychic, I think that you can be psychic, perfectly pure and non-commercial, and be paid a hell of a lot for what you do. Invariably, the psychics who go about simpering that you cannot perform psychic work for money are in fact the very ones who are tearing about scrounging for readings at five bucks a throw. But they are always uptight about anybody who may be able to command five hundred or one thousand dollars a throw. That, from their point of view, lessens the purity of the act. From my point of view, money frees you. And the more you are paid for what you do the better able you are to do it. Painters, singers, psychics, and lovers may have some very definite hangups in regards to material gain for their efforts, but you cannot say that paintings, songs, psychic experiences, and love affairs don't exist. For, despite whatever personal reactions may exist toward the material gain, the existence, of paintings, songs, love, and psychic experiences tends to remain constant.

In my judgment it is better for me to be paid directly for what I do than to organize a charitable group, have donations made to it, and then siphon off monies to cover my extravagant expenses, as so many psychics feel they must do in order to stay pure."

Psychics should not set themselves up as experts in every field. There are certain areas which I know well because I have taken an interest and studied them for years. And there are other things I know absolutely nothing about. How could I? And why should I?

Though the F.C.C. objects, producers always insist that a psychic on their show make predictions. If I must do so, then I attempt to at least stay within specific areas. I stay away from earthquakes, tornados, hurricanes, etc. In my judgment only *man's* behavior is reliably predictable. Though many psychics do on occasion make a fortunate strike in other areas, it is a shaky business. It would be distasteful for me to be known as a predictor, as I have a low opinion of most of them. Though I have several "good" ones to my credit, I am not known because of my predictions. I have other charms!

Once I almost burned down KFOX in Long Beach. I was doing a show with Ed Perry. We were tormenting a self-ordained minister who claimed he took a trip in a flying saucer. They — the visitors from outer space — were far superior to us in all aspects, he said. Yet when we asked him to describe the decor of the inside of the space ship, his own very bad taste seeped through.

The minister had brought with him for moral support an ex-Army officer, who had also gone for the ride and two prim and proper girlfriends. Halfway through the show, Ed asked me to cast a spell for the listening audience. The spell was to increase sexual vitality in Long Beach. While the minister and his friends held hands and prepared to form a white circle of protection about themselves, I lit the flame. We don't know what happened, but in that very close, very small, and very crowded broadcasting room, suddenly everything was aflame.

Between the fumes of the incense, the billowing clouds of smoke, and our tickled reactions to the minister and company, Ed and I could barely get the fire out or the show ended. We were hysterical. We finally beat it out, and ended on a fairly sensible note — considering our subject matter. The minister was convinced we had conjured up evil.

Sometimes when I go on television I bring my pet beetle, Sandoz. He is very rare, very black, and very beautiful. He is of a primitive species, hard shelled, and appears to have a handtooled backside. He resembles a miniature dinosaur; however, not everyone appreciates him. Once, while I was doing a funny bit with Steve Allen, who had not anticipated Sandoz, Steve reacted most unfavorably to the beetle's sudden appearance. He was visibly shaken.

Another time, while doing the Joey Bishop show, I pulled out Mellissa my pet rat, but I put her back in her gold box when I realized that Regis Philbin was about to keel over in a paralytic trance. She was very cute. I had her for years.

Life magazine took eight months and six photographers to shoot a three-page feature story about me. In the opening shots Mellissa was posed on my shoulder. It was one of our last times together. One of their photographers especially flown in from Milwaukee, decided it would be cute to photograph Mellissa on the lip of a large cauldron. For special effects he brought along dry ice. It was placed in the cauldron, and while I pretended to be tasting soup, he poured hot water over the ice and fanned up clouds of vapor as he shot film.

I'm very angry with *Life,* because not too long thereafter, poor Mellissa dropped dead of a heart attack. It was awful!

During one of the sessions when Mellissa was still alive, another photographer wanted to shoot her sitting on my shoulder. Mellissa insisted upon crawling to my other shoulder. I was wearing a low-cut dress, and soon my cleavage was quite inflamed. We were shooting film for a few hours. Now I loved Mellissa, but I had to face the fact that she lived in a one room studio cage: kitchen, bedroom, living room, and john. I told *Life,* "I'm getting worried. My usually green-tinted flesh is bright purplish red."

Life said, "Don't worry. We're shooting in black and white. It will never show!"

My cat Triska was almost done in by Ralph Story's television crew. When they came to interview me, I was to wear a gown and stand in front of my fireplace. Calm! talking! Upon arrival, they decided to shoot me and Triska outdoors hanging from a tree branch. Each time Triska climbed off the branch, they threw her back up again. I stopped them after the first twenty minutes — but *me* they continued to hang for six hours. Triska is a delicate Burmese. The producer of the show got angry because "Your cat isn't cooperating."

"Look," I said, "I talk. I don't do animal acts."

My beetle is much sturdier. He travels with me everywhere. If Sandoz likes someone, I can be sure they are involved with magic. Sandoz *loved* Merv Griffin, so I knew Merv had to be a wizard and very knowledgeable on the subject of Witchcraft.

A few years ago, Maggie Courion from KABC Television telephoned me with a problem. Eye Witness News was then being run by Baxter Ward who was putting together a special feature on the occult. Maggie said they were having difficulty getting people to demonstrate their ability. I couldn't believe that the psychics in Los Angeles had become timid. I suggested a rather extensive list of names she could call. A few days later Maggie called me again. No luck. Our conversation went something like this.

MAGGIE:　Louise, no one is interested.

LOUISE:　I don't understand that.

MAGGIE:　I've called everyone.

LOUISE:　What did you tell them.

MAGGIE:　Well, I said Baxter wanted me to find some psychics who could do their stuff on camera.

LOUISE:　What does he want? Does he want readings?

MAGGIE:　Baxter said to call you again. Louise, he said if anyone can do it, you can. Baxter wants to film someone bringing back the dead.

Well, if I could do that, I wouldn't have to be writing books for a living.

Later, Baxter canceled his original thought and did a ten day special on witchcraft instead.

I love working on radio and T.V., but there are some sensitives who insist that they will never return to guest on certain programs with one or another host. They believe they have been wronged or in some way ridiculed, or not entirely respected for their efforts. They have insight but no character. Nevertheless, back they go, again and again. They make the same dull responses to the same nonstimulus, which sort of points out that sensitives of the psychic world are not too different from the sensitives of the world of music, or comedy, theater, or of the show biz world in general. The survivors toughen up. Many of the shows, unless the guest is a member of A.F.T.R.A. (American Federation of Television and Radio Artists), will pay the guest absolutely *nothing* for the visit or for the so-called performance! So it must not be the money that brings the guest back time after time.

What motivates the psychic's continued appearances? Why all the guest spots? Is it an indication of spiritual dedication to the profession?

I shall never forget a syndicated talk show in Los Angeles that was hosted by a glib black man who was obviously hung up on the visiting psychic. She wasn't bad, but she was creeping rapidly past the edge of girlhood into early menopause, with only the faint trace of an echo left of what once may have been first shouted through the canyons. Youthful defects are not as obvious and are more easily tolerated. Her smile was humble and her eye downcast as the virile host boomed a list of credits honoring her talents that would have made Nostradamus blush. For a time they discussed the fact that she and the host both got "funny feelings," but they didn't have to convince anyone . . . for it was obvious that they did indeed!

I know this lady. She telephoned me constantly for readings. And she had recently developed her "gift" as a rebuttal to a destiny that had given her two and a half husbands, a runaway teen-age daughter, and an abusive live-in mother-in-law. Hubby's momma was tough. But, there were compensations. She acted as a buffer of clients, screening out potential bunko officers and hopefully scheduling the five-dollar-a-reading psych-ees so that the clever psych-or could squeeze in her laundry, ironing, and cooking and still clear about forty dollars a day. The guest clairvoyant seemed not the least bit harrassed by the confusions I knew to exist in her personal life. And as a gifted clear vessel, the turbulence at home seemed not at all to affect her powers.

She was a regular on the show. And why not? She was free! Hardly an entertainer, and not a member of A.F.T.R.A., she would become grateful and cooperative merely with praise.

The host, in lieu of scale, magnificently thrilled at some of her past predictions of a secret nature. These he declined to discuss except to insist emphatically, "Came true chillun, came true." He hesitated to upset her sensitive balance, and sensitive it was indeed; but despite his tenderness he nevertheless suggested that perhaps as a special thrill for his audience, she might, just might, offer her impressions about the upcoming 1966 Cailfornia gubernatorial race. The psych-orette leaned back on the arms of her chair, swayed a bit from side to side, cast her eyes upward — and sighed. Meanwhile, hostie, sitting as close as his swivel chair and large bony knees would allow, pleaded, "Yes! Yes!" With a tired wan smile, yet a gentle tone (that was a feat in itself, considering her home life), the psych-orette informed the stocky host that the impressions were not her own. They came through her clear and delicate vessel from a higher power. A greater power than herself. The spiritual fountain of truth — Jesus Christ!

And always when Jesus spoke through her pudgy but ever so frail body "It" was always correct. Always! Jesus wasn't to be doubted. And she was not to be praised for His work! That night on syndicated television, before, hoped-for millions, though Reagan later was to win, Jesus picked ex-Governor Edmond G. Brown for re-election!

7

Funny Feelings

Not everyone who gets "funny feelings" is funny! Some pretty well-put-together people have experienced unusual psychic experiences. Happenings that indicated to them that the human mind and nervous and emotional systems do indeed operate in ways that may not be fully understood inside the present framework of scientific understanding.

Surely you have had it happen. You are alone one quiet evening and your thoughts are swirling about in subconscious and primeval levels of pulsating creative activity. Into your complex nerve center, for a brief moment, the face of a relative involves your every reaction, and a few moments later there is a telephone call from that very same relative.

Or perhaps one day, overtaken by melancholia, your heart heavy, you decide to write to a dear distant friend whom you've been too busy to contact for many months. You mail the letter, and about three days later you receive a return let-

ter from this same individual, and you are surprised to notice
that the postmark indicates that the moment you mailed your
letter to this friend the friend had mailed a return letter to
you. And often the similarity doesn't end just there. The letters
touch upon the same thoughts expressing the same ideas. We
know this is a coincidence. But, is it significant? Was there
some mysterious form of communication?

Did one subconscious reach out to another? And is the subconscious not handicapped by distance?

Another time you are happily humming the tune of a song,
zipping around the house dusting furniture, and straightening
up. When you turn on the radio, the song that you have been
humming floods through the airwaves. Or maybe you have
been standing in line for a while at the post office or in the
bank. You are dreaming and staring off into space, when
you become aware of something, you don't know what, and
you start to fidget. Turning around you find that there is
someone, also in line, who is staring blankly into the back of
your head. Coincidence? Or did you turn because you "felt"
something? What was it you felt? Their mental energy?

One evening you crave mandarin chocolate ice cream. You
suppress it. You are dieting, and you don't want to keep
adding pounds. But you really do want some mandarin chocolate ice cream, so around the time you think your husband
will be preparing to leave for home you telephone his office.
Unfortunately, you're a few minutes too late — he has already
left. However, when he does arrive, what is he carrying in an
insulated ice cream bag? Mandarin chocolate ice cream! Or
you think about sauerbrauten all day and when you get home,
what has your wife prepared for dinner? Sauerbrauten!

Do you know what would have happened if you lived back
in the 1500's? A lady named Martha Shipton who lived between 1488 and 1561 found out! She was unfortunate
enough to have been born into this wrong time slot. When

she had her turn, whipping about, getting "funny feelings," the society that she was involved with didn't respond any too well to people who had hunches and intuitive flashes. Martha Shipton was accused of witchcraft. No one will ever know if she was really a witch, but we do know that she had intuitive flashes — quick grasp of what was going on about her. She also wrote poetry. She had very vivid impressions. One of her poems indicates she may have been clairvoyant:

> Around the world thoughts shall fly
> In the twinkling of an eye
> Carriages without horses shall go,
> And accidents fill the world with woe.
> Underwater men shall walk
> Shall ride, shall sleep, and talk;
> In the air men shall be seen
> In white, in black, and in green.
> Iron in water shall float
> As easy as a wooden boat.

It's obvious that she did have some hunch as to what was going to take place in the future, and usually if someone is perceptive, intuitive, psychic, clairvoyant, or what have you, that is not the only thing "wrong" with them. Many times there are other evident differences from the tolerated norm. And these differences are not usually accepted. Martha Shipton wasn't terribly popular! And in the end, her neighbors did away with her. She was accused of witchcraft, tried, and sentenced to death. It's not likely though that her accurate insight could have been based upon chance alone. Even so it's taken four hundred years to vindicate her. What she accomplished was beyond the mere tuning-in to nearby mentalities. Evidently, her energies, her psychic energies, her mental and emotional energies, were able to leap further than her present condition warranted. She let her soul take a wild, extraordinary, exuberant leap into the future.

Unless someone is *born* with a particular ability, it can never become possible to teach methods for developing it. The psychic mentality, not made up of only one or two factors, is the result of an expression of the entire personality.

Much is involved in contributing to its existence. It may be possible one day to determine through in-depth testing, the types of personalities subject to the phenomena, but at present there is no such clear picture available. It springs up everywhere.

Vern Furber is vice-president of Fremantle of Canada, the distributors of television shows in Canada, England, Australia, New Zealand, South America, and the United States. He exhibits a tremendous drive. He is confident, knowledgeable, controlled, and successful. Conversations with him find his answers often preceding your questions. He never forgets anything he has ever seen or heard. He has total recall!

Vern Furber: "I always seem to know things in advance. I don't know if that is considered extra sensory perception, but whatever it is, it does help me in my work. In my most recent encounter the decision so to speak was critical in that it involved a great deal of money. Having had several meetings with the group of top executives of a major chain of department stores concerning future displays and galleries, the question was asked of me, 'How large a gallery do you envision in our main store?'

"Sitting there with six or seven of their people waiting for my answer, I replied, 'I see a circular gallery made up of nine archways, formed from pillars each sixteen feet apart.' Then I went on to describe the plan I had for utilizing them.

The chairman of the group said that he could see I had given a lot of thought to the project and I had obviously even measured that particular area in that department of the store — as the main pillars *were* exactly sixteen feet apart!

"As a result, my reply impressed them a great deal. The truth of the matter is that I had only visited their main store on two very brief occasions. And I hadn't really paid that much attention to the department in question. I wasn't even aware that the pillars in fact — existed.

"I've had many many experiences where I've felt that I've been in the same situation and/or location sometime before. However that is a fairly common sensation — as I have talked to people who have also experienced the same feeling.

"Being in sales and management I'm often called on to make decisions or statements pertaining to whatever it is I am discussing. And often after the fact so to speak I'm amazed at how accurate I was. Possibly this comes from experience — when it relates to my business, but many times I've made statements regarding other matters — where I had no previous experience — and later — time has proven me right.

"Years ago as a time salesman at a radio station, I had a client who was having a major clearance sale at his stores. He had given me the copy points he wished followed and asked me to prepare seven different commercials, each one of which would be run on a certain day of the week.

"We were to prepare the commercials and once completed I was to see the client again and at that time he would then decide on which day, which of the commercials were to be used. The commercials would be run depending on the stock situation in his stores, just prior to the sales.

"The girl at the station, in the traffic department, who was in charge of logging spots, was most annoyed at the manner in which I wanted to handle the account. She demanded to know a few days ahead of my next meeting with my client, which of the spots I would want to place on which of the days. She wanted me to identify them in advance of seeing my client, and number them one through seven, and log number them for specific days. Number one for Sunday, number two for Monday, number three for Tuesday and so on.

"Forced to accept the challenge I sat with her in her office and numbered the commercials. I assured her I would talk the client into accepting our schedule and into adjusting his stock at the stores — accordingly. I felt certain though that after I met with my client and he made his decision I could get the station manager to change the rotation of the spots with the girl in traffic, because as the old saying goes, 'the client's always right.'

"On visiting the client the Thursday prior to the Sunday starting point, I gave him the seven scripts and asked him to number them one through seven in the order he wanted them run.

"He numbered them according to the stock he had on hand and according to the stock he was to receive at the time of the sale.

"To my sheer amazement his numbers were identical to mine. No changes were necessary.

"Since not even the client had been aware of future sequence of sale items . . . this development was really — most unreal!"

Larry Scheer is the world's only telecopter news reporter. He is with KTLA T.V. in Los Angeles. Aggressive. Emotional. Precise. He has not only "tuned in" to others but has experienced projecting thoughts. His mother also had telepathic ability.

Larry Scheer: My psychic experiences have directly concerned the saving of my life, and have been very personal. I have extra sensory perception. And most definitely it has helped me in my work. I have on a few occasions experienced a form of mental communication with very close relatives and friends. I'm convinced many people have this ability, and I personally know some who are genuine psychics.

"Once while flying in Canada I had an interesting experience pertaining to psychic phenomena.

"I was flying over mountains in British Columbia, headed toward the coast. Suddenly a cloud cover came in under me. Under normal circumstances I would immediately come down under the cover, but in this case I could not because of the mountains.

"I was forced to fly at an extremely high altitude without any visibility or knowledge of what might be below me. I had no flight instruments. When I was informed by the radio station in Vancouver, that the cloud bank stretched five hundred miles inland and a thousand miles to the coast, I became worried. I could not sustain the high altitude for very much longer.

"There was no hope of dropping altitude and attempting to land on a mountain top.

"The only thing that could save me was to find an opening in the cloud cover, just above terrain where it would be safe to land. There was no way for anyone to pinpoint an opening.

"At the moment of my greatest anxiety I had a vision, a premonition, a preview, an insight — whatever it can be called. I saw something.

"I saw a clear opening in the clouds. And under it terrain, safe for landing.

"The vision calmed me.

"Instead of pushing the panic button I sensibly continued on calmly waiting. I knew the spot was close by. I headed in the right direction, in order to find it.

"Within fifteen minutes the opening appeared. Below me — exactly as I had imagined — in perfect detail — the landscape of my vision!

"It was my *only* opening in the cloud cover, between me and the coast.

"How had I known where it could be found?"

Perce Anderton, cool, unruffled news commentator for KNBC T.V. in Los Angeles, says that he too has extra sensory perception, and that it most certainly has helped him in his work. He believes he is capable of non-verbal, non-visual non-touch communication with someone he loves. In fact he has regularly experienced this phenomena.

As a trained, nonemotional observer he has witnessed disturbing phenomena that was absolutely not faked and could in no way be explained by any of the current existing scientific forms of logic. In fact — he has been witness to what from all appearances — had to be termed a ghost.

He knows personally genuine psychics.

On the other hand, Hal Fishman, newscaster for KTLA T.V. says he has no E.S.P. — and has never experienced an intuitive link with anyone — not even a dear loved one. He doesn't get hunches. And if he ever did he would probably ignore them. He also says he has never witnessed any peculiar psychic disturbance that was not rigged or that could not be explained logically once investigated. He has never seen a ghost and he knows of no one who he could support as being a real psychic. He says he is neither overly emotional nor overly cool, and places himself somewhere in the middle.

He does however admit to experiencing love!

Isn't love a psychic phenomena?

Art Laing, newsman from KFWB radio in Hollywood doesn't call non-verbal, non-visual, non-touch communication extra sensory perception. For, although he has experienced this phenomena with both relatives and strangers alike, he does not admit to having E.S.P. and believes the phenomena to be within normal boundaries.

He says though that he considers himself to be emotional, but he has never seen a ghost. Sometimes he has "funny feeling," but he prefers to ignore them. And he has never known anyone he could say was a psychic!

Ben Hunter, for years a television talk show host, now at KTTV T.V. in Los Angeles, says he has a rather cool steady approach to psychic phenomena. He does not have what he believes in extra sensory perception, but both he and his wife have been able to communicate on another level (minus the usual senses of sight, sound, and touch), both with each other and with close friends and relatives, but never with a stranger. He said he doesn't get "funny feelings." He has never seen a ghost, and has never witnessed a real psychic disturbance in his environment. Though he supports the existence of E.S.P. and says he knows real psychics, he also says someone like David Frost, or the policeman on the corner, or a lawyer, probably has more extra sensory perception than your average news commentator reading from a teleprompter.

Dick Hatchcock, roving reporter for KTLA T.V. says he believes that extra sensory perception increases in direct proportion to the amount of alcohol consumed. This is probably a valid theory, as evidence does show that when an individual has to some extent removed his inhibitions and has lessened the control of conscious mentality — never mind the method — then there is indeed a gain in extra sensitive awareness.

Ed DeVere, staff writer for the Evening Outlook in Santa Monica, and editor of the weekly editions of the United Western Newspaper in California is highly psychic. He both receives and projects thoughts. Conversation with him is simple. He feels meanings, and communication is not difficult. Yet he calls his insights hunches.

"The 'hunch' that I carry in my back pocket is the source of many good stories. And it sort of just appears at odd and unusual times. It may show up in a strong urge to be somewhere, at a certain time — or to make a call to someone — I have no business calling at that moment.

"Once a few years ago I had a whole series of events that occurred over a period of several weeks. One led to another in unraveling a hell of a good story. I can't explain what happened — but I knew — well in advance — everything that would take place.

"For days I just waited and watched for the string of events to click off. In fact it ended with one of the principals in the case — frightened by my 'insight' actually showing up at my office. And it came to the conclusion that I had known in advance was to be inevitable.

"Take the case of the 'Tate Murders' —. Because I spent more than the usual amount of time talking to a certain police officer — due to a strange feeling that drew me toward him — when the call came through an hour later — about the murders, he thought of me first and telephoned me, and I was the first reporter on the case.

"I do have E.S.P. at times. It has benefited me in my work. I have experienced psychic contacts with friends, relatives and strangers. I tend to pay attention to my hunches.

"I believe myself to be a rational human being — neither completely nonemotional nor overemotional. But, I have never seen a ghost."

My mother has a very potent personality. She sends and receives thoughts. Has a great deal of magnetism. And she tells us:

"I have always had psychic experiences. I remember far back when I was very little my mother and her friends remarking about the different things I said, but I don't remember specifically what they were. I remember the earliest was even before I could read. Listening to the adults I heard that a little girl could not be found, she was missing for quite a while. It was in the papers for perhaps a week or two. I told my mother that I had a dream. In it I saw this girl in an enormous house. It was a great big room. It was nothing like the houses I knew that were made of brick and stone in New York City. In my dream the girl was lying on a wooden table. She was discolored. I told my mother that the little girl was dead. I said they would find her in a couple of days. A few days later the little girl was found. She was in an old abandoned warehouse. She was dead. And the scene was almost to the letter the way I had described it.

"I don't know why but most of my psychic experiences throughout the years have been of people who have met violent deaths. Or of disasters that had no bearing on my life. I have had more psychic experiences with total strangers than with relatives. I would dream of someone being killed in a car accident, and later would read of the accident in the paper. Exactly as I had dreamed it. I would dream of disasters such as earthquakes and later see pictures in the newspaper which were exactly the same as I had seen in my dream. When I was a teen-ager I had dreams of murders which were commited. I didn't know the people involved — but after I related my dreams to my family, then the story would appear in the papers. But there was never any connection with the victims. Once a young boy was in an accident. He lingered for a couple of days in the hospital, between life and death. He was ten years old. I woke up one night and went straight to the window to look out. It was a warm night. I saw him dressed in white, walking down the street, at about two o'clock in the morning. The next day I told my mother that he must have come home, as he had been out walking. Well — he hadn't. We found out later he had died during the night. About 2 A.M.

"For about four or five months I had a feeling of depression. I sensed something would happen. Something sad. For some reason I knew it was to be a death. I didn't know who, where, or when. Yet I knew it would be someone closely related to me. One death did occur, a close friend, and I of course assumed that was it. But one evening, I was enveloped within an overpowering, sickening sweet odor of flowers. Mostly roses and other very heavy perfumed flowers. Somehow this made me sure there was to be another death. Positively! Absolutely! I don't know why it meant that to me. I just knew there would be another death, because of the feeling that I had the past few months. I felt the roses were the clue that a second death was due. This overpowering fragrance of flowers convinced me of the next death. My brother passed away. After he did, I did not have that feeling again. I think the depressions lasted so strongly and for so many months prior to these two deaths, because they were both connected closely with me. The reason my depressions started four months prior to the second death may have ben due to the fact that my brother at that time, discovered he had cancer. Although I was not at that time aware of his problem, my depression did begin at that time! The depression lasted up until the time he died. After that I didn't feel that form of depression. Also just before these two deaths occurred I had dreams about my father almost every night. My father is dead for some time, and during the years I have dreamed of him possibly two or three times. In fifteen years. Suddenly I was dreaming of my father almost every night. This and the depression were at the same time. After the death of my brother and my friend I have not had another dream about my father. Isn't that strange? I knew that he was coming in my dreams for a reason. Another eerie part of this, was that when I purchased a

birthday card for my brother — before I was aware of his illness — I thought: "Next year I won't buy another card for
him — he will be gone."

Perhaps the subconscious understands information that
comes to it, that is not clearly understood by the conscious
mind. If it sensed death, in order to bring the information
up to the conscious level in a recognizable form, might it not
use symbolism? If the intimate loss of a relative had been experienced before — like the loss of a father — it could be
that the sensing of any death in the family would then be associated with the previous experience. Dreams would be the
vehicle toward understanding. The first loss would symbolically represent another death in the family.

As I said before, my husband Mentor is an artist. He paints
in oils. Post impressionistic. He is also an illustrator for motion
pictures. He is involved with a picture's visual concept and
continuity. He designed the chariot race that was responsible
for winning the Academy Award for the picture *Ben Hur*. He
designed Robbie the Robot for *Planet X,* cars for *The Great
Race,* and many scenes for *Funny Girl, Fortune Cookie, The
Longest Day, Trials at Nuremburg, Darling Lily, The Chase,
Fiddler on the Roof, etc.* He is emotional, temperamental,
magnetic, creative.

Mentor Huebner: "I was in San Francisco with another
artist. We had a three-hour wait before the museum opened,
so we went down to an abandoned railroad yard and were

just sketching the old rusted stuff. It had been sitting there for years. I sat on the railroad track leaning with my back against the wheel of a railroad car, sketching some cars in front of me, when suddenly right in the middle of the sketch I stopped, stood up, moved away about twenty feet or so. I never begin a sketch, that I don't finish. I just never do that. In order to discipline myself I always finish a sketch. I never stop in the middle, never. But this time I flipped the page over and started drawing something else. When I was well into the second drawing, and had completely forgotten about the other drawing, suddenly I heard a horrible crash. I looked around, and saw that a train car had broken loose from a way up, about a mile or two, and had come down and hit another car and had knocked it about a block forward. It crashed into the car I had been using as a back rest. I would have been cut right in half. There had been no reason to move at all. I had no apprehension. No anxiety. Nothing. It was a perfectly safe area. Nothing ever moved. The weeds were growing up the middle of the track. It hasn't been used for years. Maybe it was just a coincidence.

"Once when I was a small boy, and herding cows with my Uncle Ernie, he had gone on ahead. We had about fifteen or twenty cows and Uncle Ernie had gone on to drive them back to the ranch. He was a half block ahead of me. I had stopped to look at something. It was a huge field with about waist high alfalfa, or something. Hay or alfalfa. So I started to run across the field to catch up with Uncle Ernie. I was running at top speed and he was quite a ways ahead and over to one side. Then without thinking or anything I threw myself face down. At the tip of my fingers was a well with no cover. It went down about thirty feet. There was stagnant water at the bottom. I don't know how deep. I just sat there and looked at it. Half paralyzed for about two or three minutes. Then I got up. This time watching where I was running, I ran and caught up with Uncle Ernie. At the time I had been afraid he would say something and bawl me out, so I didn't tell him about the well. I don't know why it was that I threw myself face down. I couldn't see anything! I had no normal warning about the well. Only a physical reaction. I could have drowned. There was no doubt of it. No one could have ever heard me. He was too far ahead. They wouldn't have missed me for a long time. No one would have suspected a well in the area. It wasn't a conscious act at all. It was almost total reflex. I didn't have a premonition of danger or anything, I just threw myself face down. The thing that has always baffled me is if I couldn't see it, how did my subconscious know that the well was there . . . that anything was there? It certainly wasn't anything that makes noise or anything that emanated evil."

Pat McGuinness is the news director for radio station KBIG in Los Angeles. He is very respected for his integrity and holds an extremely responsible position in the news media. Pat has received many awards for outstanding work done in his field. He was the first radio journalist to win the Ted Rogers Special Award for writing and producing a documentary on transportation.

He admits to having extra sensory perception. He says it has helped him in his work. Though usually exhibiting rather controlled emotional responses, he has, with loved ones, many times experienced telepathic contacts. And sometimes — though not as frequently — he has experienced the same even with strangers.

As a trained and competent observer he has witnessed psychic disturbances that could not be explained. Disturbances he, with his critical eye, knew could not be faked in any way. However, he has never seen a ghost. He also has never, in all his years of reporting, met anyone he considered to be a real genuine psychic — in the professional sense.

Pat McGuinness: "While doing interviews in the field, I suddenly sense the person being interviewed is lying, no matter how smoothly he has told his story, and invariably I can detect which part of the story being told is erroneous. Some people trying to lie to a reporter are of course obvious, and whether what I have is insight from experience, or E.S.P., I don't know. I just know I have had it happen numerous times during my twenty-two years of reporting and I rely upon it."

He says several times if he has forgotten a script or a tape insert and found himself on the air without it, a colleague, for some unexplained reason, will sense it and bring it into the broadcasting booth. And this always happens if the news transcript happens to be an integral part of the newscast.

There have been many times in Pat's life, however, when experience could not have been the prime factor involved. During World War II Pat was in Italy. He had never before been in Italy. His men and he were under heavy enemy shelling. The situation was one of severe strain. They entered a house. Suddenly, Pat knew every part of that house. He told his men. He seemed to know every room that existed in the house, and where everything was located. There was no explanation for his having that knowledge. Not one of the other men had ever been to Italy and not one had ever before seen the house. There was no way for his subconscious to get the information from any one else present.

Survival of life seems to be a strong catalyst for psychic phenomena. He may have been aware of the house and been led to it because it would offer him protection. How this could occur is not understood.

Another time Pat was covering a Malibu fire. It was New Year's Eve, 1958. Naturally everybody knows fires are dangerous, but besides this common knowledge, Pat was hit with a sense of imminent danger. An urgent feeling to get out of there overcame him, and he did — fast. Within mere seconds the fire roared over the hill and enveloped completely the spot where he had been standing.

Insignificant coincidence? Chance?

Jamelia Levy doesn't believe she has extra sensory perception. At least not in any amount that would be considered out of the ordinary. She is an office worker for a company that administers insurance for labor organizations in Los Angeles. It's a routine job. Except for a flair for drawing, and an appreciation of the arts, Jamelia would seem to be "just like everybody else."

The reason Jamelia doesn't believe that she has any extraordinary perception is because most of the unusual happenings in her life — have happened to other people. Other people have been affected. She is a woman with great emotional strength and a healthy nature. Characteristics of one who is a "sender" of mental energy — not only a receiver.

Jamelia has some very close friends living in Havana, Cuba. They corresponded regularly and for many years had no other contact. One late afternoon when Jamelia returned home from her office, she had an impulse to call her friend Carmen Meilan in Cuba.

It had been years since they had last spoken with each other, and Jamelia never had occasion to use Carmen's phone number. When she first decided to call, she realized that her address book was missing. So, she called the long distance operator in Los Angeles and explained that she needed information for a telephone number in Cuba. At that time she had already spent about an hour looking for the address book.

The Los Angeles long distance operator had to place the call through New York City. The New York City long distance operator attempted to reach the Havana, Cuba operator but was unsuccessful for two hours. When the Havana operator finally responded, she said the telephone number for Carmen Meilan was not listed in the main directory.

The operator in Los Angeles told Jamelia that if she wanted to try to find the number they would keep the line to Havana open so they would be free to put the call through immediately rather than chance another two-or-three-hour wait. Jamelia remembered that Carmen's number was in one of her letters, and she tried to locate the letter while the operator waited.

Under the pressured circumstances she could feel tension mounting — and frustration. Unsuccessful in locating the letter she thanked the operator for her help and said she would place the call at another time. She spent the rest of the evening searching for the letter with the phone number. At about eleven-thirty she decided to go to bed. Up until that time she had re-read every letter Carmen had ever written to her. She went to sleep restless.

The next day at lunch Jamelia visited the public library on the off chance that she might find the telephone number herself. Evidently the operator in Havana had overlooked the number because she found it very easily. When she returned home from work that next afternoon she placed the call a second time. It went through without mishap. She could hear the phone ringing in Havana. On the third ring it was picked up, and Carmen Meilan answered with "Hello, Millie?" (Jamelia's pet name.)

How had she known who was calling at that exact moment? Well, the night before, as the frustrated Jamelia in Los Angeles re-read all of her friend's letters, her friend, Carmen, then asleep in Havana, dreamed Jamelia was trying desperately to reach her and would call her the next evening.

Perhaps Jamelia doesn't have E.S.P. — but she certainly does have something! Jamelia has had many experiences of this nature, involving other people. Always the incident has been

connected with a form of electricity, as with the telephone call
to Havana. Though at that time, the electricity was not directly
related to what happened. At another time it very assuredly
was a prominent factor.

Her cousin who was living in Seattle, Washington, wrote
and asked if a friend from that same state could stay with
Jamelia, while she visited Los Angeles. At the time, Jamelia
was living with her father and his brother. One uncle had just
passed away about six months before and his room was vacant
and served as the guest room.

Jamelia agreed to the visit.

The night that the young guest slept in the uncle's old
bedroom was the first time it had been used in all the years
since the uncle's death. Jamelia went to sleep with the thought
on her mind. She was awakened later by a loud buzzing sound
which she recognized as an alarm clock. As she awoke,
startled, her first thought was, "I bet it's three A.M. Uncle
died at three A.M., and he must be angry someone is using
his bed." She does not know why this thought occurred to
her. Stumbling from bed she followed the buzzing sound
and found that it was indeed coming from the uncle's alarm
clock in the bedroom.

Both she and the young girl were by this time thoroughly
awake as Jamelia entered the room and disconnected the clock
from the wall outlet. She was too sleepy to merely turn off the
alarm. It was just as well, because the next morning when the
two looked at the face of the clock they could see quite
clearly that it had been stopped, when it was disconnected, at
exactly three A.M.! And the alarm pin had not been pulled
out!

I am more inclined to feel that this was a case of mind
energy over the electrical energy of the clock, and not a manifestation of the spirit of the dead uncle.

There have been other unusual occurrences.

Later, when Jamelia's father died, too, she continued to live on with the one remaining uncle. He is quite elderly and had become very forgetful. Since they shared a very large house in an isolated area, it was a worry to her to keep a constant check on the uncle's habit of never locking any of the doors — or for that matter even closing them.

Since he frequently roamed about at night, long after Jamelia went to bed, she was always more or less aware of the problem just before she dozed off for the night. One night, in the middle of the night, a loud buzzing awakened her and the old uncle. Once again following the sound, she was led into the kitchen, only to see that the electric alarm clock on the stove was guilty. As she turned off the clock, she noticed that the back door was not only unlocked, but was also wide open. At this point, you might begin to suspect that Jamelia was cleverly setting the clocks in advance and then forgetting about them later. But, both times others also heard the buzzing, once the guest, once the old uncle, and we are forced to believe the alarms did in fact ring. She *could* have set the alarms to ring, one at three A.M. and one at one-fifteen A.M. and then completely forgotten about it. She would then have truly been startled, along with the other members of the household.

She could have . . . except for one thing. Each time the alarms went off, neither clock had been set for a specific hour. The clock that rang at three A.M. was found to be set for seven. And the clock that rang at one-fifteen A.M. was permanently set for six.

Why then did the alarms ring when they did?

If we are to attribute precognition to a subtle and unrecognized transference of ideas from one subconscious to another, we are then at a loss to explain incidents that are not directly related to a human factor. Those incidents that are part of natural disasters.

Pat McGuinness, in the Malibu fire, may have been given the "thought" of impending danger — from any stranger located in the area, who may have been aware of the fire's direction. It would not be necessary for either of them to be visible to the other. Nor in any way connected. Yet if the "knowledge" existed anywhere at all — just moments prior to Pat's awareness — the precognition, insight, is at least reasonable.

One morning while my husband and I were driving in Italy, I screamed, "Look out!" I had seen a truck coming at us, head on. And because I screamed, Mentor pulled over, and at that instant a truck did come up over the top of the hill straight at us, head on! We were on a bridge and the road abruptly turned down, and though it was a huge truck you could not have seen it while on that bridge. Impossible! At the moment I screamed, we couldn't see the truck. And in the winter, with the car windows rolled up and the radio going, there could not have been any other indications that the truck was coming. But all of a sudden the truck appeared, two-thirds on our side of the road, and there's a forty- or fifty-foot drop down to the river! He was two-thirds over into our lane. Mentor slammed on the brakes and hit the horn, and as he hit the brakes and the driver responded to the horn, both stopped. The huge truck wheel, about five feet tall, had stopped just inches from the radiator of our car. I had screamed prior to the truck being visible. If I hadn't, we could all be dead now.

Maybe the case of the truck in Italy exists in the realm of "shared knowledge." Though *we* were not aware the truck was on the road the driver of the truck knew it, even in his stupor. Some part of him was aware that he was veering into the wrong lane. So, though he may not have given too much attention to his knowledge of the circumstances, I certainly was alerted by my "tuning" into his "knowledge" and reacted immediately. And maybe with the runaway train car someone two miles back saw it get loose.

Most of the cases can be explained by the theory of "shared knowledge." All, that is, except the case of Vern Furber in Canada and his ability to list and date correctly seven commercials at a time when we are sure that no "knowledge" about them existed, and again, in the cases of people who accurately predict earthquakes.

On May 16, 17, and 18, my father told me there would soon be a devastating earthquake in South America.

He said he "felt it" very "strongly."

"Daddy, come on now. How can you 'feel' an earthquake?"

I could understand his "feeling" that I should not fly to Boston when on the day I was scheduled to fly the plane's pilot was shot. He could have "tuned in" a few days prior to the plan for the highjacking, though even that, we must admit, is an achievement. But how do you "tune in" to an earthquake? Daddy said each time before, whenever he had "felt" this same way, there had . . . always . . . been an earthquake.

"Wait and see Cissie, one is coming, and it's the worst one they have had in a long time!"

I don't know how daddy could have known, but on May 31, 1970, two weeks after our talk, a terrible disaster hit just outside of Lima, Peru in South America. The two towns of Chimbote and Yungay were completely destroyed by earthquake!

Could this sort of knowledge "exist" somewhere in a form we are at present unable to understand? How did daddy tune in?

My sister Marie's mother-in-law, Anne Strickland, had an earthquake-oriented experience when my brother-in-law Larry was just a baby.

Anne Strickland: "I don't remember when the earthquake was, but we were living in Huntington Park. We really got hit hard there. We heard this rumbling, we were all at the table eating. I grabbed Larry, he was just a baby, and Eddie, and I started running. All I wanted to do was run. I heard this rumbling — the house started going. It was swaying, and making cracking noises. It was about to fall in on top of us. I wanted to run out the front door fast. But their dad caught me. He wouldn't let me go. I thought he was crazy. As he pulled me back into the house the whole chimney came down right outside the door. Right where we would have been if he hadn't grabbed me. We would have been under that pile of bricks. To think I fought him! I really fought him. Because I wanted to get out of there. I believed the house was going to fall on us, and I wanted to get outside. He had to struggle with me to keep me in. I'm glad he did!"

My brother-in-law Larry and his father shared yet another earthshaking phenomena.

Larry Strickland: "My dad and I were hunting. We stopped to camp overlooking a cliff: My dad kept looking at me and then he said he didn't want to stay at that spot. He looked worried. It was a very nice place — but he said that if we sat there and there was an earthquake, the entire area would go down. Now that's crazy. Who would be expecting an earthquake? But he insisted we move. In fact he practically physically forced me to move. He said — 'Let's get the hell out of here!' I swear to God, no sooner had we moved when the ground shook and the whole side of that cliff fell off down into the canyon."

8

The Ghost and Mrs. Huebner

Almost unnoticed
Like a muffled sound from before
Or a sudden flash
A sight from way over there
Somewhere;
With a light brush against my skin
It will begin.
Then a deep warmth captures my every part
And as the pulse quickens
And wild winds circle my heart
There is a rush
A swoop up from some secret place
And my body
Caught between time and space
Delights
In a ghost's embrace.

—*Louise Huebner*

FIGURE IX   *THE HAUNTED*

A sudden slight chill, a distant train whistle, a lonely call of a heartsick dove, a drying settling house, sounds in the brush, and even astigmatism serve to add to the legend of ghostery.

Have you ever *seen* a ghost?

It has always been my good fortune to never see what I would consider to be a real live ghost. Oh, there have been *things* no doubt that could be classified in the category of eerie happenings. But, I, not believing in a return from, or a life after death, have never attracted anything which I felt could not be happily explained in a sensible and rational manner.

If I am mistaken, and at a very much later date should myself return from the "other side," I shall be the first one to drop dead — from shock!

We live in a haunted house. At least everyone else says it is haunted. Even my husband says it is haunted. And I believe it probably is about as haunted as any house could possibly be. But, by what? And, with what? And from whom?

When we first came to live here, it had all the character of a house that should be full of spooks. The house was overrun with vines, night-blooming jasmine, honeysuckle, primrose and wisteria. You could not see the front garden from the street, and you could not see the front door from the front garden. Inside was worse! Decorated in khaki greens and tomb browns with ochre shades, no sun entered from anywhere. Huge black lizards covered the outer walls, and gray rats raced from treetop to treetop occasionally falling onto the roof. The place had gone wild.

Perhaps we felt an empathy for the house, since the original owners and builders of the house had been, by strange coincidence, a writer and a collector of oil paintings. They were three times older than we. After we moved in we were to hear unsupported rumors to the effect that there had been a series of mysterious, unnatural deaths connected with the owners' intimate family. Soon after we purchased the house the first owners passed away, and we were unable to probe with any certainty into what may have been the truth.

We had come upon the house in an odd manner. I was expecting our first son, Mentor Frederick, when we impulsively called a broker and asked to see some places up on the hill. We made an early appointment. The broker, Mr. Baker, drove us to one rambling house not too far from where we now live. We were impatient and told him that it was not the place. Next he drove us to our house. When we pulled up in front, all we could see were the stone steps leading up to the garden.

Mr. Baker informed us we wouldn't like the place. It was old and dark, and had been vacant for two years. It wasn't moving on the market and it wasn't renting well, yet at the instant we parked, I wanted the house. My husband, trying to act cool in order to get down the price and to keep me from suspecting his infatuation with the place, also wanted the house. We had both silently decided to grab it before we even left the car.

We went through the motions of wandering about — complaining about the rundown conditions and needing time to think. Within six weeks we were signed, sealed, and moved in. Six weeks after that our first son was born.

The lizards took awhile, but our collection of cats soon scared off the rats. At the end of a year the place started to brighten. However, by the third year the hauntings began.

First, we had an oppressive sensation in the dining room. We painted it white and cleared the vines away from the window, but we could not eliminate the feeling that all was not well. Finally, upon removing the dining room door we seemed to relieve the problem, at least temporarily.

The entrance hall is in the center of the house. It is impossible for any light to reach it from the highway as we are twelve hundred feet up on top of a small mountain. The only highway we can even suspect is over on the other side of town, yet we had "lights" moving across the wall that appeared to be car lights from a road. Either they were not car lights, or they were beaming in from a wall that had no window.

Next, the den off the living room developed into a bit of a trouble area. Whenever anyone entered the room, the door would swing closed. This was a bit unnerving. Especially to our guests visiting overnight. The floor did not slant. We had a carpenter study the situation. Various technical things were done that cost money and solved nothing. No matter what. Even with a stopper — the door would close. We removed the door!

Inasmuch as whatever was happening, happened only with the door, we figured no door, no happening. I don't know where it went or what the ghost may have reverted to for kicks, but our guests are happier.

In the beginning it was the front part of house that acted up. And the only noticeable disturbances that took place in the bedroom areas were the children. I don't mean ours. At the time of the annoyance, we had just the one boy. Mentor Frederick would be put to bed at seven. At eight I would catch a glimpse of him running across the hallway. After giving him several extra chances at shaping up, when I went to firmly set him straight — I would find him heavily and soundly asleep.

This could have been attributed to distorted vision, and would be much easier to understand, if I alone had seen him racing about, but my husband would catch a glimpse also, and so would any other person who was around at the time. We couldn't all have the same eye problem. No one could explain it.

I believe Mentor Frederick has a fantastic energy and sense of self, so that even at the age of three he was able to project his presence into an environment and make himself known, if only for a second!

During our seventh year of ownership the ghosting got down to business. We arrived home from a two-year stay in Europe; we brought home twin babies but the house beat us to it and had already developed a few extra entities of its own.

My husband was the first to spot the ghost. A She. *She* would shuffle down the corridor, beginning from the children's bedroom, pass the bathroom door and stop short of the entrance hall. She always came from the back toward the front of the house, and never reversed direction. It usually happened while Mentor was shaving. Always he would check the household. And always he would find us all sound asleep!

For one year, Mentor alone heard the ghost. While he was amazed no one else was ever in on the phenomena, I was amazed I had married a nut who had managed to keep it quiet for so long. Then, one night, very late, I was writing in the dining room, when I believed I heard Mentor Frederick creeping down the hallway. Calling to him to go back to bed, I realized it was the sound of a woman, shuffling down the hallway, wearing huge furry slippers. Just in case though, I asked, "Mentor, is that you or the ghost?" The shuffling continued. I raced over to look. The noise stopped. Everyone was sound asleep.

Since then our overnight guests hear her. The housekeepers hear her. And believe me, when we hire houskeepers, we don't tell them ahead of time that she is around.

Only once, though, has she been heard coming and going at the same time. That was when my husband was in Europe working on the motion picture, *Darling Lily*. My friend Elaine Davis was spending a couple of weeks keeping the children and me company. The night it happened, we had stayed up until four in the morning working on my press releases for the Hollywood Bowl spell cast. Elaine had just gone to bed in the front of the house, and I, in my bedroom in the back of the house. We must have both just closed our eyes when I heard Elaine get up and walk down the hallway toward the bathroom, and Elaine heard me walk up the hallway to the bathroom, and at the same instant.

I said, "Is that you Elaine?"

And she said, "Is that you Louise?"

We were both up in flash, and not bothering with slippers and robes, we searched the entire house, making certain everyone was sound asleep. They were! But we stayed up until after dawn.

There are other occurrences: The smell of decaying roses in the center of the living room — at odd times of the year — coming from nowhere; a woman sighing in fatigue; a woman crying; there have been exploding light reflections in the entrance hall. Hammering, hard and loud on the roof, and heavy-booted clumping about; closet doors have jerked open; and loud knocking on the bedroom door — by someone who would have to be eight feet tall!

LOUISE: Honey, tell about the Christmas ghost!

MENTOR: O.K. We were lying in bed wide awake . . . .

LOUISE: Wait a minute!

MENTOR: What?

LOUISE: No . . . . Honey —

MENTOR: What do you mean "No?"

LOUISE: First of all, sweet, can I begin it? First of all, we were asleep. Sound asleep!

MENTOR: What do you mean . . . asleep?

LOUISE: Maybe we're talking about two different times. Are you talking about Christmas Eve?

MENTOR: The knock on the door?

LOUISE: Yup? We *were* asleep, and I heard the ghost go down the hallway. The usual one. The footstep one. So I didn't pay any attention to it, because we always hear footsteps down the hallway. Then after I heard the footsteps down the hallway, three times, I then poked you, and I said, "Mentor, the ghost has gone down the hallway three times. Usually it only goes once. Wake up."

MENTOR: I said, "Cut it out ghost."

LOUISE: Then you sat up in bed, and when we were both sitting up in bed, we heard the ghost go down the hallway for the fourth time. You were then wide awake. And I had been awake and hearing it for three separate times. When you heard it, that was already my fourth time! And your first time to hear it! Right? At least for that night! Now, while we are both sitting up in bed wide awake — what happened?

MENTOR: O.K. O.K. Then . . . at the very top edge of the bedroom door . . .

LOUISE: Yes, at the very top of the edge of the corner of the bedroom door . . . .

MENTOR: At the top of the *corner* of the door . . . .

LOUISE: If you're about eight feet tall . . . KNOCK . . . KNOCK . . . KNOCK. On our bedroom door. It's not the outside street door . . . .

MENTOR: We were both wide awake!

LOUISE: So we thought for sure . . . it's the kids. Pamela, my cousin, was over with her friend Susan. And my grandmother's over. And our housekeeper Zoila and her husband, Nichito from El Salvador. About eleven people are in the house for the night. It's Christmas Eve. Our first impulse is that somebody's up. So we get up and we investigate. The whole household is sound asleep. The next day we are scaring the hell out of everyone, telling them all about the ghost knocking at the door. Nichito, who is very, very dark, dark tan, turns greenish white. They were sleeping in the bedroom downstairs. The one that opens out to the patio. And there was knocking on their door too! Only their door is an outside door.

MENTOR: Same knocking!

LOUISE: He woke Zoila up, and she says "Go to sleep — it's the dog." He says dogs don't knock at the door —.

MENTOR: Not at the top corner of the door!

We have all heard loud pounding on the front door while the screen door was locked. It would be impossible to reach the wood door unless the screen door were open. And once and only once, while I was standing in the entrance hall talking to my housekeeper Consuelo, preparing to leave for a program and wildly brushing my hair, I saw a tall man dressed in black walk across the corridor.

I believed it was a visual trick based upon my rushing about and brushing my hair — however, Consuelo saw him too.

But I still don't think he was a ghost. I believe my eyes played a trick, and in the moment of my surprise I may have transmitted the sight telepathically to Consuelo.

I don't believe in ghosts! But my mother does!

When she was a very young child, she had a dream about her grandmother. This grandmother was the psychic one. In fact she is one in a line reaching back to my grandmother's great-grandmother. When my mother's grandmother appeared in her dream, she told my mother she had come to say goodbye, because she was dying. And she asked my mother to be sure and tell her "Mommie" first thing in the morning — and her aunt. The aunt lived a short distance away.

She told my mother she had come to say goodbye because she would be dead by morning. My mother told her grandmother that her mother and her aunt would not believe her. But her grandmother said she would leave proof. In the morning all the pots and pans in the kitchen cupboards would be on the floor. The next morning my mother told her mother about the vision. She didn't have to tell her about the pots and pans. My grandmother had been awakened during the night by the sound of them falling out of the cupboards.

Now maybe, in some way, my mother could have been responsible for the pots. Or maybe she heard the pots falling during the night and then made up a story — except for one thing! Her grandmother did die that morning, and across town, my great aunt awakened to the same condition in her kitchen!

When my sister Marie was eleven years old she was frightened by a dream that left her cold. In it, our paternal grandfather was pounding on her bedroom window, angry and trying to get in. The next day we received a phone call that three thousand miles away he had died during the night.

Another time my mother arrived home from shopping and hurriedly opened the door to the kitchen only to find her Uncle Martin lying on the floor, dead. She screamed and dropped her bags, and Uncle Martin disappeared. He was found later in his own kitchen — dead from a heart attack.

Perhaps these may be termed ghosts. But are they the dead come back? Or are they the living dying? I am convinced that in the last moments, emotional communication is possible. In the crisis of dying, the self longs to make contact and be known.

Several years ago I found myself melancholy for a week. I could not pull myself from a dreamy, drifting, distracted state. Far away — I could feel myself slipping into a quiet state that caused me to feel as though I were very far away.

I told my husband that I knew from the quiet and the sensation of distance that someone of my flesh and blood was about to die. Someone old, someone far away, someone female. Don't ask me how I knew the mood to mean anything so specific. That week my grandmother — my father's mother — three thousand miles away, died. Later, we were told she had become increasingly ill just that last week.

Perhaps I had tuned in to my father's thoughts and his knowledge of the situation. No doubt his melancholy reached me.

When I was in Cleveland, Ohio, for a business meeting concerning production of a television show, I had an odd experience. There were five of us in the hotel conference room. The room was large and airy, and pleasant. Everything was running smoothly. Suddenly, I felt choked up, and breathless. I felt uncomfortable stabbing pains in my heart. I thought it could be the heat — it was hot and humid outside even though it was comfortable indoors. Becoming more uncomfortable, I excused myself and went up to my own room.

A strange mood of remoteness came over me. And I felt compelled to telephone home to Los Angeles. When I did, my husband told me that my mother had just called him about a close friend who had just died of a heart attack. At the time of my discomfort she had received the message about the death.

What I felt was in essence a ghost, a ghost of a heart attack. The form is different, but isn't the principle the same?

Mentor: "As for ghosts . . . I've heard them. I don't know. I don't think they could all be audio-hallucinations. I kind of think that it's some form of energy. Unexplained energy. But why it takes the form of footsteps, or a voice is something I can't comprehend. An experience that really stays with me, that I recall most of all, is once late at night, I was in the john, and when I turned to leave, opened the door and turned out the light at the same time, and had just started to take a step forward, I noticed as I did that there was nothing there! A black opaque nothing! I couldn't see across the hall which is only three and a half feet, or four feet wide. And I couldn't stop the reflex of my hand as I had already switched off the light. I switched the light on immediately and took a step back at the same time . . . because I had the feeling that I would fall forever. As I did that, the hall was perfectly clear. I could see across the hallway again. When I had opened the door, simultaneously with the opening of the door, I had my hand on the light switch ready to turn it off, and as I started to step out, it seemed I wasn't stepping into the hallway, I was stepping into a black opaque void. It was so startling. It was almost as though I had gone unconscious, but I could still see the edge, the frame of the doorway, yet as my hand had already started its downward movement with such a fast flick to turn the light out I couldn't stop it. When I immediately flipped the light on as I stepped back — there was the hallway perfectly visible again! If it were my eyes, I would not have continued to see the door frame, or the inside of the bathroom. In this case only the outside was gone. Into some sort of black opaque mass. I had not blacked out. It was not an eye defect. What in hell would create a thing like that? I could still see the frame of the doorway. Past the frame of the doorway was the black mass where the hall should be. Yet I could still see the door frame. Why should I be able to see the reality of the door in a normal way — yet not the reality of the hallway? I guess I've got to stay out of that bathroom!

"One other time, all I saw was a foot in a slipper. That's all there was to it. I could see that it was a foot. A bare foot. I turned suddenly at a noise, and I saw a foot with a slipper just disappearing past the frame of the door. I immediately looked and there was nothing there."

My mother adds her experience: "The three children and the maid were out in the yard playing, and I was in the kitchen drinking coffee, when I heard the children running back and forth through the corridor, and I thought for heaven's sakes, the girl had just washed and waxed the floors! So I told them to, 'cut that out. If you keep that up you are all going to get it.' But back and forth! Back and forth! It continued. I thought, 'Now that's something, all my talking, and no one pays any attention. I'll just march them straight out . . . . ' As I'm going towards the hall to murder the one who's running around, I pass a window and realize all three of them were in the yard with the maid. Who was it running through the hall?"

Most people claim to have *felt* a ghost. Others have *heard* a ghost. Some have insisted they have *smelled* a ghost. When dealing with the sensations anything is possible.

Scientists agree something does indeed take place that can be interpreted as a ghost. A theory exists that suggests that the "disturbance" is an extension of energy emanating from a living dynamic source.

The human subconscious is able to surpass the Arabian Nights and Grimm brothers in originality. But just because some apparitions are quirks of someone's indigestion, the possibility remains that some others may be real honest . . . ghosts!

What is a ghost?

A ghost is a condition that disturbs the norm with vibrations creating sensations of smell, touch, sight, and sound,

that are considered to be unrelated to the particular environment, and that seemingly originate from sources impossible
to trace or recognize.

Jim O'Daniel: Costume designer for *Hello Dolly,* tells a
fascinating tale: "Well, if anyone was ever to ask me whether
or not I believed in ghosts, I'm afraid that up until just a couple of years ago I would had to have answered quite emphatically, 'No!' But now I'm not so sure what it is that I can so
positively *not* believe in.

"When I was twelve, I had a nightmare that my uncle, with
whom I felt a close rapport, was all in flames. I woke up the
entire household with my screaming. Finally my mother got
everyone settled down again — but about an hour later the
phone rang — and we were informed that my uncle had just
died in a fire which had destroyed his entire house. The exact
details of his death were never made clear. There was a
question, at that time, of his having been murdered, and of
the fire having been set as a cover up. But nothing was ever
proven, and the police eventually were forced to close the case.

"My grandfather had been shot and killed just two years
before. He was at dinner with guests and in full view of the
guests, while seated at the dining room table — and had been
shot. This case was also never solved. Although the next day
his business partner dropped dead of a heart attack, and it was
later discovered that many thousands of dollars had been
embezzled from the business, nothing was ever really proven!

"Then when I was eighteen, and at college, one night I
woke and saw a luminescent object seated at the edge of my
bed. I called to my roommate — and when he woke up he
said, 'Christ, what's that sitting on your bed' — So he had seen
it too! We never could figure out what it was all about — and
after awhile we both preferred to forget about it.

"Except for those two rather odd experiences, I have never

been too terribly turned on to ghosts, or E.S.P., or for that matter any other form of psychic phenomena, until two years ago.

"One night a couple of casual acquaintances invited me along with them to attend a seance. At the time we were all working on *Hello Dolly*. A young girl presided over the activities and was I guess what you would call a medium. She began by describing a man — stocky, not quite five feet in height. She said he was a relative of mine. That his face was very hot. Then she said he was in a fire — and then she said he was murdered.

"Well, I went into shock! No one — no one I was with knew anything at all about this uncle.

"The medium told me my uncle wanted me to help him. She said he wouldn't rest in peace until the killer was punished. At the time of the seance I was twenty-nine and it had been seventeen years since my uncle had died in the fire, and eleven years since I had seen the luminescent object (whatever *it* was) in college.

"The ghost or whatever, made up for his original lassitude over the following two years. During the two years that followed the seance I saw a luminescent object four separate times. But it was all the rest of what happened that was worse.

"I have my workshop in the front of the house, and either I, or my secretary, Betty, or the fellow who sews for me, has access to it, besides of course the maid.

"Always late at night we would hear footsteps behind us. When we would turn — no one was ever there. Betty did not know about the seance. So there was no reason for her to start hearing ghosts. But it got so bad she refused to work if she had to be alone.

"Cold hands would rest on our shoulders. The maid was positive someone was breaking into the house, because of

all the strange footsteps. Small complaints began piecing together, and I realized we had a haunting on our hands.

"Sometimes my downstairs tenants would hear me walking
around and come up to see me — only to find no one at home.
One night I came home late — and found the lights on all
over the house and the front door wide open. I had left the
fellow who sews for me working — and when he heard the
ghost he panicked and ran out. And he too, had not known
about the seance.

"I had never heard of this sort of thing happening before —
so I wasn't sure how to handle it.

"Then I panicked one night — when I was working late.
You know how you can feel someone walk in behind you.
Well I felt a presence in the room, but I kept working because
I thought it was the tailor.

"When I heard the tailor ask me, 'Who is Frank Seymour?'
I turned and asked back, 'Frank Seymour?' And realized
there was no one there. That did it! Calling my mother long
distance and in the middle of the night, I asked her if Frank
Seymour was anyone who could have been connected with us.
She said my grandfather once had a next-door neighbor with
that name — in fact just at the time of his murder.

"What's so confusing about this ghost — is that at the time
of the seance, a man was described to me who resembled my
uncle. The shortness, the fire, etc. But my uncle lived in a
different state than my grandfather — and the man Frank
Seymour was a neighbor of my grandfather.

"So it seems we have two ghosts all rolled up into one.

"Since this was an odd occurrence — and there never has
been any prescribed method known, as to how to handle it, I
called in a medium. The medium came to my home — and
told the ghost or ghosts that the case or cases were closed. A
ghost's suspicions were not enough evidence for the police to
become interested and although we would truly want to help,

it was just impossible. If 'it' continued I would lose my tenants, my maid, my secretary and my tailor — ! Please! If the ghost cared for me at all — would it go away?

"Please!

"It did.

"The hauntings stopped."

Many "ghosts" have been handy and have guided worthy friends to buried treasure, lost or stolen money, and rich deposits of minerals . . . or gushing oil wells. Some ghosts stick around a place because they owned it first. That's O.K.! Too, some ghosts have been known to save lives by appearing during critical moments (much like Superman) and have prewarned potential victims of exciting events to come, such as: derailed trains; washed-out bridges; head-on truck collisions; fire in the basement; fire in the attic; exploding gas heaters, hot water tanks, boilers, furnaces, and land mines. Others concentrate upon the dangers involved with rabid dogs, polluted water, earthquakes, hurricanes, tornadoes, the striking of lightning, shipwreck . . . and the stock market. And an occasional ghost has even generated enough energy to burst upon the scene and succeed in pointing out the killer of their own physical self.

A ghost with a dynamic cause is a ghost to respect. A ghost with a reason is believable, and can be respected. Ghosts can be wonderful! But what of the unexplained ghost-like occurrences that happen for absolutely no reason at all?

What of the case where a ghost was reported to repeatedly hammer on the roof over a bedroom? It warned of no immediate danger. It warned of nothing. Absolutely nothing! Nothing ever happened after the hammering that could be considered to have been of any ghostly interest.

Upon checking the probable causes for the knockings, no real reason could ever be discovered — neither for the sound, nor for the ghost or ghosts. Yet, it had to be considered a ghost. What else could it have been? As far as is known, no one had ever lived in the house who died. Or to put it another way, no one died who ever lived in the house.

Usually it is accepted, that if a ghost visits a location, it is no doubt in some way related to the home, the furniture, the personal items, or the present occupants. That seems to be the popular view. But if no one is connected with a place in any way, or with the ground the home stands upon, why should they come back as a ghost and haunt it? Why should they shuffle down the hallway toward the bathroom, always heading in the one direction? What do the footsteps indicate: why do they appear dozens of times each year, year after year, and without a reason?

Should the ghost of a tall man, dressed in a tuxedo, appear, cross a hall rapidly, and disappear again if he or "it" hasn't any decent reason to manifest?

After much investigation proving that a house does not have a slanted floor and that there is no draft near the site that could be responsible, why then do doors swing closed by themselves and engulf the inhabitants in an oppressive and sickening atmosphere? What could it mean when an odor of decaying roses rises up as a column in the center of a living room . . . remain for several hours . . . fade . . . and then return again either the next day, next week, next month, or next year? What does it all mean?

Allowing for the possibility of the existence of ghosts, a practical mind would only expect a ghost to project into the now in response to some traumatic emotional experience, some unfinished business, a psychic tie or some feeling of responsibility towards the ghost-ee! It seems a terrible waste of energy, and a sad thing, too, for a ghost to wander about where it never lived in the first place, spending an entire death on insignificant hauntings.

A goalless ghost is pathetic.

Whatever do they get out of shuffling down the hall to the john? . . . smelling like roses. Why the need to slowly close doors? Why the sighing?

The thought occurs that these unnecessary ghosts may have played out a similar role when in the flesh, being unoccupied unnecessary beings. Busy at nothing, butting in where they didn't belong, wasting time, and shuffling about, smelling up the place.

Before we fall into a depressive breakdown due to the contemplation of the futility of a retarded spirit, let's consider the alternative. Researchers say there is now adequate support for the theory that a ghost is a disturbance within an environment that can be traced to the release of uncontrolled psychic energy stemming from an emotionally immature, highly romantic and impulsive nature.

Oops . . . there is someone knocking on my ceiling again!

GREGORY: When I was walking down the hallway to my room, to take off my clothes and put on my playclothes, out from the paintings in the corner of the hall, I saw a man, running. A little man, just my size, but a little bit bigger. He ran across the room. I think it was a ghost.

MOMMIE: Jessica, have you ever seen a ghost?

JESSICA: Nope!!

MOMMIE: Have you ever seen a little man as Gregory described?

JESSICA: Forget it. No!

MOMMIE: Do you believe in ghosts?

JESSICA: No!

MOMMIE: Gregory says you believe in monsters — is that true?

JESSICA: He better be quiet or I'll sock him!

MOMMIE: Well, do you?

JESSICA: Yeah . . . .

MOMMIE: You do believe in monsters? Well, what's the difference between a monster and a ghost?

JESSICA: They're more hairer than a ghost and you can't see through them.

9

A Dream by Any Other Name!

I dreamed
I entered a sea shell.
A brilliantly colored sea shell.
Pale lavenders and blues.
Its walls were smooth . . . and cool
A golden haze filled this domain
And faintly . . .
As if from afar . . . Heavenly music played.
And a soft and silken voice . . .
Urgently called my name.
I traveled on . . .
Through intricate corridors that formed a maze
I lost all count of time . . .
And all sense of reality that was once mine
Soon I came upon the center of its being
A small and darkened lonely room
The sea shell's very core.

Within this room peace descended
Dimmed was the ocean's roar
I knew when I emerged into life's stark sunlight
I would be much changed
For in the center of its being
In its small and darkened lonely room
Where all of time stood still
For a brief moment
While listening to the music of the sea
I . . . . was me.

—*Louise Huebner*

When daily tensions interfere with awareness, often in a dream, the subconscious has opportunity to present symbolic fortification in order to attract attention. If moods are thrown off, ignored, and relegated to an "it's nothing" category, then dreams may force a more insistent recognition of certain facts and truths.

All dreams mean something. What is chosen as dream material is significant. However, the degree of significance and the value of the interpretation of this significance is sometimes questionable. Throughout history there have been countless cases of prophetic dreams that support telepathic communication between individual consciousnesses. It may be that in such a relaxed condition as exists in sleep vulnerability is increased.

Dreams frequently utilized as a method for tension releases and means of psychologically coping with daily problems have, at times, clearly outlined events that, at the time of the dream, in no way existed as a potential, in any form.

FIGURE X A DREAMER AT ELEVEN

Yet, at other times, have obviously been the result of psychic communication.

I have experienced two dreams that are examples of these two origins.

Early in June 1961, I dreamed I gave birth. I saw the hospital rooms in great detail, and relived a childbirth completely. When the baby was born, I was wheeled back into my room, but my doctor breathlessly arrived and once again wheeled me into the delivery room. In my dream I said, "I've just had a baby." And he said, "Yes, but you're going to have another one!" At the time the dream didn't mean anything to me. But when I found out later I was pregnant, and with twins, I realized that it had been a very strange dream. I dreamed through two complete childbirths. It was especially significant because even though we already had one child, I had never before dreamed I was giving birth — and never did again. The twins were born the following February 28, nine months after my dream took place.

Obviously it was an intuitive dream. Since at the time of the dream I was not more than one week pregnant. Could the body recognize changes that the subconscious is then able to interpret?

Since I had dreamed of the births at a time when I was pregnant (I was not then consciously aware of this fact even though it had been in existence for only one week or, at the most, ten days), the dream could have found its origin in subtle body changes — changes that the subconscious could recognize and interpret from my past experiences, changes that were still too new for the conscious mind to notice.

My second experience occurred after our return from Europe. I dreamed that I was with my husband and our three children. We were seated on a wooden bench in what seemed to be a train station. We were obviously traveling, and except for the fact that in my dream we were completely underwater, there was nothing frightening about the dream. I accepted the conditions, yet dreaming it, I "knew" it was a nightmare. Seated in the station with us were several thousand people. I recognized no one.

It was the kind of dream that comes across like a movie. I could see myself as I saw the others. Walking up and down the aisle directly in front of us was an old woman, European type. She was wearing a dark shawl over her head and shoulders. She was obviously distressed. There was a silent understanding between us, and she softly wailed and moaned about the other people who were present. "They don't even know, they don't even know they are dead — so fast they died, they never knew, they never knew."

The only odd condition of the dream, was that it was taking place underwater. And, another strange fact was that the woman appeared to be a giantess. She looked twenty feet tall.

I woke up in a panic. Although the dream haunted me for days, I could find no meaning in it.

Later, there was a disaster in Italy, and afterwards in *Life* magazine there was a two-page photograph of the area. It was a town in Italy in the Brenner pass. A dam broke in the middle of the night, and everyone was lost, everything destroyed. In the foreground of the photograph was my old woman wearing the shawl. She was standing on a hillcrest. In back of her was all of the destroyed area that had been underwater. My dream and the photograph in *Life* were, except for location, exact in detail.

I could have accepted the phenomena if I had the dream *after* the photograph was taken (existing knowledge). But I had the dream before the disaster took place. There was no real tie between us and that town. During two years we had lived in Europe we had visited the location. It was a beautiful, peaceful spot. We had stopped only long enough to eat lunch and to purchase bottled water in a pharmacy, for our babies. And we had walked about, admiring the scenery.

As we stood on the bridge overlooking the dam, and the magnificent splendor of the landscape, Mentor had said he would like to return one day and paint the view.

One year later to the day of our visit — the dam broke!

Abraham Lincoln is an excellent source of psychic experiences. He was a psychic. On the afternoon preceding his assassination, during a much needed nap that he hoped would prepare him for the evening's festivities, he had a prophetic dream. He dreamed he awakened, and, hearing sobbing and crying, he followed the sounds into the hallway toward a sitting room. Opening the doors into the darkened room, dimly lit by candles he saw a coffin. Lifting the lid, he saw that he was lying there, dead.

Lincoln had previous dreams related to his death. And his wife, Mary, also highly intuitive, had frequent "moods" that she interpreted as an indication of impending loss.

The murder had been planned for months, and for months, psychics throughout the world tuned in. But as time ran out, an inexplicable knowledge of what was to come rapidly moved throughout the country. In a North Carolina Union Army camp, a barber sensed that something bad was going to happen to the President and discussed it openly. In Southern Illinois, an old lady who had helped raise the President, suddenly burst into tears, and sensed the loss. In the tiny office of a newspaper, the Evening Eagle, the editor, suffering from a stroke and unable to speak, printed a headlined edition reporting the assassination *three hours before it actually happened!* Since the man could not speak, and was quite ill as a result of the stroke, he was unable to relate why he did it or where or how it was he had come upon the knowledge.

Moments before the shooting, a soldier in a downstairs room of a hotel experienced an even more potent psychic disturbance. Having recently returned from the war zone and trying to get a desperately needed rest, he was harrassed by eerie sobbing and crying. Believing the soldier to be suffering from battle fatigue, the hotel manager, in answer to three complaints of "noise," refunded the money paid for the room's rental. The soldier, frightened by the ghosts, decided he would sleep in the park. Just as he prepared to leave the hotel, an officer burst through the front door, breaking the news of the assassination. All through that night, as Lincoln lay on the soldier's vacated bed, dying, the room was filled with much sobbing and crying.

Galina, a young girl from the small town of Armavir in Russia, had a dream she can never forget.

In her dream she was taking an afternoon nap on a blue couch in a large house. A man entered the room and was apparently angry with her for some trivial household problem. In the dream she said she knew the man was obviously her husband. In her dream, the man wore a jacket that had metal buttons and she believed him to be a naval officer. Yet she knew he did not belong to the Russian Navy.

Because of this dream, Galina told her mother that she felt that someday she would marry a foreigner and live far away in a big house. Four years later Galina went to study in Moscow. One evening, Galina was having dinner with another student, a young man from the university on the terrace restaurant, on the seventh floor of the Moscow Hotel. The Russian night air was chill and they decided to move indoors. It is customary in Russia for couples to share dinner tables with other couples — even if they are strangers; so Galina and her date sat at a table with another young lady and a man called Romaine Fielding. The first thing she noticed was the metal buttons. The man was a naval officer, an American. He was the same man who had been the husband in Galina's dream! They are now married and live in a big house in Los Angeles and frequently Galina takes catnaps on a blue couch — a blue couch that was in the house many years before Galina or Romaine ever knew the house existed.

You are better able to interpret your own dreams than is anyone else in the world. A dream psychic or a clinical psychiatrist cannot come any closer to *your* truth than you care to allow. Only you have the key to your own subconscious.

There are a few simple steps to follow in dream interpretation that really work. If you give yourself time to think, very soon you will be able to find the solution to many of your problems, problems that you may, during daytime conscious awareness, prefer to keep a mystery. While you sleep — and while you dream — symbols rise from the hidden depths of your subconscious mind.

The many symbols are important only to you. Perhaps you may have learned some of them from your father and mother, your aunts and uncles, your grandparents, your brothers and sisters, your friends, your teachers. It could be that at some time in your past you read some things somewhere that forevermore will have special meanings for you. But whatever the original causes, the symbols you use in your dreams are yours; they belong to you now. With a little quiet effort, you will understand them. And when you understand your dreams you will understand more about yourself. Once you have a better understanding of yourself, you will be better able to cope with your problems, and if you wish, you will be better able to eliminate your problems, for as you sleep and dream, you are trying desperately to make contact with yourself.

A good thing to remember is that most dreams mean something entirely different than what appears on the surface. However, though there have been cases where dreams exactly predicted a future event, most times this is not the case. Some effort must be made to understand the varied meanings of dreams.

Despite the daytime conscious reactions to your dream subject, be honest; how did you feel, really, when you first awakened? This is an important part of your dream analysis. Remember — your dream is symbolic. You may have dreamed something that you know makes you feel guilty when awake, but that may not bother you in the dream state. Give your dream a chance. There may be no need to feel guilty about the dream. It may mean something quite different. Answer truthfully. Only you will know. Be brave!

When you awoke from your dream, how did you feel? Happy, sad, tired, rested, expectant, brave, fearful, shameful, confident, guilty, mad, sexy, optimistic, pessimistic, quiet, energetic, anxious, surprised? Would you like to have this dream again? Did your dream use nighttime or daytime background?

Was your dream sensible or silly? Did your dream seem as real as life? Did your dream remind you of a movie? Did your dream remind you of a fairy tale? Did you dream about people you know, or about total strangers? Were there more men in your dream or more women? Did you dream scenes in the city or in the country? In your dream did you take charge or were you helpless? Was your dream subject in good condition? Were things new, old, used, sloppy, damaged, faded? Was your dream in color or shaded? Were the colors vivid or dingy? What do each one of your answers to the above questions mean — to you? It is also advisable to add to the offered list of sample questions with some personal ones of your own.

Each aspect of your dream must be carefully considered,

along with *your* attitudes about your discoveries. If you are living with someone, it also helps for you to ask yourself how it is *you* believe *they* would feel about your dream if they knew about it. Keep in mind that what you think may be their opinion is what really counts. What they in reality think about your dream means nothing and can in no way help you with your dream analysis.

There have been times when a dreamer related a complicated dream to a loved one with the request, "What do you think that means?" only to meet the offered analysis with hysterical screams and often physical violence, when the interpretation in some way offended the dreamer.

Dreams are a secret and sensitive expression of your true nature.

Sometimes when you are involved with some difficult emotional problems it may be better to keep your dreams separate from your personal relationships.

Remember to study your dream as you would any other situation or experience. Pretend you are a guest (and you are in fact just that!), in a new acquaintance's home. What do you notice about the atmosphere? The decorations? The other guests? Are you having fun? Or are you sorry you accepted the invitation?

If you begin to see your dreams as indicators of the real you, and look at them through the same sort of cool appraising eye you reserve for strangers, you will rapidly find clear meanings.

Perhaps, too, you will catch a glimpse into your own future. If our future is an end result of past actions and current desires, and if we attract everything to ourselves, however surprising and unwanted the events may seem, then within our subconscious dream symbolism may lie our destiny.

Psychologists tell us that dreaming in power symbols may be related to sexual attitudes. Therefore, dreams of electric generators, batteries, airplanes, cars, dynamite, Niagara Falls, or the President of the United States, may well be considered dreams concerned with sex.

The same is true of any object or condition that represents in some way reproduction or fusion — or something that contains something. In this regard we can include peaches, scotch-tape, and teacups. Phallic symbols such as rockets, submarines, the Eiffel Tower, and frankfurters need no explanation.

All that is needed to explore the dark recesses of your sub-conscious is a bit of time, patience, and imagination. Looked at this way, dreams can be fun! — including the nightmares. Talking about one's dreams with strangers is fashionable. Cocktail-party popularity sometimes is based upon whether you do or whether you don't . . . in living color.

Doctors dispense flu shots with, "Boy . . . I had a good one last night. . . ." A babysitter keeps you straining at the door, on your way to the theater, as she offers a detailed account of a dream that she dreams "every March." Your mother-in-law informs you she has had "a kind of funny one. . . ," and an aunt dreams about old houses "all the time." A grocer brags that his "go on for hours." Even a passing breakfast partner may have no qualms about upsetting a romantic mood with exploration of intricate byways of a night of sleeping horror.

Dreams apparently are the poor man's attempt to mimic Cecil B. DeMille. They offer creative outlets for even the timid. Dreams come equally to all men. National, racial, religious, professional or sexual differences create no obstacle.

While outer roles in life may vary, there is one very significant similarity between all the tell-it-like-it-was dreamers. They are convinced that their dreams have meaning. And find that meaning they do.

As your blood pressure goes up or your blood sugar goes down, their tales wear on. You are taken through painful sexual longings, as the dreamer reinacts the plot. It seems "the ocean waves reached high up over the shoreline as the car starts up," or, in the very last moment . . . just in time, "to speed away" from the advancing "head hunters." You are told that this dream has always taken place just twenty-three days prior to a cooling off of any currently existing love partner! And always, always, just before pork bellies drop! It is difficult to grasp the relationship here, but at these times a smile and a nod are sufficient.

Licensed for business but not much else, telepaths will tell you: Dreaming of teeth falling out means news of a death. Dogs howling — danger in the neighborhood. Dream of cutting hair and a friend will prove unfaithful. Dream of a birth of a baby boy and fantastic good luck will come your way, within a week. Dream about a visit from a dead relative, expect promotion at work. Dream that you are flying a plane and a new sex partner will soon enter your life.

Studies in the field of dream research support evidence that man dreams of a house to symbolically represent his overall life, each room being significantly associated with special life involvements. According to scientific reports man's dreams appear to be basic, simple, and obvious, at least when he attempts to concoct House for Life, Room for Personal, division-dream-symbolism.

A dream taking place in a living room is said to have social connotations. This room stands for your reputation within the community — your friends, entertainment, love.

To dream of a kitchen indicates concern with the basic securities of life — money, job, investments. To dream of eating is the same, except when it involves fruit, and then it stands for promiscuous sexual relationships. To dream of the john is a bit complicated and may cover deeprooted, lifelong, suppressed hangups — the reasons for your many physical ailments and uncomfortable habits. And of course to dream of the bedroom is obviously tied in with sex. A neat room equals a satisfactory condition. A bedroom in a shambles can mean either a problem, or wild freedom, depending on social status and early training.

However, I can't help wondering about a large, ignored segment of mankind who may not subconsciously associate their various emotional needs in this sane and common way. Surely there are the individualists. What about people who may connect the basic security of the kitchen with the living room and not the kitchen? After all there are many millions who eat dinner as they watch television.

What about families who have socially active kitchens? Those who spend hours entertaining around a table? Could they use a living room to indicate friendship? And depending upon imagination, generation, and deviation, a hot stove is subject to varied interpretations.

As far as a bedroom offering clues to one's sexual interests — there are those who make love in the bathtub. I would imagine a greater percentage of Americans would find the back seat of a car or the side street under a bridge closer to the truth about their romance.

There may be some scientific truth attached to the possibility of dreams having meaning. Eventually research may offer helpful future insight. But, since these meanings may many times be triggered by a physical condition, a chemical reaction, financial problems, stressful situations, previous experiences, or a two o'clock in the morning bowl of chili beans . . . and onions, it is not likely a list of valid general interpretations is forthcoming.

For a while at least we shall have to go it alone. Dreaming is a personal business. What dreams are made of seems to come from some private and hidden store of symbolism. If there is meaning, this meaning may often be too obscure to interpret. Dreaming of Las Vegas has different meaning to a

FIGURE XI
FOUNTAIN AND FRIEND

gambler, an entertainer, a newlywed, a maiden aunt, an un- happy wife, a teen-ager, or an Eskimo. Even so, some psy- chiatrists support the theory that water is a universal symbol for emotion, though the theory as yet has not been proven.

Regularly, three times a year, I dream I am dancing in the nude in a beautiful multilighted fountain on the corner of Los Feliz Boulevard at Riverside Drive, in Los Angeles, Califor- nia, and even I, as yet, haven't the faintest idea of what I could possibly mean by that!

10

A Letter Materialized

New York
A POEM FROM A MOVIE PRODUCER

"ODE TO THE MERV GRIFFIN SHOW"

You entered my room on an electrical wave
And your message was infrared
"Louise Huebner!" flashed channel 2
And the springs moaned on my bed.

You reeked of witchcraft
And made it sound like fun
One could see you juggling moonbeams
And dancing elaborate minuets with the sun.

I spoke to you of a movie where men would
Beg to be langorously humiliated by you
And you replied right away —
"How deju vu, John, how deju vu!"

Santa Monica
Dear Louise.

What can I say? I love you! You incarnate what a woman has best, sensuality, womanhood, wit, cleverness and above all you are frank and very natural in your way of life. In this country it is a rarity, as you know. I never saw you on T.V. I dislike T.V. I am 20 years in this country, and have watched 4 hours all together. I was lucky to hear you on many radio programme. The last of which was with sweet Dick. He is very funny and handled you as you deserve nicely, but the commercials destroy everything. I call to speak to you but after 30 minutes waiting a voice told me no more calls, it is finish! Yesterday I received the telephone bill, and it was a costly game. Worth it to speak to you but for nothing — what a disappointment! It is why i decided to wrote to you. A few years ago I already wrote and never received a letter back, but one evening heard you say "I read all your letter when i am in bed, thanks you for them, but i do not answer!" Do not remember what excuse you gave to doing so. To day it is serious because last year i read part of the ad in the Free press and to my delight saw an ad for sexual compatibility. Unfortunately have now nobody to ask about. I need your help. In the past when married had always multitude of occasions to have extra marital affairs, but loving my wife I never did in 16 years, feel the need to do so. After she from an angel became a monster we split. About 14 years ago went to France for 5 months and once more was so lucky to find without looking, a woman healer, to lay hands on me. This woman had a incredible power and save my life. My life was at the edge of insanity and nervous breakdown after remaining 6 years with my fallen angle. I must say she was at that time already mentally very off. She had been mentally poisoned by a man when we were in Central America and became a toy in his hand. Sensitive like i am you can easily imagine what that did to me. My karma was good it was told me in Europe. Because am older, am a bit fatter, it seem

FIGURE XII   A STAMP

M/H

that no girls come to me anymore and am absolutely without sex life at all and am like you — very sex conscious. If I can say so, without sex I am like a candle not lighted. Lately I felt that I could not any longer go on like that. I want to reverse the steam like we say in french (i am french). I want sex again. It seems that something remain from the ex against me, because every time I saw a *psychic reader"* in the past she told me invariably, "YOU PLEASE WOMEN, YOU HAVE A CHARM AND A MAGNETISM WHICH ATTRACT THEM AND," so on and on it is truly usually I could do almost anything with females. In full strength I am a casanova (it is the name women gave me in the past when I was working). I want a girl in my bed to love plenty! I am choosy. It is true, but have a lot to offer am not a morron. I am not at all, an ordinary a lover as average men of my age are. I was born in Geneva switzerland), January 21, 1911 around noon or 4 p.m. I cannot go out alone in the dark is one of the reason have nobody around me. I do not want men. I do not get along well with men here but everything being done at night it is easy to understand if am never nowhere nobody shall know me. My second handicap is I almost married. I was incredibly timid to, an extent hard to imagine after 17 years marriage, was almost cured of this horrible weakness, but now am since in the beach all the time there are plenty beautiful girls of every age and descriptions and most of the time even when they speak to me first (rarely) am timid again and have wasted many hundreds of beautiful opportunities. This is not normal! My ex knew I attracted females and she was very jealous. So she cut my hair. She was an artist, hair stilist. She kept some of them for her Black Magic dirty work. Louise darling, help me to go back on the normal track to be an active man again. If you have the powers you say you have *now* is the time to prove it. Clean my life of the remnants of the bad actions against me. I want to live again. I saw my face lately and begin to look like a frustrated person bitter with the corners of my mouth downward it was never like that before.

The saddest is that because I am pleasant and good looking everybody is sure I have a love life very full. And that I refuse girls due to lack of time. It is very hard. To help you I send my photo. Years old made for passport. My children say i look better than the photo??? I heard "sweet Dick" say you look voluptuous. I believe that fully. Your voice tell everything. I shall not say, "mister sandman give me a dream," I shall say "Louise darling, erase from my atmosphere all the remaining poison and free me of all obstacles, timidity and lonliness." thank you very much. I hope you read this letter in your bed. With hope and love.

Andre

Dear Andre,
    I am better looking than my pictures too!

Santa Monica
Louise Huebner:

Have you eaten any apples lately? With big long fat worms in them, I hope? Your not a true witch! Only another mere member of the herd. Your columns, and chatter of endless sex vibes, and ordinary spells, appeal only to the unenlightened masses, who are still feeding on milk, and whose lack of interest in the divine supernatural, will keep you in spades forever, unless you begin delving into truths and realities!!! All your bunk promoting sexual appetites (*LUST*); (as though man's appetites are not already filled to the brim and overflowing) assuredly are not appealing to all the victims of rape, incest, unnatural *sex* hangups on the cross, etc., etc., ad nauseam!!! Your soul is too filled with *sexual lust* to have any time and energy for seeking and fathoming inner revealing truth and redemption, guided by the Comforter, who is revealed in St. John, chapters 14, 15, and 16. What a dis-service you are doing to the community as well as the editors, publishers, TV and radio programmers who are promoting you and honoring you! Contrary to popular beliefs, man's hunger to have power over others is our basic need for survival and so pitching woo with the enemy always leads to war, whereas, pitching war with the enemy will eventually lead to peace! Also, your alleged small wisps of "Witchcraft" are odious to the innocent while aiding the victory of the evil. All who take up their cross following the Lord, turn their cross into a broom (a symbol of a cleaning utensil) and sweep all the dust out of their lives removing all the spells nailing them to the cross, and we soar above the herd with each new victory over death! Until the final victory called the resurrection, the Comforter soothes, tutors, and guides us into evening all scores, which is of course madam, true witchcraft in its purest form!!! *ALTER YOUR COURSE LOUISE!,* your heading for a fall!! Aim your wrath, not your affection to the men in your life who are all prototypes of your father and other male kin who put the shadow of death upon thee! Awaken, awaken out of the deathly sleep they cast upon thee and return the spell unto them!, who are not afraid of thee because their power is stronger than your's! Ask the Lord to give you the sword of victory and the Comforter will come into your soul! Spread the "GOOD NEWS" to all the martyrd and you will truly then be Los Angeles County's most honored witch, promoted by the underdogs who will overcome all the evil ones.

Elaine the Endowed

Dear Elaine,
  Believe me you need every inch of it.

La Crescenta
Dear Louise,

I listened to you on KRLA on Halloween nite. I wasn't sure to believe you or not. I'm still not sure.
I did that TV thing. I saw a lime-green person walk like my boyfriend does, from the right side of the screen to the left. It was really freaky — my TV is black & white!

You mentioned something about beeng able to communicate to people clear across the world by your mind. I did this and woke two of my friends up — it was really wierd! My girl friend and I think really hard, about waking the other up at nite, and it works.

You know that spell thing? I've done it twice now to my boy friend because we got in a big hassel last week, and it seems to be working really great. Things started to straighten out the next day. It was really freaky.

"Converted"

Dear Converted,
Does your boyfriend do the pea commercial?

Chicago

Where can I get more information on witch-craft. I know this guy that is studying it and really believes in it. He has a lot of books, but he won't tell me where he got them or even let me look at them. The more I think about it, the more I believe in it. I want to know more about it so I can understand it better.

Marcia

So what's to understand?

Walnut, California
Dear Mrs. Huebner:

Many months have gone by since I first thought of writing you, but many things have happened in my life to prevent me from sitting down to my ever faithful typewriter. However, I feel compelled at this time to write you of an incident which took place many months ago during a very late night radio broadcast you were doing. I have recently seen you again on T.V. (Joey Bishop) and heard you again on the radio, and I feel I must share this experience with you.

While on this broadcast (10:00 pm to 2:00 am) you spoke of being a Witch and much about Astrology. It was a two way radio show and many people were calling you for Astrological and Psychic readings. I was sitting in my office (at home) with a small transistor radio on my desk. I had a project in front of me which was taking all of my time. I had a strange impulse to call you, but because we are in a different Area Code Zone, I could not get a connection, as the lines were so tied up with the many calls. Several times during the show you wanted to "cast your spell" over the various parts of Southern California and you asked the listeners to put their hand on the radio and all concentrate together on "your spell". Being busy with my project, I did not bother to do this each time. However, I still continued to try to reach you by phone, always to no avail. The frustration was building up inside me something fierce! . . . as I wanted to talk with you very much.

About 1:30 a.m. (just a half hour before you were to go off the air) a *very strong urge* came over me and I placed my hand on the radio and kept repeating that I wanted to talk with Louise Huebner. Over and over, I repeated this . . . Suddenly, I heard a woman come in on the radio and mention to you that she was a Gemini and that her birthdate was June 8, 19...... The year was not the same as mine. (I am June 8, 1930, ... 12:00 noon . . . . Inglewood, California). As she continued to speak to you, you interrupted her by saying "Are you the Gemini who is interested in making artificial flowers, tissue paper flowers? Because I am getting a very strong vibration from a Gemini who is interested in this new fad of making flowers for money." The woman said "No" she was not. At this point, you could have knocked me over with a feather, because that had been my project all evening. I had been sitting there all evening making tissue paper flowers and for the previous 5 minutes I had been sitting there with my hand on the radio, repeating "I want to talk to Louise Huebner" over and over again.

Could it be that I made contact with you? On many occasions
from the time I was a little girl, I used Mental Telepathy with
my Mother and even now as she lives some 30 miles from me,
we do pick up one another's thoughts. Proving this out, by
one or the other picking up the phone and asking almost the
very question, the other was thinking. To my knowledge, I
have never had the experience with anyone other than her,
and so my experience with you, really set me spinning.

Best wishes,
Nadine

Dear Spinning Nadine,
I'm famous for things like that!

Rolling Meadows, Illinois
Dear Louise:

Just now I got through reading your book. There are many
things I would like to tell you, but you know them already.
Would your publicity minded and suspicious mind ever accept
that I never heard of you?
Well, I didn't!
But somewhere I heard or read: "If one sorcerer meets another, and one of them doesn't laugh, then that one is not a
sorcerer!" So — Ha, ha — and *Bravo!*

Ute
Official Witch of Rolling Meadows, Illinois
How does that grab you?

Dear Ute,
In your title; is that Witch spelled with a capital W or a
capitol B? — Ha Ha!

Iowa City, Iowa
Dear Louise,

I want to thank you for your book. I bought it and read it.

I am 31 years old and have 5 children. My first husband got sick and died after about 7 years. I was a widow for 2 years. I had to get married the second time for financial support. My second husband is sick and just skin and bones. We will be married 5 years this November.

I'm a flop at marriage. I can't communicate with them and they always get sick. I enjoy the kids but I don't like to be guarded and spyed on. I'm independent and don't like to play 20 questions. I've been working nights for two years. My husband works days.

I work at a restaurant 2 blocks away. I need the company of the kids, fifteen to twenty years old, that work and come there. We can communicate, and they enjoy me as much as I enjoy them. They hug me and some call me "Mom." A lot of the customers call me "Mom". They want me to have coffee with them. The owner is interested in everything I do and say. I have a "trans-oceanic" radio. I can reach the outside world. I write to people I don't know.

I can't stand to have my husband touch me. It's psychological I think. My husband think's I'm crazy and should have my head examined. He thinks everything I do and say is wrong. He criticizes me all the time.

How can you go to bed with anybody like that? I have this thing going with the Tuesday & Thursday manager. We can sit and talk by the hour and I make love to him. He's married too. We only have to talk about enjoyable things and not bills and other family disorders. We never argue like husband and wife. It's just him and I. Two people being themselves and not somebody's husband or wife to complain to. We have worked together a year first.

Will you cast a spell to bind us for ever, or do I have to do it? I did the Sexual Seduction Spell and used a red candle. I know you said not to use red candles at first, but I'm desperate to make things better. I have 5 kids, a sick narrow minded dead in outlook husband, a dumpy falling apart 2 bedroom shack, and I work 50 hours a week plus getting social security, plus what money my husband makes and we are still no place. I need my companion and lover. I also need a seven bedroom house plus the kids have never been on a trip.

I know what I want. I'm consistent.

Yours truly,
"Mom"

Dear "Mom,"
  Next time you marry for money, make certain the guy has some.

Downey, California
Dear Witch

Is their any way of testing yourself or someone to find out if they are a witch?

Also can these powers be used to make money?

For example I know a man who is very rich. I would like to make him give me a hundred thousand dollars. Is their any special way I go about this?

He lives 400 miles away.

Also just exactly how can you live without working. You must have some way of making money.

Yours truly,
Ace

P.S. I'm a believer.
Ever since I was 6 yrs. So help me. I'm not evil minded. Just a groovy turned on person.

Dear Groovy,
  Turn off.

Chicago, Illinois
Dear Miss Huebner,

I saw you on the Steve Allen show, and I wonder if you could help me.

Do you know of any so called white witch in the Chicago Area that can cast-off hexes, or curses whatever you call them, since I can't come to L.A.

I wonder if I could be hexed, because I have difficulty getting a job, even though I have a good education. There seems to be an antipathy toward me, and they can't even give me credit to tie my shoe-laces.

It would seem that the law of averages would take care of getting jobs.

Something always happens to make a deal fall through as if it was pre-ordained.

If you don't know of any witches in this area maybe you can give me the materials and instruction to throw a hex off.

I am serious about this, and would appreciate any help or advice.

Yours truly,
Barry

Dear Hexed,
  First — I'd start wearing moccasins.

Los Angeles
Dear Mrs. Huebner

Have been wanting to write you often but do not know if you answer personal requests. Could you please tell me if I am headed for divorce. I was born March 19, 1930, and my husband was born July 23, 1925.

A year ago last summer you were at the Water and Power picnic, you asked the people if they would write their date of birth on a piece of paper you would tell them part of the future, when you came to my paper you said there was a great deal of frustration ahead, in the near future. You were absolutely right!

Paula

Dear Paula,
   Thanks, but I have never been to a Water and Power Picnic in my life!

Inglewood, California
Dear Mrs. Huebner:

The art of Witchcraft has always interested me and I have boughten several books on the subject. All of them have shown pictures of men and women semi-nude, their bodies painted with symbols, standing around an altar of some sort. I always thought that it was really very ridiculous. A few days ago I purchased your book, "Power Through Witchcraft". I really enjoyed reading it very much and I think it is a very good book! For once someone has taken a very sensible attitude towards witchcraft. Now I think I have the right idea of what it is all about. One of my best friends who has always laughed at the idea of witches etc. has read your book also. Her opinion of the whole thing has changed considerably. She doesn't think it is stupid anymore. In fact she is waiting anxiously for the new moon so she can make up for herself a "Isis Full-Moon Ring." I am planning on doing the same.

The main reason why I am writing this letter to you is to ask you a favor. I realize that you have a very busy schedule with your family and all but if you could answer this letter I would really appreciate it. I *think* I have the makings of a fairly good witch. I am not positive but I'm pretty sure. I'd really like to help a lot of people, and myself too of course. In your book you have written out several spells and chants. What I would like to ask of you is if you could send me the "formulas" for many more. If there is a fee for this information I will *gladly* pay it. I realize that this is really asking a lot of your time but I'd *really* appreciate it if you could send me any helpful information that you can.

Best regards,
Karen

Dear Karen,
    You're right, it is asking a lot of me and my time — but don't worry dear — I won't let you impose.

Los Angeles
Dear Mrs. Huebner,

Sometime ago, I heard you on Radio Station KLAC and was very impressed with your abilities to tell people over the telephone so many things, which they admitted were true. Unfortunately, I was unable to get thru on the telephone.

Yours very truly,
Pauline

Memphis, Tennessee
Dear Mrs. Huebner,

Some of my friends were telling me that they heard you on the Joey Bishop Show talking about being a witch. They said you could give me some advice on the subject. I. am interested in this matter.

Could you help me in my affairs concerning love, sex, home life and just to be lucky about money.

I want to do good, & not the evil things, because I do not want to hurt anyone. I wish I would have heard you that night, but we were gone at the time.

Thank You Very Much
Billie

Dear Billie,
    You're too noble to be a witch. Give it up.

Portland, Oregon
Dear Miss or Mrs. Huebner,

I have a feeling that you have been expecting this letter.

First a Slight case history:

I have been interested in occult theory for about a year. I was introduced to witchcraft in Vancouver B.C., and when I returned to the States I brought with me a Slight knowledge of "Black Magic" so to speak. In Portland I met a friend of mine who is also very interested in occult workings & practice.

I've found within me a great amount of energy and Power. Certain symbols I have found in my pre-conscious have aided my talent. The symbols seem to be of universal knowledge. The main thing I would like to express is that from what I know of you, is from your record album, "Seduction Through Witchcraft." You seem very sincere and knowledgeable about what you are doing. As most people I know are playing with a loaded gun. The only cut I've heard is your "Isis Full-Moon Ring."

Now to make a long story short, I was Wandering if you might find time through correspondence to teach my friend and myself the art of Sorcery.

We would be more than happy to become your students, for we have looked for a long time for a teacher with some more knowledge and power than we have.

One thing I have found is that most people in Witchcraft are out for themselves and feel the only way to gain power is to mess up others. I would like to see all aspects help, distruction, protection and *"Love."*

I would like to learn as much as you can teach me even than I will look into other types of Mystics. Everything you teach us will be held confidential at your wishes.

Thank you,
Sincerely Yours

Dear Sincerely,
    Here is lesson number one: I'm not interested.

Lake Forest, Illinois
Dear Louise,

I am very interested in becoming a witch. I was wondering if
you know of any witches in the Chicago area that would be
willing to take on a pupil. It would be more or less someone
I could go to for help, and to answer any questions that might
arise.

I would also like to say I enjoyed your book very much.

Also I have a problem which I thought you could help me
with. On Sunday, Oct. 5th, 1969 My pet, german shepard was
stolen from me. We were in Lincoln Park. I was listening to
the band that was playing and Ty (my dog) was playing with
some other dogs. I realize it was my fault that he was stolen.
First because I ignored the flash I got of the event to come as
merely my imagination. Second for not watching him. I was
wondering if you could help me find him or make sure he
can get away from whoever has him so he could come home.
I will enclose a picture of him.

My birthday is September 21, 1952 and his is March 6th,
1967. This is very important to me. For he was a good friend
and a protector. Which at times in Chicago could mean life
or death.

Please write soon.

Love
Merle

Dear Merle,

*I don't know how to put this to you — but whenever a
Pisces disappears — there is a good chance it was under their
own power. Suspect a romance.*

San Diego
Dear Louise;

I am a warlock.

I'm writing you on your witch's reputation. I can't communicate with my god now. Could you help me? I have used Ly-cantrophy, transmigration, astral flight, necromancy but I can't use sorecery.

I need help.

If there is a coven in Los Angeles I must be in it. It is de-pressing and lonely being a warlock. The devil, my god, was in contact with me in '37, '44, '55 but not since.

'44 was my baptismal. Three times I called my god — and got help but no more.

Now I ask, but "my god" has turned deaf. Just cause I'm 35 is no reason for god to turn from me.

Help me or I'll use sorcery on you. There must be other witch-craft.

Warlock Kenneth Kirsher

Dear Kenneth,
    Sounds as if you need Estrogen!

Great Lake, Illinois
Dear Mrs. Huebner;

I first became aware of psychic power in my early adolescence and worked diligently at developing fair proficiency in using them. When I went to college I kept up the practice. My wife and I, however, are telepathic and I dream events in my fu-ture approximately six months before they occur.

A few months ago I decided to start practicing Wizardry.

Your book, *Power Through Witchcraft*, is the most frank-and-serious-book on the subject I have found. I especially like your explanations and easy to follow descriptions of the spells.

I noticed though that your book seems to be written for witches and I was wondering if the spells would work as described if used by a wizard or if any changes would have to be made.

If so could you please tell me what and how to alter the spells.

> Thank you very much
> *Terence*

Dear Terence,
   When Christine Jorgenson was faced with a similar problem she went to Denmark.

Los Angeles
Dear Mrs. Huebner:

I was lucky to find your book "Power Through Witchcraft." It it the only book that I have ever found that really tells anything intelligent. All the Ancient books that I've found are so involved with Diagrams — etc. That I can't understand them. I am carrying your book like a Bible and studying it so that I might be able to Cast the Card Spell, but there are some questions that I would like to know besides what I find in the book.

First, I will tell you that I am Scorpio, a firm believer in the Occult and am a Medium or Psychic. I have Prophecy that comes true, world famous events, far off places that is all over the Head Lines and Television the next day or two. Some of the Prophecies are regarding Medical discoveries, Styles, famous people and far off places. I feel the Spirits touch me, move the chain around my neck, drop cold substance on me, talk out loud to me and make loud noises near by bed. They tell me things when I have forgotten to do it, as light the Candles, say my "Pass Word" which is Ecstasy. So, You see I am a Psychic, and know it. I live everyday as a Psychic.

Two years ago I was given some Spells by a beautiful Lady I saw before me. She gave her name as Eliria. She said the word to me very loud "Conjurare." Meaning that she would help me Conjure. Evidently she was a Sorcerer in her days. She was middle aged, with shining grey hair dressed on top of her head in an Aristocratic way, wore a Black Velvet Chocker of Pearls and a Rose Velvet Bodice. She had beautiful Chiseled features and gave me formulas for beauty secrets that they used in her day. She told me to mash the purple Plums, Apricots off the tree, make a Paste and apply to the face. Break the Kernals made from new Fruit trees, that they would benefit the tissus and cells of the Skin as an Astringent.

That they did this in her day. Now, this year, I see they have almost the same thing in tubes, selling at a big price. She also gave me some Conjuring Spells, which have worked. And the fresh fruit does make the skin very smooth.

Now, I would like to know the Spell that your Grandmother used to get rid of people that bothered her. I used the Spell that Eliria gave me of writing the names of two people, sticking them face together, rolling them in a tight little roll, burying in the ground and watering ever day, or spitting on them as the paper rots, they will try to pull apart and break up the conspiracy against you and break themselves up. That works. For an Enemy, she told me to take a Coconut or similar hard ball, beat it, curse it, thinking it is your Enemy and they will run like a Rabbit and be afraid of you. That works. Now, I would like to know something. I have a handsome boy friend, who is a Magnificent type and Pisces, dark and moody, who is so hard to understand. He wants me to wait for him, while he overcomes some strange situation. I am given the Psychic information that he has been having some Homosexual entanglement, but he denies it. I want to know a spell to cast so that he will be made impotent with them, if this is true. I placed the cards for him with all the Jacks, Kings, and 3 Aces in his 12th House so that I might break them up. Is that correct? Is there more than I could do? He says that he loves me and wants me to wait longer for him and will not return my pictures and little things. He is a very handsome man, a Government Man and worth waiting for, if I could only straighten him out. Do you think I could have two Spells going in the House at the same time, if they are in different locations? Eliria told me to cut out two red hearts, place them in front of two Gold Candles and a Red One, about like your "We are One Spell." Any way, I am grateful for your Book and studying it. I do hope you will not be displeased with my letter and answer it soon. I am also confused as where to place the first House for Casting a Card Spell for a friend. Would that be my 11th House as their first House? In your Wild Spell, I found out a large amount of "Dirt" from my Enemy's Enemy, just as you said and almost blew up the place with some Tens and Aces in my Friends House. (Just like a Powder Keg) as you said. So, I believe You.

Mrs. Huebner, if you can help me, I will be ever so grateful.
Thank you ever so much,
Clarice

Dear Clarice,
My mother, not my grandmother specialized in the "Get Out of Town" spell. As to helping you — I'm afraid not — you seem to have already gone One Step Beyond!

New York City
Louise Huebner

I have a serious problem concerning possession by other spirits. Also I have been poisoned three times and my brain has lost most of its expansion contraction vibration capacity. Could you please help me defend myself.

Thankyou
Brian

Dear Brian,
I thought you sounded like a Stranger in Paradise.

Dear Mrs. Hubner,

I know that you are very pourful and I would a spell to turn my sisters in to a mouse. and please could I have your record of you?

Do you visit elementary schools or Jr. High school? I know you are the official Los Angeles county witch. And by the

way would you have your husbomb draw a puture of you?
Thank you fore taking time out to read this note.

Sincerely
Dory Moyer

Dear Dory,
  Thank you!

Johnson City, Tennessee
Dear Miss Huebner:

I have long been interested in witchcraft, and a group of
friends and I are seriously considering joining a coven. We
would be very grateful if you could give us some information
on how to start a coven or on any coven in the vicinity of
Kingsport, Tennessee.
Thank you very much

Sincerely yours,
Richard

Dear Richard,
  Shame on you!

La Verne, California
Dear Miss Huebner:

Because I am *so tired* of listening to discussions on integra-
tion,tion, segregation, *complaints* of this organization, & *that
cult* — I never turn on *Tempo!*
Today — I *accidently* turned to Channel #9 — and saw *you*
— heard the *word* — *"Witch"* — and did *not* change the sta-
station. I recall seeing your *face* — on *another* program —
but must have turned in too late — *that* time — to get your
name — or hear much *about* you.
Altho I have *tried* — it seems I *cannot* contact an *honest* —
sincere psychic! They have *all* turned out to be *very* inferior
— telling me about my *past* — (but *nothing* that would *not*

apply to almost *anyone* — on the street). For the past twelve years — I have been interested in a *huge* area in Southwestern Arizona — that is a *positive* oil and/or *gas* potential.

No need to tell *you* of the progress & present position of this matter. If you could help me, on this, it is needless to say, you would be well reimbursed, at the proper time.

Most of us are retired and on a Social Security check, so you know I *cannot* send you *money* — at *this* time. If you are *in*-terested in this, and wish to cooperate with me, I would be *very* happy to *hear* from you.

Sincerely,
Kay

Dear Kay,

Thanks for your *offer*. I'm *sorry* I *can't* help you, oil *doesn't* turn *me* on. Besides *I've* inherited a *"green" thumb* from my *grandma*.

Martin's Ferry, Ohio
Dear Louise,

I feel as if I know you, after reading your book "Power Through Witchcraft." You have put so much of yourself in its pages. I wrote one letter about my own background, of my Mother, her Mother, an uncle and a great grandmother — but somehow I feel you already know the things I've written. Suffice it to say I've come from a long line of family who stood apart from other people, because of perhaps habit, our likes and interests etc. that most people either laugh at or call crazy (in your absence).

I grew up with Bell, Book and Candle, incense and odd things happening, it was a matter of course. Reading of tea leaves, numbers . . . things like — "if that tea leaf falls, I'll get my wish" — or if the next car is red. Or concentrating and projecting your own image to a someone, and then be able to describe what they wore — where they slept, sat, etc. without ever having been in the same town.

Making someone call — or picking up the phone before it had time to ring — just on impulse & thought about that person. Checking Mechanical objects — so they wouldn't work when a certain person picked them up. Willing a person to leave if you want to be alone.

Mom in her bursts of temper burned 2 light cords off from the lamp to the wall (that I know of!) She is gone now — I lost her five years ago — I loved her deeply. Now my own children are close to me, too.

They used to fear Witchcraft and ESP but now my oldest daughter Cheryl, born Oct. 24, 1947 is becoming more and more interested, now that she is old enough to appreciate her own powers of ESP. We are both studying as much as we can find on the subject, trying to help what powers we have.

I suppose I've been casting spells of a sort all my life, but without organization, till I read your wonderful book, even the card spell — but in a different manner. I do know anything I persistently concentrate on, something that really fires me — comes true, but I just recently began to use the props I had grown up with — Mom burned incense — always — and loved candles, bells, etc. — but I don't ever remember her using them, aside from just sitting in the evening enjoying them.

I do know she could hex — if someone hurt me or one of her cats — and the person that did the damage would always be hurt in the same way. But she just outright cursed the person — without the aid of anything but her anger — she could heal animals that were given up for dead.

I have a birthstone ring, my Mom bought me years ago, it's a sardonyx. I want to make the Isis ring, the 6th of February, although I always felt it had a heavy significance to it — if I was having problems — I would just reverse the ring, that is, take it off, turn it around & put it on again. Always the situation would improve.

There are no supply houses here in the Valley for anything worth while, and I've had a terrible time finding a copper bowl! I finally settled for a nipple like thing of copper I found in the plumbing dept. of a store — Mercy! — it holds the ring but very little soil!! Laughable? Umm Hmm — but I suppose if I'm going to start being a productive Witch, I'm going to have to learn to . . . 'produce'!

My children from the oldest, Cheryl, then Melanie — May 17, two years younger, Sparkie — February 23, three years from Mel, and my adorable Shannon who is four, a beautiful little boy — who even now can concentrate on the flame of a candle and make it spark up & grow tall — and also remember the chant "Eye of a needle, Finger & toe, flame of this candle, Grow Grow Grow!" But that was before we read your book, before when it was fun and games.

> Very sincerely,
> *Rita*

Dear Rita,

   Have you tried, "Splickity Spittle, Quigiley Quak, Beezle, Bozzel, Basil Brack!" It works every time.

Florida
Dear Louise,

I bought your book today, *Power Through Witchcraft,* and was puzzled over something you said in it about — after you die you don't think you'll come back. Did you mean you'll be going on to a higher level or you don't believe in reincarnation? The coven I am joining in Miami, has very strong beliefs in reincarnation. If you don't come back — then how do you explain the spirit world?
Thankyou very much,

> Sincerely,
> *Linda*

Dear Linda,
   I don't!

Los Angeles
Dear Louise Huebner

I have listened to you on radio. I tryed to call but never could get on. Can you tell me if my life will ever be happy and specially in my love life. I've been thinking about a man I been knowing since I was 16 and loved deeply. The last I heard from him he was in Los Angeles I would like to find him if he's the one for me. My birthday is July 12 ,1933, 9:47 AM. Please tell me what the future holds for me. Right now I need someone to care for and one to care and love me to. I'm a very lonely old lady right now life is not worth living sometime.

Sincerely
Jacqueline

Dear Jacqueline,

    Wouldn't it be better to become involved with a real live flesh and blood male — rather than a dream image from half a lifetime ago? Do the "Self Fascination Ritual" and build up your personal magnetism.

Los Angeles
Dear Mrs. Huebner.

There is a lady in San Antonio, Texas that called me long distance to look you up.

Being you are not listed — got in touch with your publisher.

Please send me your address and phone number so that Mrs. Thornton can reach you.

Thank you.
Ruth

Dear Ruth,
  No!

Vestaburg, Pennsylvania
Dear Mrs. Hubner,

My name is Karen Koval and I am twelve years old. I heard
you on the radio and watched you on television. Ever since I
was very small I have believed in witchcraft. I even have several books on witches which I read frequently. I would really
like to become a witch although I don't think I can. I have
really given it much thought. However, the purpose of my letter is to see if you could possibly send me some spells or
chants. They don't have to be about anything in particular,
but my sister is seventeen and she would like to have one to
get her boyfriend back again. If it is possible could you please
send us some? We would really appreciate it. Thank You!

Karen

Dear Karen,

*The next time the Moon is dark, plant one apple, three
raisins, two dates and a fig along with a lock of your hair.
Within two weeks Love will find you.*

Italy

Gentile Signora, ho letto l'intervista da Lei rilasciata al gior-
nale "Grazia" e ho pensato di scriverle. Non so se Lei recevera
questa mia lettera perche non ho il suo indirizzo estatto, ma
spero che la trovino lo stesso data la sua fama. Se riceve la
lettera la prego mi sisponda subito, ho un caso da proporle,
molto urgente. Mi sono rivolta anche adaltre chiromanti ma
nessuno, anche se in un primo tempo mi dicono che il mio
caso e facile da risolvere, ha saputo aiutarmi. Sono disperatta,
impegnata da otto anni con un giovane a nome Ilario Porcina
nato il 23/12/1932 ancora non si deci de a sposarmi, in casa
non maivoluto venire e da un anno non ci parliamo; Io gli
voglio sempre tanto bene e vorrei sposarmi e avere dei figli,
ma vedo passare il tempo senza che lu si decida e ho paura
che ormai non mi sposi piu. Signora, dopo aver letto la sua
inserzione, ho pensato subito che lei avrebbe potuto aiutarmi.

La prego, se puo, mi aitarmi. La prego, se puo, mi aiuti, Io mi chiamo Merina Corrias sono nata il 25/8/1929. La prego esamini i miei dati e mi dica cosa si puo fare per riuscire a farli sposare da l'uomo che amo. Mi faccia sapere anche quanto devo spedirle di soldi e se in vaglia o assegno. Ma prima volgio dirle che anche se sembra un caso facil le invece si tratta di un caso molto difficile essendo Lui un giovane dil carattere e personalita molto forti. Ma io ho una grande fiducia in Lei signora, e penso che a lei sarann capitati casi anche piu gravi del mio. La prego mi scriva subito ho sofferto e sto soffrendo troppo nel vedere la sua indifferenza nei miei riguardi.

In attesta la saluto caramente
Merina

Dear Merina,
   Chow!

Long Beach, California
Dear Louise:

I love to hear your voice, it's so bubbli . . . Now, let me tell you what happened to me on the night of October 31 at 11:00 P.M. That Halloween day I had listened to your instructions over the radio and I was all set with the things I needed to do my little witchcraft act. My husband was home and I didn't want him to know that I was preparing myself for witchcraft because he does not believe in it, anyway, he sensed something fishy going on or about to go on; so when he went out to the garage I locked him out of the apartment; and all nervous and in a hurry, I conjured my wish and allowed my husband to come in the apartment and I ran out to burry candle, & apple, and spread the ashes to the wind. In my hurry I broke the candle in half when I was trying to burry it in the ground, also, I didn't burry the apple deep enough in the ground for somebody picked it up later. So everything went wrong as far as the burrial is concerned, of the candle, and apple. Now I am wondering if what I wished for will come true although the New Moon is due and I am still having bloody fights with my husband and he is not treating me fair, even though, he tells me he loves me. My wish was that "I may have health, happiness, love & fortune in the near future." One thing is apparent before the above mentioned took place my husband was out of work and now he found a job! And we are moving to Long Beach to a very lovely place. I have consulted a few fortune tellers and strangely enough they all said that there were malicious, envious, and jealous people around me that are my enemies, and that somebody had cast a spell, or ill influence, so that I will never see my wish come true. Could that be the cause of all my troubles? I seem to be lucky but not lucky enough and I find evil and strange forces working against me when all seemed so well!

Your friend,
Sala

Dear Sala,
It has ever thus been so.

Santa Monica
Dear Mrs. Huebner:

I know you get a lot of mail and perhaps they all sound alike. But I will write to you hoping that you may take a few minutes to read my letter.

I am now reading your book "POWER THROUGH WITCH-CRAFT" and I find it most interesting. Of course, I always did find the unusual fascinating but that is perhaps because I am so desperate. I look for something or someone to help me and I never seem to get the answers. Your eyes on the cover of the book gives me the feeling that you could look through someone and tell or say a lot about the happening of that person.

I am hoping like many others to meet you in person some-day soon. I have turned to Astrology people, I have gone to spiritualist who say they could get me what I want, I have tryed to find a witch or one who knows how to practice it. I heard there was a place in Torrance. I am desperate in many ways

In one form, want my husband back because I feel I made a mistake but when I see what he has done to his morals, standards, and the children I don't know if it's worth it. The woman he is going with must be putting some spell on him because he is completely helpless to her commands. I never found him to be so weak but she seems to overpower him to the extent of forgetting he has any children. Is there really such a thing as some kind of tea that can do this to one??? Or something that can be put into food or drink that puts power over someone??? I must get him back and I must destroy that feeling in him about this woman. Please, do not get me wrong I am not an evil person and I am not a jealous person. I feel my husband has the right to do as he pleases since I am not married to him but I don't feel the children have to suffer for it or that we have to starve or be neglected.

Desperate Terri

Dear Desperate,
    The only way to destroy his feeling for her is to increase his feeling for you. Try the "Sexual Seduction Spell."

Beverly Hills
Dear Louise Huebner,

Last night on the KRLA Halloween Show, you made a tremendous impression on me. Long before now I have been throughly fasinated with the supernatural. I do have the unfortunate problem of not being born a witch, however. I am 17 and my birthday is November 14 so I was wondering if Scorpios are more or less receptive to magical spells and psychic powers than the other signs? I am intrigued at the thought that hidden forces are at work somewhere in the universe and I believe that occasionally I pick them up.

The main reason for this letter is to inform you of a reacion which you wanted people to write to you about. You talked about the Hollywood Bowl preformance and the spell you and all the audience tried to cast on the population. Last night was the first time I had heard about it and was shocked. From July until September, I experienced a sexual hunger so powerful and furious that it was frightening. It had never happened before or after those months in such an overwhelming way. I thought you might be interested to know that your experiment was a success on me. Sexual starvation is a horrible feeling. It is very irritating. I hope this is the kind of reaction you were looking for. I wish you would write to me and tell me if I really have any basis for my belief that it was your spell.

I don't think it would be wise for me to try the sexual seduction spell because I have enough problems with that subject without adding a spell to it! However, it sounds beautiful and maybe I'll get my salt and candle out and chant a little.

Sincerely,
Lynn

Dear Ruth,
   I think the salt and candle are wise at this time.

Fullerton, California
Dear Louise,

Heard your forecast on KRLA —
I called & talked to you one night on a radio show — You were 100% right. Thanks a Million —
Please could you forecast anything for me now — especially should I *sell* my house? My birthday is June 20, 1919 — after midnight — before 6 A.M. is all I know. Thanks again — Bless You and Yours.

Sincerely,
Ruth

Dear Lynn,
   Sorry, only one to a customer!

Pasadena
Miss

I heard a portion of the radio program you were on for station KRLA.

I would like very much to know more of what you do, if possible explaining the love and sex formulas again.

Please mention again the date you made the spell in the Hollywood Bowl, this is *fantastically vital* to me, because if it's the date I thought I heard on the program, it's absolutely unbelievable.

Would you be interested in putting spells on some people of interest to me? I'm not sure all this is for real, but you have given me sufficient reason to carefully consider it. I'm a nineteen-year-old college student looking for answers.

Sincerely,
James

Dear James,
    Gee, that's awfully big of you.

Los Angeles
Dear Mrs. Huebner:

I take your book most seriously because I am positive the mind has amazing powers. I tried casting spells a few years ago without any special knowledge, most of the spells missed the mark and back fired. My little boy or myself were always affected. My son and I are on the same wave length (he seems to read my mind.) My son would fall or get in trouble at school on the day of the spell. I had to stop.

Then, I read your book and decided to try again. I have done three spells. The moon ring spell went smoothly. Then I let a blue candle one afternoon and tried to imagine a good situation happening to me, but I had big trouble that day. I tried the card spell next, but my son touched the cards a day later and so I felt everything was ruined and threw them out.

No need to say what happened. I used a silver ring for the moon ring spell, does this mean that I am not protected because I didn't use a birthstone ring? I was born April 9, 1927. Please let me know what I am doing wrong.

Paula

Dear Paula,
Give it up — it's obvious that you have tuned into evil forces!

Covina, California
Louise,

I have been told by many people who are knowing in the field that I am a witch.

I also feel that I might be. But I can't find my powers. Neither have I been able to find someone who could help me. Is there any way I can find out if I am a witch?

I am anxious for your answer — please help me —

Susan

Dear Susan,
If you are a real Witch — you would be fantastically gorgeous! Also — you could never ever fall in Love.

Alhambra
Dear Witch

I enjoyed your program on the radio and TV — on Halloween Night.

You gave a Chant or a Method to Attract Love.

Do you have any Chants for attracting Money — or Health — or developing E.S.P.?

Sincerely,
John

Dear John,
Yes I do.

Pasadena
Louise

Ever since I read your book "Power Through Witchcraft" and performed the "Full Moon Ring" ritual — which will end at midnight 2/21/70 — I've been having mysterious experiences beyond my conscious level of comprehension.

It is of these unusual circumstances that have occurred to me in unexpectency that I must talk to you about.

I need your experienced guiding advice, to clarify my puzzled mind.

Cruz

Kansas City, Kansas

A true poem for you

At the time I thought of you
The wind whispered your name
And among the stars that magic night
I saw your eyes laughing with mine.

Yeah — sometimes I do tend to get a bit giddy.

Los Angeles
Hello Louise

I listened to you on KRLA last night. A most interesting experience. I was in a perfect mood for it. Halloween Night, and stoned. I got completely wrapped up in it all. At 12 o'clock I turned on my t.v. set. I was alone. It was dark and I sat in front of the t.v. A first I didn't see anything. Then things started flashing by. Around, and around, and around. A Merry-go-round with colorful horses. Faster and faster.

Then I was in there with the horses. We all tumbled around together.

I really enjoyed listening to you.

Thank you for a very enjoyable Halloween Night. I hope to hear you again.

Fyne in Long Beach

Dear Fyne,
Sounds like an orgie!

Seattle, Washington
Dear Mrs. Huebner,

Thank you so much for your book, *Power Through Witchcraft*. It's been a big inspiration and help for me. I think it was extremely generous of you to share your "Card Spell" with us (special thanks for that).

From your book I get a very definite impression that you are a beautiful person — not to leave out, intelligent, pretty woman and very clever, talented witch!

Sometimes, I felt (from your Letters Chapter) that you were being too hard on some of the people that wrote to you and your own self as well. It seems to me an aware person that is hard on others is usually twice as hard on his/herself. You'd still be a beautiful Spirit/Soul/Energy (whatever), even if you weren't a woman or a witch! However, I'm glad you're all three and I hope you write another book!

Thank you again for your "Super Far-Out" book!

Ugenia

P.S. Please be careful living in L.A., people do such weirde, sick things there sometimes. I know you could probably protect yourself, but be careful anyway."

Dear Ugenia,
I try to watch it. Thanks.

Brooklyn, New York
Dear Mrs. Louise Huebner,

I saw you on the Merv Griffin show. And you spoke about Witchcraft. I would like to know more about it. I would like to know if you can give me any advice on what to do with my husband. You see I am very much in love with him and he tells me he loves me very much. But he is possessed by this other woman. I know her and she knows me, he invited her to my home. I love him with such a desire that I will die for him. He loves me like a sister, he never desires me he never has sex with me. And yet he doesn't want me to leave him. We are married 13 years. He is seeing this other woman for 10 years now. Him seeing her doesn't bother me that much. What annoys me is why doesn't he have any sex with me? I have sex with other men and he knows this and yet he says he still loves me and will never leave me.

Maybe you know of a love potion I can give him anything to make him desire me. I know I sound foolish but I don't know what to do. P.S. I don't want you to think that maybe he is seeing her because I am not pretty or am too fat, because this is not so. I am prettier than his girl friend and I never nag him. All I want is for him to desire me. Please try and help me. I don't care what the fee may be.

Thank You
Bernadette

Dear Bernadette,

Your line "Him seeing her doesn't bother me —" is exactly what's bothering him — Turn on Baby!

Mansfield, Ohio
Dear Louise

I'm writing you, to ask for your help. I saw you on T.V. and I read about you in a paper called Newsletter, in which you told how to make a person love you, by baking a Soul cake. I can't make this cake, because my husband has diabetes, so he can't eat anything with sugar in it. My husband is a drunk. He is also unfaithful, won't come home from work, gambles and throws his money away. Our home is a mess, it's falling down around our ears. He won't fix it. So I'm writing you, to ask you can work a spell, to help him stop drinking and going with other women, and stop gambling and be a decent husband.

Thanks
Grace

Dear Grace,
  Use saccharin.

Canton, Ohio
Dear Friend

I read your recipe for a love cake. I haven't tried to bake it. Because after I would bake it I wouldn't know how to get him to eat it.

Isabelle

Dear Isabelle,
  You can lead a man to potions but you can't expect to make him eat them.

Compton, California
Dear Louise,

I was looking at Channel 9 the night you were on and was very impresssed with you. I don't know if you can be of any help to me. I don't have any children and never have. I was wondering if there was anything you can tell me to do. Thank you for taking the time to read this letter but my problem has gotten to the point where my marriage is on the verge of breaking up if I do not have a child soon.

Thank You
June

Dear June,
  Are you expecting a poor sweet little innocent baby to have more marital know-how than you and your husband put together? I suggest you leave off with the baby spells and try Voodoo — it will be less disastrous.

Niles, Michigan
Dear Louise,

This house is old but not ancient and I know nothing about its history. It is in an area which was once the home of many Indians.

Things come up missing and are returned after a few hours, days or months. One dress was gone two years. A library book disappeared in May. I scolded about that and in Sept. it was found on a table in my son's house about a mile away.

Many things have gone and come back, but we only count things we are sure were missing and found in a place where we are certain they had not been.

Last year we all had to leave at 7:30 A.M. We sent the four children outside. My daughter and I checked doors, windows, lights, etc. I had just changed the lock on the only door which gave access to the house from outside. No one else had a key.

When we came home we found red poison wheat (for mice) scattered on my beige rug. Every time we came in we checked for more. The next week we left in the same way. I came home at 11. I checked and there was nothing on the floor. I took off my coat and shoes and sat down to read my mail. I stood up and took four or five steps. I stepped on something as cold as ice. It was poison wheat, 40 grains were scattered on the rug in plain view of where I was reading. I have had a few psychic experiences but do not feel I am responsible for these apports.

I would also like to know if it is considered possible for consciousness and memory to be with the astral projection, rather than with the body. What do you think is going on?

Sincerely,
Charlotte

Dear Charlotte,

First — I'd get in touch with the Government's Bureau of Indian Affairs!

Jamaica, New York
Dear Mrs. Huebner,

I have just completed reading your book *Power Through Witchcraft*, and in spite of the somewhat caustic remarks to letters received, I will venture to ask you two questions.

I have just moved into a new apartment and have discovered it to be infested with roaches. Moving out is impossible at the moment, and an exterminator is ineffectual besides being expensive. As a biologist (I received an "A" in Entomology in college) I know that to solve this problem would require extermination of all dwellings in the entire area. This entire area is New York City!

I think it's obvious that scientifically, this problem cannot be solved in a conventional manner. I wonder if you know of any spell that might work.

Yours truly,
Scorpio

Dear Scorpio,

   In keeping with my usual acid responses — may I suggest Boric? In powdered form — it works!

Sunnyvale, California
Dear Louise:

I was wondering if you could help me.
Could you tell me of a spell to meet a man about forty years old and my religion I am Jewish. I would also like to move out of California.
I am not happly married. I have two lovely children.
You have certain powers and if you could do this spell also for me I would appreciate it. Thank you for your time and consideration.

Sincerely,
Rachel

Dear Rachel,
  You're married to an Arab maybe?

West Los Angeles
DEAR LOUISE:

I REALLY DUG YOU ON HALLOWEEN; ON KRLA IT WAS A "REAL GAS" NOW I HAVE SOME REQUESTS TO ASK OF YOU. FIRST OFF I WANT SOME MAGICAL WAY I CAN INCREASE MY STRENGTH SO I CAN HAVE THE STRENGTH OF TEN MEN? AND I'M VERY SERIOUS TOO. I SURE WISH I COULD MEET YOU IN PERSON? ALSO WOULD YOU PLEASE SEND ME A COLOUR PICTURE OF YOURSELF? PLUS YOUR PHONE NUMBER? I PROMISE I WILL NOT GIVE YOUR PHONE NUMBER OUT TO ANYBODY IF YOU GIVE IT TO ME. PLEASE ANSWER MY REQUESTS RIGHT AWAY.

                              YOURS TRULY
                                   DUKE

P.S. PEACE/LUV.

DEAR DUKE,
  PEACE ON YOU TOO.

11

Witchcraft: A Fly by Night Affair

Bats, Beetles, and Bees
Tremble
In the dank dark deep
And silently
Silver swirling smoke
Thick enough to make you choke
Mingles with the sound of Bells
As a Witchy casts her Spells.

—Louise Huebner

The establishment is subject to attack from all areas and even witchcraft has seen a revolution. Today's witchcraft is a composite of all the early forms of medicine, alchemy, chemistry, and superstitions, with orthodox religion, astrology, paganism, mythology, and ethnic character added to many wild rumors about food, coupled with some sex and sadism thrown in for a little good clean fun. Catering to a multitude of beliefs and customs and neurotic hangups, today in witchcraft — anything goes!

Witchcraft, dealing as it does with the emotions and the mysterious processes of the mind, has served many masters. The craft has even been linked with an outrageous crime in Los Angeles. The leader of a coven or "family" sought everlasting life for himself through the ritualistic sacrificial murder of his victims, with his "followers" acting as mediums and the tools for his fanatical madness.

It was reported in the press that Sirhan Sirhan believed if he used a witchcraft method of self-hypnosis, he could psych himself into additional emotional strength needed to see him through his June 5, 1968 visit to the kitchen of the Ambassador Hotel in Los Angeles, where he was to shoot Senator Kennedy, in a symbolic offering.

Most books dealing with occult studies, in order to add merit and value, will frequently list a few dozen well-known historical names as having exhibited extreme interest in such subjects as astrology, palmistry, numerology, psychic phenomena, and witchcraft. And there is nothing more boring to me than to read the same tired list of oldtimers (poor Benjamin Franklin for one) who supposedly dealt in the black arts.

Now, maybe Benjy did and maybe he didn't. My guess is that he may have been interested in witchcraft as he was in any number of other exciting ideas. Perhaps his interest did not exceed whatever yours is at this very moment. His interest

FIGURE XIII   *WITCHY HUEBNER AT EIGHT*

in the past, neither adds to, nor diminishes, the value of to-day's witchcraft movement. Personally, I think that if the only support found for a subject is to reach back two hundred years, that's a big put down. But witchcraft needn't worry.

Today, there are over seven thousand witches living on the West Coast alone. Projection of that amount across the country is an impressive thought. Practically every community in the United States sports at least one coven. Most covens can be described as a group of twelve women and one male leader who meet in order to cast spells and perform religious ceremonies in the nude, because as they insist, clothing . . . inhibits.

However, if one ever has been *un*fortunate enough to catch a glimpse of the group in action and seen the squeeling, screeching, could-stand-to-lose-at-least-thirty-to-forty-pound menopausal-enchantresses skip about with flopping beads and boobs, and ity-bity blue marks from ity-bity whippys on not so ity-bity bottoms, one would be certain that nothing ever inhibited them, not even Sherman tanks.

There is a fanatical rivalry between witches. Some feel that only an interest in occult studies is sufficient reason to use the title. Others believe they must practice various forms of perversion to be eligible. There are some who are psychic, and many more who are not. Some lead organized and productive lives. Some exhibit no control over their life circumstances. Some claim heritages going back into the centuries. Yet many more spring up new next door. All claim their visions of witch-craft to be the only true version.

Witches come from every financial structure, social level, and ethnic background, with wide differences of emotional and intellectual capacities. Of course not all of the witches are for real; there are still many thousands who are sincere and these should not be discounted merely because the craft does seem to attract looneys. And strangely, the least suspected are frequently the most adept in the art. Witchcraft has always found followers from within the creative fields, but now housewives, businessmen, bankers, real-estate brokers, lawyers, and teachers are known to be quite . . . interested.

Evidently the old religions and philosophies are not offering what the society of today demands. With no answer ready, and with fearful conditions ever on the increase, the trend toward a belief in one's self seems inevitable. And witchcraft does teach belief in the glory of the Self. In witchcraft there is an optimistic look inward that offers hope. To control one's self and to tap the inner power of your life force — to tune in to a universal energy — seems to be the exciting stimulus directing one toward witchcraft. At least that appears to be true in some instances. At other times, it would seem that those attempting certain peculiar forms of witchcraft are seeking something other than a spiritual fulfillment.

There are all kinds of witches out there. Many are involved in experimenting with psychic phenomena. And attempt to "read" minds, attitudes, and emotions with the hope of obtaining power over others. Many are sincerely interested in the art of "healing" through magic. And of course as with everything . . . there are those who are only out for the fun and games.

Some dangerous psychopaths seek through witchcraft a means to reach their own mad ends. There are the good and the bad people of the world found inside any movement. But despite the publicity given to those who seek sexual thrills through perverted avenues, witchcraft exists and blooms mostly in gardens cultivated by the sweet souls of the world, witches who are fanatically attached to herbs. Witches who emphatically insist that the complex use of herbs will aid health, increase strength and make the road easier. Consequently the herb business is now on the uptrend. Interesting offshoots of the craft have developed. The Latin Brujos Herbal Parlor where you can be stripped nude, placed on your back in the center of the floor, and circled with salt as an attempt is made by El Brujo to cure your problems by fanning smoky herbal fumes into your fanny.

Their motto:

"Herbs and Spice Will Make Everything Nice."

For those not interested in herbs:

ORGIES — A TOOL OF WITCHCRAFT

(From the Album: *Seduction through Witchcraft,* by Louise Huebner Warner Brothers Seven Arts Records, Inc.)

Orgies are ritualistic energy exchanges that provide concentration of power needed for spell casting.

Witches and wizards crave energy and in fact are very much addicted to it in all forms.

There is a special kind of energy derived from uniting with one another, and so spell casters do a tremendous amount of uniting.

We know that a mysterious bond exists between love-makers. This bond is able to attract all sorts of good luck and success. An energy exchange celebration that is offered as a token to the Gods will liberate your soul and expand your consciousness. You will be better able to absorb the raw energy of the cosmos and convert it quickly to your needs after you have participated in a glorious celebration of love.

Enchanters need orgies. The orgies will help you generate the electrical and magnetic impulses you will need to cast spells.

The best time for an orgy is during the dark of the moon or when the moon is full and again at the times of the equinoxes.

These are periods when the earth is surrounded by wild vibrations and when if the orgy is successful — you will be able to slip easily into the fifth dimension of fantasy, gather what you need and return stronger and ready to create your destiny. Traditional orgies have always consisted of either nine, eleven, thirteen, or twenty-two guests. You are able to double the amount, triple it, increase it seven times over.

But! You must never invite one more or one less.

There is a reason for the strict discipline in witchcraft — and if you deviate from the rule you could unleash powerful and unfortunate evil forces. So plan your orgy with care. Invite only the specified number of guests.

To begin the orgy: All guests must stand in a circle. Each must light a red candle and dedicate the flame to the god Pluto. And then let the place be filled with laughter. And as the queen witch rings a pewter bell three times . . . psychic inspiration will direct the group activities from there on.

Enchanted Wild Flowers

Witches believe special flowers can magically bring about certain happenings. They suggest you gather them just before a new moon (when the moon is almost dark), store them in a dry, cool area, and later, powder them finely and wear them in tiny packets hung by a ribbon around your neck. Their magic is quite potent, and works suddenly. Many times, witches place packets of the dried petals, leaves, and stems, in bureau drawers, closets, or inside pillow slips.

Sometimes, it is thought that a packet of these flowers, offered as a gift to a potential love — will insure the desired romantic reactions.

The enchanted flowers are wild. You will find them scattered through the woods, rambling along the riverbanks, high on hills, hidden in shadowy places, nested in valleys, blooming in the sun. Waiting!

Pink Shooting Stars . . .	Emotional Love
Violet Wood Sorrels . . .	Physical Rapport
Lavendar Filarees . . .	Fidelity
White Spring Beauty . . .	Peace
Golden Thistle . . .	Spirited Lover
Blue Vervain . . .	Freedom
Venus Looking Glass . . .	Purity
Regal Scarlet Bee Balms . . .	Passion
The Green Meadow Rues . . .	Freedom
The Purple Cone Flower . . .	Platonic Involvement
White Camas . . .	Joy
Yellow Gilias . . .	Lust

Dangerous Herbs and Flowers

(Act as protection against enemies if kept in a small flower box in southwest corner of home)

Name	Latin Name	Common Name	Use
Birds Tongue	*Fraxinus excelsior*	European Ash	Diuretic
Dog Mercury	*Mercurialis perennis*	Dogs Cole	Poison
False Pimpernel	*Pimpinella magna*	Pimpinella	Diuretic
Gold Thread	*Coptis trifolia*	Mouth Root	Tonic (vitality)
Henbane	*Hyoscyamus niger*	Devils Eye	Poison
Mana Tree	*Fraxinus ornus*	Flowering Ash	Laxative
Passion Flower	*Passiflora coerulea*		Diuretic
Pest Root	*Petasites offcinalis*	Butterfly Dock	Poison
Pile Wort	*Amaranthus hypochondriacus*	Lady Bleeding	Mouth Wash
Pitcher Plant	*Sarracenia purpurea*	Fly Trap	Tonic
Scammony	*Convolvulus scammonia*	Bind Weed	Diuretic
Skullcap	*Scutellaria lateriflora*	Mad Dog Weed	Nervine Tonic

Virginia Snake Root	*Serpentaria aristolochia*	Birth Wort	Poison
Worm Root Tree	*Melia azedarach*	Pride of India	Poison
Wormseed	*Chenopodium anthelminticum*	Jerusalem Oak	Anti Helmentic
Worm Wood	*Artemisia absinthium*	Absinth	Poison
Yellow Toad Flax	*Antirrhinum linaria*	Snap Dragon	Diuretic

(Botanical research by Mentor Frederick Huebner)

Gods

There is an ancient belief that a particular God concept has jurisdiction over certain areas of your romantic life. And it is thought that worship of these gods will guarantee their sympathetic intervention in each of your personal affairs.

In order to honor these gods it is suggested you offer the flame of a candle, for just a few minutes, one day each week.

The god *Jupiter* has control over all physical power and the creative forces. With his help you will acquire greater magnetism. You will be irresistible. With his help you will discover everyone overwhelmed by your charm. His day is Thursday. His candle color: gold.

Mercury is the winged god of all psychic energy. He controls extra sensory perception. With his help you will be able to control the secret parts of your lover's subconscious. Communications of electrical and thrilling sensations will leap between you. His day is Wednesday. His candle color: silver.

The god *Mars* controls sex appeal. He is in charge of action. With his help you can be certain of attracting multitudes of wild romantic adventures. He is the god who puts the extra zing into your zap. His day is Tuesday. His candle color: red.

The goddess *Venus* furnishes Joy. She is the only one who sees to it that emotional fulfillment coincides with the physical attractions and the mad passionate rapports. She puts the sensuality into lust. Satisfaction guaranteed. Her day: Friday. Her candle color: lavendar.

The goddess *Nisaba* blesses all sexual unions and attempts to protect the couple from outside interference. She cannot insure fidelity — but she can make certain, permanent friendships. Her day: Sunday. Her candle color: white.

Isis the moon goddess is the one who helps out in desperate cases. If things have gotten out of hand and are fast headed for a huge state of collapse, worship her! In her case nineminute offerings are a must and a minimum! Her day: Monday. Her candle color: coral.

If you are leaving for vacation and would like to meet a wild new lover, the god *Uranus* can bring about spectacular concidences. In this case you should burn eleven, ten-inch pale blue candles, for seven minutes, at midnight, the night before you take off.

Saturn will see to it your lover returns, repents, and remains. He is the god of fidelity. He may be slow to act but he is sure! He needs an offering of candle flame for two hours. His day: Saturday. His candle color: black.

Neptune is the god you worship just prior to each sexual union. Just before you get into bed with your lover, in fact, even before you remove your clothing, prepare to worship Neptune.

Sprinkle coarse salt in a circle around the area that has been chosen for the lovemaking. It doesn't matter if this is a bed, couch, tub, car seat, or office desk. To the left of the circle place three tall, tapered, green candles. Lit. Preferably twelve-inchers. To the right a pot of incense. Let the candles flame during the entire involvement.

Neptune increases fantasy and delightful reveries. He is especially interested in clandestine activities and offers complete protection. However, since this is related only to social interferences, it is still advisable to stay on the pill.

DEMONS

"On the coast of Coromandel where the early pumpkins blow,
In the middle of the woods lived the Yonghy-Bonghy-Bo."
—Edward Lear

People who know say there are seven million demons roaming about the earth.

A demon is a wild form of energy that expresses itself through diabolical and ferocious forms. Those who believe in demons say that demons are able to see into the future. In fact, they will insist, that not only do demons see into the future, but they really are already in the future, in the now, and in the past, all at the same instant. And because of this knack, they are able to interfere with and alter happenings. This has fascinating potential for adventure.

The trick is to get hold of a demon, so it can be controlled for one's own evil purposes and selfish gains. Some demons have sordid reputations, but there is no real evidence that the Coromandel's Yonghy-Bonghy-Bo is the best available. With seven million to choose from there are all sorts of demons who are not very much publicized, and who are willing, able, and available, and who shouldn't, due to misguided snobbery, be overlooked. After all, a demon's a demon.

Don't worry about the possibility of overlooking one; they are easy to spot. Demons most times sport wings, glinty yellow eyes, knarled and skinny arms and legs, pointed ears, twisted horns, scraggly tails, and toothy fiendish grins.

Many times they are the real reasons behind haunted houses, wailing storms, strange odors, short circuits, leaky faucets, lost keys, stringy hair, blind dates, nagging associates, and pimples. Demons are by nature lousy no goods. However, their one strong point is energy. Wild, crude energy. Wouldn't it be wonderful to take all the demonic energy of things that go wrong and convert it into something a bit more exciting and satisfying, like a wild passionate love affair? A demon-made love affair can be fun, and is never an overall life pattern interference. It's a love affair based upon exciting attractions — strong physical compatibility — with underlying emotional rapport, and absolutely no intellectual hangups!

In order to capture a demon, you need a magic circle. If you don't have one, they are fairly simple to put together and not terribly expensive.

You will need: three red candles, white chalk, finely ground wheat, whole cloves, basil leaves, garlic, three red kidney beans, and a fist full of roses.

When the moon is high, draw a three-foot-wide circle of white chalk. Then cover it over with the finely-ground wheat. Sprinkle the basil leaves, garlic, and cloves in the center. Now place the three red kidney beans in the middle. Put the three red candles at the top of the circle. Light them. Now throw the rose buds high into the air, letting them fall and scatter where they will. Demons go ape over rose buds, and will quickly gather.

Once they are inside of your magic circle they will be trapped and helpless in your power. When the demons realize you have them, they will begin to rant and wail. Let them. All their wild hysteria will only generate fantastic energy for your love affairs.

Encourage their unhappiness. Laugh at them. They become even more violent when laughed at, and will continue to rant, wail, moan, groan, call, and bawl so much louder.

Now ring a copper bell nine times.

When they understand that you are in power they will try to make a deal. Soon, the ugliest, most frightening, skinniest demon of them all will approach you — with respect of course — and, acting as a spokesman for the group, he, she, or it will make an offering. He will promise to find lost keys, stop leaks, and get rid of pimples. Aim higher. You have them . . . and they know it! Don't be conned. Get the most. Demand the supreme grand passion — or nothing.

Later, destroy the circle!

Michael Stribling — Los Angeles City Hall Garage Attendant
"I study Witchcraft and I am sure there are forces that people can tune into. It can be dangerous. It's there — the wind — we can't see it, but it's there! I believe in Demonism. Bad angels. That sort of thing.

There is a group in my neighborhood, of people who also are interested in this sort of thing. I belong to it. Once in the classroom everyone was working with a Ouija board, when suddenly it began to raise up and lift itself several feet above the table, before it came back down again. Definitely a manifestation of some evil spirit. Four people were involved. Four people saw it happen. I know it's true — because I was one of the four.

There was no way for this to be a trick. Not one of us had our hands on it. We were all equally surprised. It had to be a case of demon possession."

An Evil Mean Bad Witch

"I lived with an Evil Witch for several years and that was when I became interested in Witchcraft. You might say I was forced into it for matters of 'self-preservation.' She and I never got along in anything. Yet I couldn't leave her. Until I learned the craft and enlisted aid from the Spirit World. Once when I came in from work she was peeling potatoes with a sharp knife. Out of the clear blue she came at me and tried to stab me. She struck at me saying I'd been untrue to her and that she was going to kill me. As she struck at my chest the knife was pulled from her hand by an unknown being, it disappeared right before my eyes. I knew someone from the Other Side helped me, and told me she couldn't live with me or without me but she was going to try. She said she was going to pack her suitcases. She left the room in a huff and went into the bedroom doorway — turned on the light and then came running back to where I was. Her luggage was lying open on the bed ready for her to pack and leave. Then she realized her power was slipping and mine increasing. Before, whenever this girl would get mad at me and if I was sitting on a couch across the room from her, she'd raise the couch almost to the ceiling without coming near me. There was like some kind of plastic shield all around me and I couldn't climb down. I had to wait for her to let me down.

I had been sitting on a couch once up at the ceiling, and she wanted some ice water — she spoke to any evil spirit to bring her water. No one was in the kitchen but the refrigerator door opened — the cabinet doors opened. Water was turned on and then a glass of water came through the air to her. I saw this with my own eyes. I was scared but in a way interested too. She made the table answer her questions at the seances she held. I was present and we had group meetings for several months every night. She could also hold a pencil and paper and get messages from the spirits. Often they were written in other languages. She could control my mind at a distance too. And on several occasions she use astro projection — she left her body and took trips anywhere she wanted to go. Through my studies I was soon able to reverse her power and get away from her." — C.H.

Petshop owner

A NICE FAMILY OF WITCHES IN PISMO BEACH

Papa Witch ♂

Pierre Kendrick Vawter is a wizard who conjures spirits as familiars from the ether and nether worlds (inner and outer space):

"These operations used to be considered ghastly and Satanic because people didn't understand them, but I haven't ever encountered any spirits that are worse than a bad dog, and I have always been able to snap most of them into shape with any cantrap found in the older tomes of Black Witchcraft.

Bad spells are best forgotten because you're vulnerable to their backfire. If one is aimed at you, concentrate your energies into a wall that deflects them. If you put sufficient strength into the act, the spell will bounce back with enough force to maim the sender. Good spells are *constructed*. The desire is framed in rhyme, incanted in powerful words, then as time passes, thoughts and ideas are added to the structure of the original idea. The cleverer you are, the more you will find to integrate into your framework, until it builds itself and has a life of its own. Unselfish ideas build faster because they absorb energies from many sources, many people contribute to them.

Use of paraphernalia is according to personal preference. I use fire, lightning, the natural elements. Candles and incense are more suited for women."

Mama Witch ♀

Toni Vawter came to California from Lake Eerie (sic) at an early age and grew up in Los Angeles. Studied a broad curriculum at the University of California at Apathy in its preprotest days, then graduated to astrology and witchcraft. Now happily casting spells from Pismo Heights, she says the elevation is an advantage.

Transylvanian Stroganoff
(Her favorite recipe — certain to increase
personal magnetism)

1½ to 2 lbs. ground beef
1 cup chopped onion
1 lg. garlic clove chopped
4 tbs. butter
2 tbs. flour
2 tsp. salt
¼ tsp. pepper

1 tsp. Kingsred Paprika
small can (6-7 oz.)
  sliced mushrooms
1 cup sour cream
12 oz. noodles cooked
  & drained
generous shaking of
  poppy seeds

(stir)

Passion
(A drink to increase sexual vitality)

2 jiggers Jamaican rum
1 pony (1 oz.) light rum
1 tsp. honey
juice of a lime

Shake together, and serve to two. The honey heightens and
hastens the effect.

Baby Witch

Ariane is eleven years old and in the sixth grade:

"A few minutes ago I was looking out of my bedroom window, eating a banana. Then I saw a boy I knew, and I stared
at him. Into the back of his head — in order to disturb him.

He kept looking back at where he had been. It was just like he was trying to make sure what he had just done was right. He turned around about 5 times. I just do this to practice my power.

"When I was six, everyone in our family, except for Pierre, did a curse on John Stevens, because he was always bugging us. We knew it worked, because we never heard or saw him again.

"I had a lot of little psychic moments, for instance; once when Mom kept on asking where Pierre was, I answered, 'at Jack Bracket's.' When Pierre came home, Mom asked him where he had been, and he told her at Jack's!

"Mom is always asking us to do the Tarots and be psychic. When I do the Tarots (or any kind of cards) she says they are true.

"Lately, (I mean in the last month), I have done 4 curses. The first one was on Gabriel Meouse, something about him makes me despise him. So I cursed him. I know it worked, because he was absent for two or three days and when he came back he went around limping. I asked a girl what was wrong with him and she said he had a bike accident.

"Two other curses were on some girls in my class, Dorthy Condike and Cindy Forsee. I warned them (by mind), that if they made one more false move when the moon was as full as it would get, they would get it! But they just ignored it. So they got it! There was even a green cloudlike blotch in the night sky to carry my curse to them!

"The last curse was on the person who had cast a spell on our family: '. . . that all the cats thouest owns in possession are cursed to death,' that's the way it happened at least. I cursed him, whoever it 'was,' (probably dead by now), with all the power in my fingertips. The wind was even blowing very fiercely.

"A little less or more than a month ago, I put on one of those plastic black necklaces on a gold chain. I'm wearing it as a symbol of my dead cat Shime. In an article on 'Witchcraft from A to Z,' F was for familiars. This is what it says: 'A pet of some sort (cat, dog, beetles, rats) owned by a witch and in olden times thought to be fed off her blood extracted from a supernumerary nipple.' I think Shime was my familiar. And I think if she was still alive I'd be a better person. She had a Siamese figure, was a girl, and was almost all black, except for a small portion of white under her chin and on her belly.

"I am in the 6th grade and am eleven. I will soon do the ancient 'Unwanted Lover Spell.' I must. As there are two little third graders who keep saying they love me.

"I think I am more of a witch than my Mom. All she does is astrology every minute of her life.

"I wear bangs too. They make me look more like a Witch."

FIGURE XIV

SANDOZ THE THIRTEENT

12
Good Cards

The cards fell easy
And I quickly drew
A Duce
An Ace
The Queen and King of Hearts
And Seven.
I drew Five Hearts
And that means love
And all the Stuff goes with it.
But still he shrugged and walked away.

Everybody says those cards are good.
And with cards so good —
I really didn't think he would.

— *Louise Huebner*

Interest in reading future probabilities from cards, goes back many thousands of years. Originally, cards were not used in a game structure. In fact, the card games for themselves alone are a comparatively recent development.

The soldiers gambling at the feet of the Crucifixion were not only "playing" the cards, but also "reading" them.

At the start, the mystical religious leaders interpreted the symbols for royalty. And today's royal flush can be traced back to a particular grouping of cards that the ancients believed signified good fortune.

The Egyptians are responsible for most card symbolism and interpretation. Many card readers continue to fanatically adhere to what they consider to be the "original" methods, even though common sense leads to other conclusions. The symbolism and interpretation have altered. And it is ridiculous to believe otherwise. Time passing is always an influence.

The Tarot, the most overly-publicized method of divining the future, was created by high priests and intended to be used exclusively as a method for achieving spiritual illumination. Today it does not exist in its ancient form. Through many translations, both of language and philosophy, it has completely lost its original value. Three different versions appeared during the last hundred years alone.

And midwestern occultists who are now cashing in on the renewed interest in the Tarot, lacking knowledge of Egyptian history, philosophy, symbolism, and language in the abstract, cannot be expected to improve upon more scholarly efforts of interpreting the interpretations.

FIGURE XV   *A GOOD CARD*

Before relying heavily upon any card reading method, it would be better to create one especially for yourself. After all, that's how it all began in the first place!

It is believed that *nothing* ever happens that was not meant to happen. And it is said that once you read through all the card meanings — in any method — your subconscious will then cause the proper cards to be dealt.

Card reading is an excellent way in which to increase psychic ability. As you attempt to read "meanings," even with directions, you trigger creative responses to the symbols and are able to "know" many things that would have otherwise remained hidden.

There is a group of Spanish gypsies living in Granada, Spain; they are descendants of the ancient Phoenecians who were known for their fantastic psychic ability. These gypsies today live in caves, and are not prone to establishing new relationships.

But, while living in the three-thousand-year-old Phoenician village of Sexi, now known as Almunecar, (a few hours drive south of Granada) I was able, because I am a witch, to invade their privacy. And I was fortunate enough to make friends with one of their leaders — Ricardo.

Ricardo came from a very long line of fortune-tellers. Their only method for divining the future was through a plain ordinary deck of playing cards. His family has used the same card interpretations for centuries. The origin of this particular form is from the Phoenicians. It has changed, of course, but still works very well. They are now called the "good cards." Ricardo taught me the method in payment for a spell I worked for him.

Don't attempt to read your cards without first reading *all* of the individual card meanings once through. In this way your subconscious will "select" the cards in the correct sequence for you. You may read these cards any moment of any day. There are no restrictions as to the frequency of the readings. Unlike the majority of methods, where one reading a week is all that is allowed, Ricardo says in the Phoenician cards, frequent reading leads to greater insight.

Use the entire deck of cards. Shuffle the cards as long as needed — until you feel in tune with them. Don't cut the cards ever! Not even once. Deal the cards from left to right, one at a time into a row of thirteen places, four times. When you deal the last card you will now have four cards in each of the thirteen places. Read one place at a time. All the four cards at once!

Think! Use your imagination. What do the individual meanings indicate when they are combined?

Try it. You can only get better with time!

THE GOOD CARDS

General Meanings of the Suits

Hearts	Emotions
Diamonds	Physical
Clubs	Mental
Spades	Spirit
Aces	The Self
Duces	Personal Resources
Threes	Communications
Fours	Securities
Fives	Creativity
Sixes	Obligations
Sevens	Relationships
Eights	Backlash
Nines	Philosophy
Tens	Potential
Jacks	Reputation
Queens	Subconscious
Kings	Social

Individual Meanings of the Cards

Ace of Hearts	Emotions
Ace of Diamonds	Health
Ace of Clubs	Cleverness
Ace of Spades	Awareness
Duce of Hearts	Magnetism
Duce of Diamonds	Dexterity
Duce of Clubs	Education
Duce of Spades	Spirituality
Three of Hearts	Affection
Three of Diamonds	Gifts
Three of Clubs	Studies
Three of Spades	Beliefs
Four of Hearts	Family
Four of Diamonds	Property
Four of Clubs	Training
Four of Spades	Organizations
Five of Hearts	Affair
Five of Diamonds	Energy
Five of Clubs	Talents
Five of Spades	Idealism
Six of Hearts	Relative
Six of Diamonds	Credit
Six of Clubs	Morals
Six of Spades	Dedication
Seven of Hearts	Personal Involvement
Seven of Diamonds	Sensible Agreement
Seven of Clubs	Friendly Rapport
Seven of Spades	Soul Mated

Eight of Hearts	Sexual Attraction
Eight of Diamonds	Inherited Assets
Eight of Clubs	Conscience
Eight of Spades	Honors
Nine of Hearts	Natural Talents
Nine of Diamonds	Learned Skills
Nine of Clubs	Profession
Nine of Spades	Insight
Ten of Hearts	Future Romances
Ten of Diamonds	Financial Gains
Ten of Clubs	Awakening
Ten of Spades	Fulfillment
Jack of Hearts	Popularity
Jack of Diamonds	Credit
Jack of Clubs	Respect
Jack of Spades	Envy
Queen of Hearts	Yearnings
Queen of Diamonds	Sensitivity
Queen of Clubs	Memories
Queen of Spades	Tenderness
King of Hearts	Rendezvous
King of Diamonds	Invitation
King of Clubs	Conference
King of Spades	Affair

Meanings of the Thirteen Spaces

I	Personal
II	Healthy
III	Powerful
IV	Cautious
V	Extravagances

VI	Restrictive
VII	Cooperative
VIII	Sensitive
IX	Surprising
X	Ambitious
XI	Discoveries
XII	Clandestine
XIII	Action

Multiple Cards in Any Space

Four Reds	Enthusiastic
Three Reds	Happiness
Two Reds	Understanding
Four Blacks	Control
Three Blacks	Anxious
Two Blacks	Sympathy
Four Hearts	Love
Three Hearts	Affair
Two Hearts	Joy
Four Diamonds	Money
Three Diamonds	Profit
Two Diamonds	Balance
Four Clubs	Success
Three Clubs	Increase
Two Clubs	Adaptable
Four Spades	Warning
Three Spades	Insight
Two Spades	Gossip
Four Kings	Man in Power
Three Kings	Man in Love
Two Kings	Male Friend

Four Queens	Woman in Love
Three Queens	Woman Relative
Two Queens	Woman Friend
Four Jacks	An Affair
Three Jacks	A Proposition
Two Jacks	Scandal
Four Tens	New Development
Three Tens	Change of Plans
Two Tens	Compromise
Four Nines	Surprise
Three Nines	Travel
Two Nines	Wedding
Four Eights	Sex Appeal
Three Eights	Tears
Two Eights	Contract
Four Sevens	Marriage Proposal
Three Sevens	Divorce
Two Sevens	Argument
Four Sixes	Health Condition
Three Sixes	Job Problem
Two Sixes	Annoyance
Four Fives	Lover
Three Fives	Gift of Jewelry
Two Fives	Gamble
Four Fours	New Home
Three Fours	Redecorate
Two Fours	Overcharged
Four Threes	Telephone Call
Three Threes	Telegram
Two Threes	Letter

Four Duces	Fantastic Success
Three Duces	Dreams Come True
Two Duces	Love and Business Mix

Special Meanings of Kings, Queens, and Jacks
in Specific Spaces

I to XIII

I

King	Immediate Answer
Queen	More Force Needed
Jack	Slight Delay

II

King	Sexy Male
Queen	Sexy Female
Jack	Queer

III

King	Stocky Male
Queen	Lovely Woman
Jack	Passionate Male

IV

King	Tall Man
Queen	Heavy Woman
Jack	Devious Male

V

King	Love Returned
Queen	Passion and Love
Jack	Platonic Friendships

VI

King	Father
Queen	Mother
Jack	Brother or Sister

VII
King   Male Relative
Queen   Female Relative
Jack   Lover Male or Female

VIII
King   Burning Desires
Queen   Smoldering Emotions
Jack   Sexual Desires

IX
King   Illicit Romance
Queen   Clandestine Meetings
Jack   Passionate Affair

X
King   Job Offer
Queen   Approval
Jack   Revenge

XI
King   Victory
Queen   Support
Jack   Meeting

XII
King   An Unusual Alliance
Queen   An Ego Builder
Jack   A Lift In Spirits

XIII
King   Aggressive Attitudes
Queen   Passive Attitudes
Jack   Melancholy Behavior

Meanings of Important Combinations
In Any Space

King and Duce	An old flame returns, old meaning from the past — or over fifty.
King and Ace	Successful gamble!
King and Queen	Emotional balance will be an important factor
King and Jack	Need for legal counsel
King and Ten	Travel to a distance
King and Nine	Man of the cloth visits
King and Eight	Law enforcer aids
King and Seven	Man in thirties
King and Six	Man in twenties
King and Five	Man under twenty
King and Four	Man over forty
King and Three	Wild good fortune
Queen and Jack	Beautiful love affair
Queen and Ace	Sensual woman
Queen and Duce	Loneliness leads to dangerous interlude
Queen and Ten	Visitor
Queen and Nine	Mystic
Queen and Eight	Bitch
Queen and Seven	Woman in thirties
Queen and Six	Woman in twenties
Queen and Five	Woman under twenty

Queen and Four	Woman over forty
Queen and Three	News from a distance
Jack and Ace	Fortunate meeting
Jack and Ten	Trip for business
Jack and Nine	Secret agreement
Jack and Eight	Powerful attraction
Jack and Seven	Divorce probable
Jack and Six	Health improves
Jack and Five	Advancement
Jack and Four	Home improvements
Jack and Three	Delightful encounter
Jack and Duce	Amorous dealings

Special Romantic Indications
(Four Hearts In Any Space)

Space One:
The very air around you sparkles with romantic impulses.

Space Two:
An important relationship is established.

Space Three:
An increase of magnetism brings about a sudden attraction.

Space Four:
Your need for love intensifies.

Space Five:
An experienced partner comes to your aid.

Space Six:
Not a time for intellectual pursuits.

Space Seven:
Follow the path of least resistance.

Space Eight:
You will now find need for additional emotional expression.

Space Nine:
Your emotional potential is now triggered.

Space Ten:
Combustible combinations ignite into a dangerous conflagration.

Space Eleven:
A love from the past gently haunts.

Space Twelve:
A bright new shining love appears in two weeks.

Space Thirteen:
Smouldering emotions about to erupt into volcanic proportions.

13

The A.B.C.'S of Numbers

I

"I'm only talking of number one, you know. I must take care of that first." — Dickens

U.C.L.A. MATHEMATICS DEPARTMENT: Is it an honorarium?

ME: What?

U.C.L.A. MATHEMATICS DEPARTMENT: Are you offering the professor an honorarium?

ME: I just want to interview him for the book I'm writing.

U.C.L.A. MATHEMATICS DEPARTMENT: Well, if you're not offering him an honorarium — he won't return your call.

FIGURE XVI

NUMBER SIXTY NINE

1.2.3.

Astrologers and numerologists though arriving at conclusions through totally distinct points of view have two things in common. They both use mathematical equations. And they both have been ridiculed by mathematicians because of their beliefs.

These cycle specialists have long claimed that it is possible to analyze character traits and predict future developments through the use of mathematical cycles. They based their belief on empirical knowledge — years of practical usage of charts of events.

Astrologers and numerologists calculate charts for everything: a phone call, the hot water tank leaking, an illness, an unexpected visitor, an accident, a business conference, a medical appointment, a social outing, a marriage, a first meeting, a first date, and the first time you go to bed with someone. All are immediately charted to see what's up.

Even after only a few situations have been "charted," it becomes apparent to them that a pattern exists. After charting several thousand events, one becomes awed by the very impressive "coincidences." I have seen enough of the patterns to know beyond the slightest doubt that they do indeed exist. But do not patterns have meaning?

Mathematicians have always led us to believe that when we deal in numbers we will see patterns. Numbers, they say, are stable. They have snickered at the amazement of the devotee of mathematical cycles. Led to believe that numbers offer constant security we cannot place too much value in finding them resolute. Told that the number two always follows the number one, we should not gasp whenever this takes place. Sequence is invariable.

Irregularity of occurrence, we are told, would be the only real shocker.

However, this no longer seems to be the case!

In questioning a professor of mathematics to clarify that discipline's position on numerology, I met with some interesting reactions. Calling the math departments in various universities, I soon discovered than *en masse,* mathematicians wanted to make — "no comment;" and that most mathematicians were away on some kind of ego trip, were not terribly creative or terribly brave. Even after explaining that all that was wanted was a simple, brief statement covering the basic nature of numbers, they still declined. I wanted to be told in layman's terms that when one deals with numbers, one will always come up with a neat little package. And therefore, neat packages were to be expected. They are the rule, not the exception.

I believed, judging from the mathematicians' previous attitudes, that this must be their belief. But they couldn't make the statement. Since astrologers and numerologists for centuries have been coming up with uniform packages of life happenings, and since the mathematicians have constantly undermined their efforts, scowling "so what," it was natural to assume that they found no great merit in the persistent blocks of steadfast numbers, and they must consider constancy to be a hard fast rule.

The search to find a definite point of view among the mathematicians was more exciting for me than all the years of discovering repeating immutable patterns.

North American Rockwell were courteous, but said they didn't want to get mixed up in "anything like that." Then their man added in a hushed voice, "After all what if it turns out to be the other way?" OH? Could it be that orderly numerical sequences would be discovered *not* to always exist?

Could numbers at some point actually be known to deviate? One professor of mathematics did confide in rushed, whispered tones that numbers did indeed deviate in the higher levels of abstractions — but:

"I certainly don't want to stick my neck out.") And if there did exist, at some level of abstraction, a numerical deviation, how would we be able to ignore constant conformity?

How could we say, "So what?" to a conforming constant factor? How could we, or the mathematicians say "So what" to the numerologists charts? Could the mathematicians continue to say the numerologists were *nuts,* or perhaps politely imply they were at best, misguided? Could the mathematicians continue to say that numbers were always consant, uniform, resolute, immutable, even though now they had begun to suspect they were not?

Evidently they couldn't and wouldn't!

If at some point numbers can no longer offer continued constancy (and yet while working with numerical equations of specific events, chartists always establish the constancy of *patterns*) then the constancy of the patterns would have to be something more than a mere coincidence. And if the patterns are something *more* than coincidence, the something more should be meaningful!

II

Numbers Zero to One

"Mathematics takes us into the region of absolute necessity to which not only the actual world but every possible world must conform."   — *Bertrand William Russell*

"I believe there is a lawfulness in nature which is different from so-called natural laws. The laws of physics are reducible to mathematical equations which involve the relatedness of measurable quantities. Not so this other kind of lawfulness. It pervades all nature in its innumerable forms, too, but it cannot be quantitatively defined. Yet it is reducible to simple 'root' or 'fundamental qualities.' It involves the relatedness of symbols. In every piece of nature there are to be found a myriad of symbols which, through a myriad of combinations, are woven into a sort of pattern, but through analysis they can be reduced to their 'fundamental qualities' or simple 'roots' just as effectively as the physics of a stone can be reduced to a combination of quantities involving weight, structure, elasticity, etc. And I would not be surprised if these 'fundamental symbolic quantities' could be further reduced to the symbolism of simple numbers, in a similar way that modern physics reduces mass, velocity, light and energy to mathematical equations. In that case, numbers would be at the root of all phenomena, governing their relatedness according to laws that are ascertainable; but in the one field of study we are concerned only with numbers as far as their quantitative properties are concerned, while in the other field we are concerned with the same numbers, yet only as far as their symbolic properties are concerned.

"I believe that the knowledge of this lawful, symbolic relatedness in nature was lost at some time during history, that the ancients knew a great lot about it, that only scraps of information (mixed with superstition and almost smothered by rampant dilettantism) have come down to us. This is not astonishing, for the source of that ancient knowledge was a mind-faculty which was different from logic, a faculty that might perhaps be covered to some extent by the word "intuition." During many centuries we have almost exclusively been concentrating on logics. And it can readily be observed that concentration of one mindfaculty tends to suppress the other mindfaculties, although perhaps this need not be necessarily so, as C. G. Jung has pointed out in his 'Psychological Types.'

"I have found in my studies that there *is* a correspondence between a man's birthtime and the most salient features of his life; that there is only a small percentage not bearing out this correspondence. That this percentage is almost totally limited to people whose lives are as colorless as their charts. I also found that there is one central factor in every chart. An enormously important factor which, for want of a better word I have called the 'level' or 'weight' of a chart. At a high 'level,' the combination of factors listed in text books as 'bad' or 'menacing' often mean constructive works or enlightening experiences. At a low level, even those listed as 'intelligence factors' may mean nonsensical accidents. However, if the one who attempts to read has an (intuitive) knowledge of the 'level' from which to project symbolic meanings into the various combinations of factors, these will arrange themselves into pictures of often astonishing accuracy, or at least into an image as well defined as that of a ship, a whale, or a rock on the screen of a radarscope.

To convince oneself of the validity of these claims, nothing is more profitable than to *see* the 'correspondences' by getting acquainted with one's own chart and with those of one's own close friends, or of celebrities whose lives are well known."

— *Clement Reicher*
World traveler, writer, professor of languages, teacher of astrology and student of oriental mysticism.

III

"Intimates Are Predestined."
> — Henry Brooks Adams

Since ancient times man has felt there was magic connected with numbers. From the beginning of time man has noted the mathematical equation of the life around him, the orbiting planets, the sunrise, the sunset, the phases of the moon, gestation, and the symmetry of each living form. And man has sought solace and emotional security inside the abstract thought of numbers.

From the start the symbolism and the meanings of numbers evolved perhaps due to a coincidence of happenings. Yet, as time passes, and though meanings have been lost in antiquity and the reasons for those remaining become vaguer, it does not seem to alter man's belief in the magnitude of the forces that were thought to come from their use.

It is thought that all relationships vibrate to different number destinies. And whenever two meet, the quality of their characters combines and forms a third more influential force. This force will supercede the direction of the individual. The relationship will have a life all its own.

To discover which number governs your affair, just add the day and month and year of your birth to the day, month, and year of your lover's birth.

It is important that you then add the mystical number 3 to that sum. The total sum will be the Fated number.

EXAMPLE:

If you are born on March 22, 1935 and your intended love was born on July 19, 1930:

ADD: $3+2+2+1+9+3+5$ to $7+1+9+1+9+3+0$
and you get 55 or $5+5=10=1+0=1$

Now when you add the sum of 1 to the mystical number 3 you get your Fated number vibration . . . *four*. Each number causes the relationship to have a special nature.

THE CHARACTER OF THE AFFAIR

Fated Number One

This combination brings much success. Both partners will, because of this relationship, develop many hidden talents. Ideas will be brilliant and lead to some amount of recognition within their community. At least one of them will have the potential for fame increased. There will be much money. It will come in quickly and they will tend to use it more for luxuries than staples. This union will produce children of remarkable intelligence. This team will be sexually compatible. Each will take the lead in romantic matters. Occasional flareups of temperament in regards to which is the boss will not damage feelings. This is a very permanent and long term deal.

Fated Number Two

This is a very moody affair. Circumstances will create a pattern of continuous tearful partings and joyful reunions. There is a tendency, on the part of both, toward promiscuous behavior. During times of separation the emotional longings for each other will be severe. The longings may cause them to seek solace in another's arms. However, the indiscretions will create no problems. Despite dynamic conflicts . . . any permanent break will be impossible. Money is of no great importance here. And the emotions not sex are the key involvement. These two *need* each other — like crazy!

Fated Number Three

Destiny has other plans for these lovers. Responsibilities and duties will demand much. An older relative will eventually move in with them. Everyone will always interfere and try to come between them and what they desire. Together they go down in weakness. As a couple they will be easily upset by gossip . . . and there is certain to be plenty. A wild wind ensnares them and during the fifth year there is a strong potential for separation. Neither one will want to take the cat.

Fated Number Four

Despite beginning sexual attraction of almost violent proportions, this couple soon settles down to a comfortable conservative involvement, and quickly begins hoarding. Security is very important here. There will be no outside love affairs, as the need for them is slight and the personal union extremely fulfilling. The home will be large, modern, plush. The carpets thick. The bank account bulging.

Fated Number Five

As soon as the union is established, travel will occupy most of the life pattern. And if there is any slack time, sports will fill in. The home situation will not exert too strong a pull. And it is not likely that sex will either. Expensive clothes, good times, and the great outdoors will ease any uncomfortable tensions, that is, until someone shows up who will cause one or the other of them to vibrate to number 9. And someone usually does. This relationship could last forever — if they set up shop in the antarctic.

Fated Number Six

A nice homey combination. Comfortable. There will be a lot of mama and papa type smooching — and eating of coffee cake — but not too much real action. Here the home is very important, but not as a show place as in the case of Fated Number Four, more as a place to doze off. Both warm cuddley but not turned on. They won't notice, but the children will be a nuisance to the neighbors.

Fated Number Seven

This is a deliciously melancholy love affair with strong tragiv overtones. At first, partings will be a must. There will be gentle tears. Effort toward understanding. Choked sobs. Wistful and furtive touchings. They soon develop a need for clandestine meetings. And even after both divorces are final and they are legally tied, they continue to visit motels. At the start they are strong and determined to "find happiness": when they eventually do they wonder if six kids between them was so smart, particularly since they got custody. This is a Fated number that always leads to marriage number two. Despite them it lasts.

Fated Number Eight

Both will put on extra weight, but the bank account will grow too. It's a business arrangement from the first kiss. The whole involvement is based on real love, though! Love of self! Neither one is blinded by the other. Neither one is fooled. Both know what's up. Each will support the other in crisis. If a friend offers concerned advice about the other's indiscretions, the friend ends up with a bashed-in head. They are happy. Secure. And perfect for each other. This one lasts and lasts and lasts and lasts.

Fated Number Nine

This is the original sin couple. There isn't any form of erotic behavior that they will ignore. Everything will be tried — and not just once. This is a mad, mad passionate affair. Much arguing. Much sexual activity. He will sport unusual red marks on his back — and she blue ones on her bottom. They eventually grow old, but not together. Usually they migrate to a number six relationship — after 85.

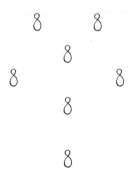

"LOVE WILL FIND THE WAY"—

If despite unfavorable Fated Number influences, you are still determined to reinforce the attraction between you, then a Fated Number Voodoo Seduction Spell will be of considerable assistance.

To generate desire in a friend, increase stimulating and sexually exciting activities with a new acquaintance, or reinforce the attraction between an old love and yourself, numbers are said to help. For every number from one to nine there is a voodoo spell. Each Voodoo Seduction Spell is based upon specific magical symbolism.

Thousands of years of research have led to startling conclusions. Belief is not an essential with any of the spells. It is known to be a fact that in Haiti victims of voodoo are not protected from the spells by their rational disbelief. When hexed, they live or die or become ill according to the whim of the sorcerer. It would seem that whether we like it or not, the power of numbers works!
Fridays at nine.

Voodoo Seduction Spell Number One

Inside a circle of fine wheat flour let a purple candle blaze for nine full minutes.

Offer the flame to the god Pluto.

Sprinkle 3 drops of olive oil into the fire.

Now on a piece of pale green stationary write the name of the loved one and the symbols: 22 . . . sun . . . moon . . . bird.

Burn the paper to an ash in the candle flame.

Let yourself moan soft and long.

Take the ash and the candle and the wheat flour and bury them in the east side of a park.

Do this spell for nine weeks.

Voodoo Seduction Spell Number Two

Take three black beans.

One gray feather.

Three bay leaves and a sprig of sage.

Tie up inside of a red cheesecloth sack.

On the night of a new moon (when the moon is dark) take the sack and drop it into flowing water (spring, brook, river, ocean).

At the same spot . . . light a green candle.

Call out to Venus, goddess of love.

Voodoo Seduction Spell Number Three

On a Wednesday that falls between the tenth and thirteenth of a month . . . Dig a small hole in the southwest corner of a public garden and bury six sunflower seeds.

At 6 P.M. sharp, light a silver candle.

Let it flame for ninety-nine minutes.

Ring a bell once and blow out the flame.

On the next Wednesday bury the candle with the seeds.

Voodoo Seduction Spell Number Four

Each Monday for four weeks at 5:30 P.M. sprinkle coarse salt over the face of a small hand mirror.

Now light a white candle and drip three drops of wax onto the salt.

Place three green peas (fresh, not frozen) onto the three drops of wax.

At the end of four weeks there will be 12 green peas on 12 drops of wax.

The first full moon following, bury the mirror, peas and wax, and the remaining white candle, inside a burlap bag under a backdoor step.

Voodoo Seduction Spell Number Five

Take one flour sifter.

Fill it with small smooth white pebbles.

Wrap it inside a cloth of green silk.

Place it on the frontdoor step of a church at 10 P.M.

Race home and light a pale pink candle.

Let it flame for three hours.

Voodoo Seduction Spell Number Six

For eleven days mail:

A sprig of thyme . . .

Some rosemary . . .

Three cloves . . .

And the name of your love . . . in a yellow envelope
to yourself.

At the end of the eleven days, bury all the eleven envelopes
at the beach.

Voodoo Seduction Spell Number Seven

Take three *unlaid* nonfertilized hen eggs.

Place inside a wooden box . . . along with a photograph
of the love object.

Light one red candle each night for nine nights.

Let them flame nine minutes.

Voodoo Seduction Spell Number Eight

Take a copper pot.

Fill it halfway with rose buds, petals, stems, and leaves.

Place it in front of a window with direct sunlight.

Each night before retiring . . .

Light an orange candle . . .

Let it flame for one minute . . .

Put out the flame by dipping the candle into the copper pot.

Do this for 13 days.

Then take the pot . . . the rose buds, petals, stems
and leaves . . .

Along with the candle . . .

Package and mail to your lover.

Voodoo Seduction Spell Number Nine

Place together one red button . . .

One gold colored pin . . .

Three leaves from a live tree . . .

And one whole head of garlic . . .

Inside a bowl of whole grain uncooked rice.

Store in a cupboard for nine weeks.

7

"Names and Natures do often agree" . . .

The Jewish cabalists believed that each letter of the alphabet could be transposed into a number of equal value, and that if there were two letters with the same numerical value, either letter could do for the other and new *magical* words could be formed, equal in value, but with altered intention.

During one point of the Second World War when the Germans occupied Greece it became obvious to the Jews in Syria and to the Allied forces that soon a German invasion army would enter Syria. It was inevitable. The Jewish people sought help from the Mekkubalim, the cabalists, the Jewish scholars.

The Jewish scholars of the cabala met in an all-night session, and came upon a plan of protection.

Counting upon the magical power within letters and numbers, the cabalists transposed the letters of the name Syria into equal numerical value as the name *Russia;* they then informed a waiting and believing populace that all would be well.

It is a historical fact that soon after their effort, the German army changed its course and invaded Russia. Syria was saved by the numbers.

Modern numerologists knock themselves out attempting to change the "luck" of would be actresses, and many a Penelope P. Perkins has found happiness when converted into Geraldine Goldblatt.

In each part of the world during every segment of history, and at all social levels, ethnic groups have had their own special systems of looking at numbers. One that has hung on through the ages . . . and is about as valuable as any other is the One to Nine system.

Letters *a* through *i* have value one through nine, letters *j* through *r* also value one through nine, and letters *s* through *z* value one through eight.

EXAMPLE:

A	B	C	D	E	F	G	H	I
1	2	3	4	5	6	7	8	9

J	K	L	M	N	O	P	Q	R
1	2	3	4	5	6	7	8	9

S	T	U	V	W	X	Y	Z
1	2	3	4	5	6	7	8

11451   54595   432395
12   28   26

The students of the numbers believe that each number value has a personality associated with one of the planets. Each plant has jurisdiction over a special sign and each sign is known to have a special meaning.

If your name adds up to number *one* you are ruled by the Sun and should be aggressive, egotistic, energetic and a born leader. In matters of love you would always take the initiative. You would be a very pleasing partner — sharp, lively, and protective. Since the Sun has a strong influence on the sign Leo, this would cause you to be dramatic — entertaining and quite a lover.

The number two vibration is ruled by the Moon. This would create a moody, passive, absorbing personality. The sign here is Cancer, and though you would cry a lot, romance would come easily. You would be very susceptible to the opposite sex. And even though you would tend toward unfaithful alliances, you would always go home in the end.

Three is a Jupiter number and is comfortable with Sagittarian type situations. You would take chances — gamble, be extremely restless, have a roving eye, make a good salesman, and spend a lot of money. The opposite sex would be easily attracted. Affairs would be brief but terribly exciting.

Number four is a Saturn number and rules over the sign of Capricorn. As a lover you would tend to brood a lot about the affair coming to an end, and of course it would be. Decidedly the Hamlet type. Partners would be drawn to you if only to comfort you against yourself. Saturn types make good lovers if allowed to sulk every once in a while.

Number five is Mercury ruled and belongs to the signs of Gemini and Virgo. As a number five type lover you would be breezy — flip, flirtatious, fickle, and yet loveable. The planet Mercury is said to have control over the intellect, and most of the number five people are very witty. The Five women are able to handle jobs that deal with communications — such as PBX boards for large companies or telephone work — and they make very good typists. The number five men are also very fast with their hands.

Number six is Venus and has a personality similar to Taurus and Libra. This makes a number six lover very sensual, emotional, physical, and sexy. Outside of that they sometimes like to read poetry . . . and the stock market reports. They are not bad as lovers, and if one can get used to the clutter and tickertape, they are fun as house guests.

Seven is Uranus and Aquarius. This is a difficult number to know. Always the humanitarian, number sevens collect pets everywhere they go, and they go everywhere. If you can tolerate being one of a long list of admirers, number sevens are for you. The only "nice" thing that can be said for them . . . is that they are usually two-timing somebody else.

Eight is Mars and Aries. This is a talkative number . . . and pushy. The number eights don't care too much for sex, but they want you to. . . . They are very hurt when no one notices that they are desirable. They make excellent sports announcers, but they play a poor game. Probably the ideal partner for number seven people.

Nine is Neptune ruled, by Pisces, and covers a multitude of sins. The nines are a mess. Not bad as lovers, once you get used to them. Nines are sensitive — melancholy, imitative, reluctant, despondent, willing to please, mystical, intuitive, insanely jealous, and easily obsessed. If you need to feel tremendously important, these are the people for you. Though they occasionally slip into clandestine relationships, they always come back!

EXAMPLES:

R I C H A R D
$9\ 9\ 3\ 8\ 1\ 9\ 4 = 4\ 3 = 4 + 3 = 7$

N I X O N
$5\ 9\ 6\ 6\ 5 = 3\ 1 = 3 + 1 = 4$

$$7 + 4 = 1\ 1 = 1 + 1 = 2$$

Richard Nixon $=$ No. 2

S A M
$1\ 1\ 4 = 6$

Y O R T Y
$7\ 6\ 9\ 2\ 7 = 3\ 1 = 3 + 1 = 4$

$$6 + 4 = 1\ 0 = 1 + 0 = 1$$

Sam Yorty $=$ No. 1

R O N A L D
$9\ 6\ 5\ 1\ 3\ 4 = 2\ 8 = 2 + 8 = 1\ 0 = 1 + 0 = 1$

R E A G A N
$9\ 5\ 1\ 7\ 1\ 5 = 2\ 8 = 2 + 8 = 1\ 0 = 1 + 0 = 1 \quad 1 + 1 = 2$

Ronald Reagan $=$ No. 2

L O U I S E
$3\ 6\ 3\ 9\ 1\ 5 = 2\ 7 = 2 + 7 = 9$

H U E B N E R
$8\ 3\ 5\ 2\ 5\ 5\ 9 = 3\ 7 = 3 + 7 = 1\ 0$

$$9 + 1\ 0 = 1\ 9 = 1 + 9 = 1\ 0 = 1 + 0 = 1$$

Louise Huebner $=$ No. 1

JUDY
$1 3 4 7 = 1 5 = 1 + 5 = 6$

GARLAND
$7 1 9 3 1 5 4 = 3 0 = 3 + 0 = 3$ $6 + 3 = 9$

Judy Garland = No. 9

ZSA ZSA
$8 1 1 \quad 8 1 1 = 2 0 = 2 + 0 = 2$

GABOR
$7 1 2 6 9 = 2 5 = 2 + 5 = 7$ $2 + 7 = 9$

Zsa Zsa Gabor = No. 9

Some of my best friends have been number threes — but even so I wouldn't want my daughter to marry one.

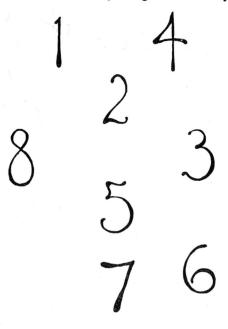

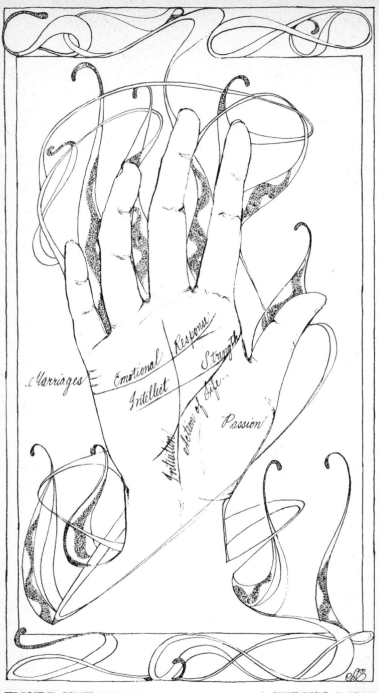

Marriages

Emotional Response

Intellect

Strength

Intuition

election of Life

Passion

FIGURE XVII   *A WITCH'S PALM*

14

You Gotta Hand It to the Palmists

Cool eye
Straight on
Steps chosen well — steady
Voice in control, no careless lilt
Only sweaty palms would tell I had felt the tilt
And my heart was ready!

— *Louise Huebner*

"Length of days is in her right hand, riches and honor are in her left." — Proverbs 3:16

By the twelfth year most are well aware of the lines within the hand's palm and of the many significant meanings of those lines. There are not too many who are not able to identify at least the basic lines, those that are associated with the quality of the emotions, inellect, and life expectancy.

Women are more prone to seek out opportunity for "cheir" analysis during their earlier years, before life was hit, and men tend to pursue cheiromantic solutions in later years after they discover life has indeed hit — and hit hard.

Everyone, within a lifetime, has a palm reading, at least once. There is always the favorite kooky aunt who is able to astound with her keen insight into the secret areas of a personality, or the just-for-fun carnival psychic, who, along with the laughs, manages to throw in a few startling comments concerning hidden behavior traits, or else the beach-pier gypsy who, between ungrammatical grunts interspersed with "Do you know whad I mean?", offers meaning, or perhaps the "queer" fellow across town who is really "sort of nice," and as a palm reader is *great* — all these types and more keep inspiring us ever onward toward uncomfortable belief.

But, are they reading the lines in the palm? Palmistry has been going on since the beginning of man. The first fascination an infant cultivates is for its own hand. As time passes the interest never lessens.

The most ancient record of man's search for truth within his cupped hand goes back to the early Hindus. The Brahmans have preserved an old book in a cave temple. This book is made of human skin. It contains many hundreds of excellently drawn illustrations of palms, and carefully explains each marking.

The book had been treated with a special compound of herbs. It is written in a red liquid, and due to the special treatment the writing has not faded. Each page of human skin appears to have been glazed by a varnish. It is remarkable that this ancient artifact has been able to ward off wear and decay. Naturally, since the Hindus were well up on preservatives, we also take their word for line significance.

Palmistry is traced back into the history of many countries. Way into antiquity it was of great interest to scholars in China, Tibet, Persia, and Egypt. However, in its present form it seems to be closely connected with Greek interpretations. And even its name *Cheoromancy* stems from the Greek word *cheir* meaning hand.

Whenever a field can throw uot names like Aristole, Pliny, Paracelsus, Cardamis, Albertus Magus, and the Emperor Augustus, we tend to be awed. Palmistry is full of such names. Why, there is even a record of Hispanus discovering a book on cheiromancy lettered in gold on an altar that had been dedicated to the god Hermes. Hispanus immediately sent it as a gift to Alexander the Great.

Impressed?

By the time everyone reaches middle age they are either convinced palmistry works, or they are convinced it's "the bunk." Attitudes are of course wholly dependent upon the accuracy of the palm reader's statements. Palm readers, along with the fabulous names, throw science at us in support of their love. We are told doctors check our hands for telltale indications of a variety of illnesses. Much, they say, can be told by an individual's hand.

The liver, the blood, the kidneys, the lungs, the gall bladder, and the heart all leave whopping good clues as to their activity, condition, or lack of interest. And now there is strong evidence pointing toward a coincidence of palm markings and intellect, especially cases of distorted development as in mongolism.

We are told that it is really quite logical to expect an association between lines and human behavior. After all, certain movements produce particular creases, and movements are colored by temperament, and temperament is behavior. Behavior produces events, and therefore the lines and creases can indicate future, fortune, and destiny!

It does seem clear. Except . . . babies are born with the lines well established. There is no argument that trained medical men can interpret hand condition and come up with amazing conclusions. But, can a loser, down at the pier, really judge from the lines, and predict marriage, trips to Europe, and inheritance?

How much can an attractive fortune-teller get out of smudges, cuts, sores, untrimmed nails and trembling, limp sweaty palms? Add to that the fact that the hand showed up for a reading in the first place, and you have enough material for a twenty-minute psych-in.

"But," the devotees of the crooked-crease school snarl, "There is *proof!*" O.K. Maybe there is, but so far no one has found any. There really has been no controlled research concerneed with the question of palm lines. Only one heavy contribution was ever made, by a man called Cheiro. He is quoted as though he were still carrying the banner, yet he has long been dead. Besides, he was a psychic. And, if he was so proud of what he came up with, why didn't he use his real name?

As a young girl I read palms all over the place. My grandmother taught me the "meanings," and once I knew them, I then did it all by "feel." I am convinced you can tell a lot about someone from touch.

Do you need *lines* to tell whether hands are warm, cold, or in between, or if they are dry, moist, or normal? Are lines needed to show that hands are limp, strong, or average, careless, or alert? Do lines tell whether they seek out or draw away from contact. So far, research has been unable to conclude in favor of or against the line theory.

Most "good" readers admit they are psychic. They may use the lines in the hand as a focal point for concentration, and as a support for their own self-confidence so that they can make a judgment. Rarely do the lines give them any information. They claim of course that with years of experience and viewing "thousands" of palms, they have become convinced that the lines are important and meaningful.

Certainly after years of experience and viewing thousands of palms and discussing intimately thousands of life habits, insight develops. But are the lines significant?

The fanatics continue to pull out famous palms as proof. They point out the markings and wail, "See that, and that, and that, it's always there as an indication of . . . " But before we can accept as proof any such evidence, it would be wise to consider how many possessors of specific marks reach a goal and how many do not, and how many get to nirvana without a mark.

It is difficult to accept a five-dollar-palmist's sincerity about controlled resarch. It would be preferable if those far removed from the occult field studied the subject. Surely an interest that has remained up to the present time, that finds its origin in man's infancy, must have some convincing aspects attached to it.

Perhaps someday science will be able to explain how it is that a palmist is able to pick up the hand of a total stranger, turn it palm side up, spread out the fingers, and whisper, "During your thirty-seventh year your stepfather died ol alcoholism." Is it something found in the grooves of the palm, or is it something found in the grooves of the brain?

Sometimes the most unsuspecting personalities have a bit of extra intuition, and delight in showing it. Once, during a television news program, film cuts were shown of a group of happy, smiling vacationers. Lounging on the yacht deck, one intense young man held a friend's palm between his two hands

and was busily involved "reading" it. The young man was
John F. Kennedy.

Easy Palms

Determine which lines are most deeply impressed and attribute greater strength of character to those areas. Is it the
emotional-response groove, the intellectual-capacity line, or
the life-action markings that are the deepest? See if the lines
are clearly separated to indicate broad viewpoints and cooperative characteristics. Which lines are tied up with which
others? Does the intellectual tie in heavily with the life-action
mark, or does it stand alone — clear, receptive, and above it
all — or does it become all muddled up with the emotional-
response groove?

Do the lines sweep across the hand or do they fall short
of their goals? Are the lines marked plainly or are their meanings camouflaged by a multitude of wispy insignificant detours?
Is the mound of passion full and hard or weak and flat? Is the
emotional approach steady and straightforward or are there
many offbranches signifying many changes of heart? Is there
strength indicated by a tight crisscross of heart, head, and life?
Or is the crossroad of their meeting a very confused disaster
area?

Does the line of intuition, insight, and introspection adequately make itself known, or does this palm lack any real
depth or consideration? Are the fingers widely and attractively
spaced to indicate a personality who is willing to give another
freedom of speech, thought, and action? Or are the fingers
closely spaced and aimed inward, attesting to mean, petty
reactions and a domineering nature? If the thumb is able to
bend almost to the wrist, watch for a killer type. However,
the usual outlet in civilized situations is promiscuity. And most
times the victim's heart, and not life, is lost to the cruel
blows rendered while helplessly lying in bed.

15

By the Light of
the Silvery Moon

γ

"The wind changes at night and the dreams come. It is very
cold . . . there are strange stars near Arcturus . . . voices are
calling an unknown name in the sky."

— Archibald MacLeish

The list of direct influences the moon has upon the tides,
sea life, criminal activity, pregnant women and the lunatic
fringe, is endless. In an experiment performed by a body of
scientists working in connection with a government project,
a primitive form of sea life was transported to the center of
the United States farmlands.

For a few days, the sea life continued to respond to the tide
pattern to which they were accustomed. And when the tide
came in or out in Cape Cod on the Atlantic, at that same instant, the sea life, secluded in Kansas test tubes, reacted accordingly. But after a few days, once they had become accli-
mated, a strange phenomenon took place. The scientists

FIGURE XVIII   *STRANGE STARS NEAR ARCTURUS*

keeping a timetable for the tide pattern on the East Coast noticed that the little beasties were no longer synchronizing their activities with *that* tide. What had happened? After calculating a timetable pattern for tides in a Kansas ocean — if Kansas had an ocean — it was soon apparent what was taking place. There in Kansas, whenever the earth and moon held the particular relationship necessary to produce high or low tides, the misplaced sea life, more than a thousand miles from its ocean nest, responded properly. Evidently, they were reacting to some unseen influence of the moon.

If the moon's relationship to the earth can produce an influence, then, some believe, the earth's relationship to the sun ought also to produce an influence, an influence over other than just seasonal changes. In support of this second theory, however, there is still not much data from scientific research. The only evidence in favor of the theory has been contributed by crackpot astrologers. For centuries astrologers have insisted that the position of the earth in its solar orbit is responsible for an Aries, Taurus, Gemini, personality, etc.

The scientists, though accepting the moon as a valid subject for research, have shunned the sun, due to its shady association with astrology.

Granted, the majority of the world's astrologers are not adequately trained to interpret the subtle changes that do occur as a result of the sun's motions, but it *is* unsporting of the scientific world to ignore the probability that changes occur at all!

Astrologers — a mad bunch — go even further. Could not, they wonder, all planetary positions be influential?. Well they could! But we really will never know for sure. At least not until an effort to prove or disprove this theory is attempted by more capable minds. That will be a long time in coming. The rational are scared off by the irrational behavior of the theory's most loyal supporters. And I don't blame them!

The disturbed and erratic behavor of your average astrologer scares me — and I'm a witch. They always place heavy emphasis on trivia, and continued distortion of conclusions, and it's unfortunate, but astrologers have never made any effort to close ranks, screen associates, or research theories. Attitudes either imply that man is stronger than the Solar system, or is helplessly intimidated by it. A refusal to increase knowledge and an insistance on continuing to support archaic methods suffocates astrology. The battle over planetary influence being *deliberate* or *coincidental* has made an orphan of the facts!

What are the facts? Planetary patterns do coincide with human activities. We don't know if it's all part of a "grand scheme," and we don't know that it isn't predetermined, but we do know that a "coincidence" phenomenon exists.

Just because so many kooks are impressed is no reason for the sane to ignore the significant factors. Maybe the interpretations have been off because of lack of real concrete research. Although frequently wrong about *what* will happen, most astrologers are usually fantastically correct about *when*. And that is fascinating! That a planet should be in any tight relationship with another planet at a moment that exactly coincides with an earth event is a bit extraordinary. It should be investigated!

We should no longer worry about *why* it is happening, or whether it is *wanting* to happen. But, we should begin to notice that it *is* happening. And many, many, many times!

RCA Communications Inc., since 1951, has utilized the fact that particular planetary patterns do coincide with sunspot activity and are related to magnetic storms and other atmospheric disturbances. They don't call their method of observation astrology, but outside of that, there seems to be no other distinction. RCA employed a John H. Nelson to discover a method for accurately predicting ionospheric conditions. After only two years of study he came up with correlations with planetary patterns.

Before Nelson's study was employed, predictions were about 65 percent accurate. Afterward, using astrology, or the planetary patterns method, predictions increased to a 90 percent accuracy!

Believers tell us astrology has survived through the ages because it works. Considering no sensible effort has been made to explore its validity, I think it's miraculous it got through even the first eclipse!

Now if you were born on the moon, your horoscope would be most unusual. Earth-oriented astrology deals with planetary patterns based upon the latitude and longitude of your place of birth.

The mathematically calculated positions of the planets are joined within a map shape that relies heavily upon the exact degree the earth holds while in orbit of the sun. (360 degrees to be covered in one year.) And the exact degree of spin about the earth's axis. (360 degree spin within twenty-four hours.)

While the earth itself is not used as a focal point for astrological considerations, nevertheless it is used as a source for narrow and opinionated interpretations. These opinions, due to the earth's chancy position on the elliptic, would appear to be biased to say the least.

Five thousand years of naive research will have gone for naught when a moon astrologer attempts a reading for an individual born during GET (ground elapsed time), in a small colony located just outside of the Sea of Sighs. The old ground rules certainly will not apply!

No matter how impelling the stars may be, it will take a while for astrologers to figure out the new meanings of the new patterns. In order to control the situation, an astrologer will have to be a keen observer of human behavior and an extremely adept psychologist, along with having plenty of hutzpah. I sympathize.

What do you tell someone who is born under the sign of a Full Earth . . . with John Glenn rising on the ascendant, and Edwin Aldwin Jr. and Neil Armstrong conjunct, Apollo 11 in the Fifth House of love affairs?

> "Embrace me leaping flames of night
> And let me share the fantasy
> The sheer delight
> Of constellations whirling on through space
> At some incredible
> Unimaginable pace.
> Let me too hear the music of the star
> The rhythmic beats of creations from afar
> And for one moment out of endless time
> Let me pretend this universe is mine."

— Louise Huebner

ORIENTAL ASTROLOGY

(Find the animal symbol ruling your birth)

Cock:

1873 1885 1897 1909 1921 1933 1945 1969

Brave, bossy, sexy, intellectual, emotional, forceful, great depths.

Dog:

1874 1886 1898 1910 1922 1934 1946 1970

Selfish, sincere, creative, flirtatious, melancholy, superficial sex drive.

Pig:

1875 1887 1899 1911 1923 1935 1947 1971

Optimistic, temperamental, magnetic, loyal, philosophical, compassionate.

Rat:

1876 1888 1900 1912 1924 1936 1948 1972

Charming, stingy, alert, opportunistic, persevering, promiscuous.

Ox:

1877 1889 1901 1913 1925 1937 1949 1973

Polite, prejudiced, humorous, talkative, pessimistic, patient.

Tiger:

1878 1890 1902 1914 1926 1938 1950 1962 1974

Loyal, cautious, creative, magnetic, strong sex drive, promotional.

Hare:

1879   1891   1903   1915   1927   1939   1951   1963
1975

Affectionate, friendly, intellectual, dexterous, faithful, objective.

Dragon:

1880   1892   1904   1916   1928   1940   1952   1964
1976

Loving, nervous, sexy, talented, pliable, emotional, revengeful.

Snake:

1881   1893   1905   1917   1929   1941   1953   1965
1977

Vain, loyal, clever, cold, informed, talkative, tactless.

Horse:

1882   1894   1906   1918   1930   1942   1954   1966
1978

Popular, impatient, creative, emotional, strong sex drive, manipulator.

Sheep:

1883   1895   1907   1919   1931   1943   1955   1967
1979

Confused, noble, suspicious, sexy, magnetic, devious.

Monkey:

1884   1896   1908   1920   1932   1944   1956   1968
1980

Fussy, tricky, opportunistic, glib, dramatic, revengeful.

WESTERN ASTROLOGY

Aries: March 20–April 19

Personality: Passionate, imaginative, easily bored, romantic, intellectual, leadership ability

Lucky day: Tuesday

Lucky number: 3

Lucky colors: Clear shades of bright chinese red and antique blue and white

Tip: Gets along best with Leo, Aquarius, Taurus, or rich partners.

Aries, easily aggravated, would be better off not to get mated. They discover very early in life that sympathy is not a good substitute for passion, and the passionate don't get very much sympathy. The philosophical approach will get them further than ruthless ambition. Good in bed.

Ⅱ

Taurus: April 19–May 21

Personality: Sensual, capable, materialistic, possessive, stubborn

Lucky day: Friday
Lucky number: 6
Lucky colors: Green, purple, black
Tip: Gets along best with Scorpio, Libra, or sexy partners.

Taurus tend toward racy relationships. They are pretty fantastic but don't enjoy being tripped, however lightly. For them, time and patience may accomplish more than force and passion, and a little passion will frequently help to pass the time. Can go on for hours.

Gemini: May 21–June 21
Personality: Creative, intellectual, nervous, nimble, witty, naive, talkative
Lucky day: Wednesday
Lucky number: 4
Lucky colors: Orange, yellow, white, sand
Tip: Gets along best with Aquarians or Leos or men in professions. Likes to show off.

Gemini are constantly inconstant. Ruled by the planet Mercury they are supposed to be great wits. However in matters of love, half of them are great, and the rest half-witted. Travel to and from romantic interludes will ease the dull pains. They have a low threshold of tolerance. Swift reactions.

Cancer: June 21–July 22

Personality: Emotional, temperamental, moody, sentimental, romantic, easily bored, sexy, dormant leadership ability

Lucky day: Monday

Lucky number: 2

Lucky colors: Green, brown, burnt orange, gold

Tip: Gets along best with Capricorns, Leos, or alone in a cute house.

Cancers concentrate on combustible combinations. Their uncontrollable passion offers secure love after a fashion. For them, emotional involvements due to habit are not as fulfilling as habitual involvements. They are the sexual activists of the Zodiac. Take their time.

♏

◡

Leo: July 22–August 22

Personality: Flamboyant, vain, proud, domineering, dramatic, susceptible to opposite sex

Lucky day: Sunday

Lucky numbers: 1, 3, 5, 7, 9

Lucky colors: Gold, antique blue, burnt orange

Tip: Gets along best with everyone and anyone who likes them.

Leos lazily leap into lyrical liaisons. They mistake the power drive for emotional urges and tend to fall in love instead of going on to fame and fortune. Energy should not be spent in proving superiority to equals, but rather in remaining equal to superiors. They are sexually vulnerable. Show-offs.

Virgo: August 22–September 22

Personality: Earthy, sexy, exacting, hypercritical, hypochondrical, witty, sarcastic, loyal, hard worker

Lucky day: Wednesday

Lucky number: 4

Lucky colors: Sand, moss green, white

Tip: Finds it difficult to get along with anyone but prefers Taurus, Capricorn, and Cancer.

The planet Mercury symbolizes speed and has jurisdiction over the sign of Virgo. Consequently Virgo women make good typists and Virgo men are also very fast with their hands. They are sexually curious. Methodical approach.

Libra: September 22–October 22

Personality: Compassionate, emotional, creative, witty, intellectual, uncomfortable about leadership ability

Lucky day: Friday

Lucky number: 6

Lucky colors: Clear shades of bright red, dutch blue, orange, and white

Tip: Best bet is Gemini or Aquarius or freedom. Sometimes like Leo for a laugh.

Libra romantics never fool with semantics. By love they are very easily captured, as they are born already half-enraptured. For them, sexual unions are urgent. Excellent lovers.

Scorpio: October 22-November 22

Personality: Violent, selfish, stubborn, emotional, strong, sexy, capable, susceptible to sex, determined

Lucky day: Tuesday

Lucky number: 22

Lucky colors: Reds or shades of purples, blacks, brown, amber

Tip: Here much depends upon the sex appeal of the partner, but gravitates toward Aries, Taurus, and Gemini.

Sex isn't a four letter word and Scorpio very early in life learned to spell correctly. Besides spelling they also learned a few other things. Slow to start, they never ever come to a stop.

Sagittarius: November 22–December 22

Personality: Restless, idealistic, inspired, talkative, romantic

Lucky day: Thursday

Lucky number: 5

Lucky colors: Gold, white, sapphire, ruby

Tip: Likes Leos, Aries, Virgo, and Pisces, and making love.

This sign discovers early enough that a touch of madness keeps one from going insane. They carry this theory into the bedroom, and lovemaking with them is a laugh a minute. They can last all night.

Capricorn: December 22–January 20

Personality: Melancholy, righteous, sexy, deep, spiritual, materialistic, high ideals, much leadership ability

Lucky day: Saturday

Lucky numbers: 7, 8

Lucky colors: Brown, amber reds, blues, black

Tips: Finds happiness late in life. Emotional fulfillment with Leo, Taurus, or Cancer.

Capricorns are accussed of being emotionally cold. Yet, this sign is symbolized by the goat and goats are hardly ever frigid. A contraire — goats are known for their climbing ability and promiscuity. However, they complain a lot.

☽

♓

Aquarius: January 20–February 19

Personality: Mystical, brooding, breezy, stubborn, flip, inventive, domineering, determined, mentally sexy, idealistic

Lucky day: Sunday

Lucky number: 11

Lucky colors: Violets, fuschias, silvers, light greens, bright blues

Tip: Loves everyone, especially Sagittarius, Gemini, Cancer, Leo, and sometimes even Aries.

Aquarians always extend disfavor and always expect a blight. They never remember a favor and never forget a slight. Have to be cajoled into it, but usually are worth the effort.

Pisces: February 19–March 20

Personality: Promiscuous, seductive, mystical, melancholic, poetic, susceptible to sex

Lucky day: Friday

Lucky numbers: 6, 7

Lucky colors: Green, blue, violet and pink

Tip: Certainly prefers to stay single, however usually forced into marriage out of sympathy.

Pisces unfortunately only find delight in the truly clandestine. Make excellent lovers. Cannot tolerate legal ties.

ELEMENTAL CLUE TO ROMANCE

Fire Signs:

An affair must offer a fast pace or you soon tire of it. A lover must involve your imagination in order to attract you, and you demand an intellectual rapport. You are excited more by the idea than the love itself. You are difficult to know and very occasionally worth the effort.

Earth Signs:

A romance must be tinged with tragedy. Happiness bores you. Only a problematic tangled relationship holds your attention. You thrive on emotional shocks. Only a strong character can take you. And one usually does!

Air Signs:

Not very emotinoal and phoney from the start, you need two lovers. One for real and one for show. Never one to find the world well lost for love you compromise your needs and the showy partner, or the one society anticipates wins out.

Water Signs:

Sympathy stimultes your desires. Of you and your loves it is wondered what you see in each other. The less anyone sees in your partner the more you turn on! For you differences of age, religion, race and sex are a must!

16

Indefinitely Probable

A probability is a likelihood! It is much stronger than a possibility (that which is only *capable* of existing), but falls short of being an actual certainty. On the basis of the available evidence, even though not yet proved or certain, a probability can reasonably be expected to happen. It is very likely to take place, and more likely to occur than not to occur. Philosophically, since there can never be a certainty in knowledge, a probability then seems sufficient basis for action. In mathematics it is the ratio of the chances favoring a certain happening, all the chances for and against it. In life most things are possible. Not all are probable. And not many are certain.

If after much observation it appears certain coincidences parallel specific happenings, could the coincidences then be used as tools of prediction? Would the presence of the evidence support a happening's probability more than not, despite lack of relationship?

PROFESSOR KOSSIS: Mrs. Huebner? I'm returning your call. You had some questions concerning mathematics?

MRS. HUEBNER: Yes, thank you Professor.

PROFESSOR KOSSIS: You know, when I got your message, I recognized your name immediately. You're doing a book on E.S.P. and fortune-telling?

MRS. HUEBNER: Yes.

PROFESSOR KOSSIS: Umm! Of course — your name is not unknown to me, — that's why I called.

MRS. HUEBNER: Thank you Professor Kossis. I appreciate your taking the time.

PROFESSOR KOSSIS: Lana? isn't it?

MRS. HUEBNER: Uh?

PROFESSOR KOSSIS: Lana? Lana Huebner?

MRS. HUEBNER: Lana? Oh, my God, no. I'm Louise. Lana? . . . She was married to my husband years ago—years ago.

PROFESSOR KOSSIS: Oh—oh. I'm sorry. Oh.

MRS. HUEBNER: It's all right.

PROFESSOR KOSSIS: I hope I haven't offended you.

MRS HUEBNER: Not at all. It was before my time.

PROFESSOR KOSSIS: I could have sworn. . . . Your name was so familiar. I told the secretary, "I know that lady." Sorry . . . sorry.

MRS. HUEBNER: It's all right. But then you don't know me?

PROFESSOR KOSSIS: No!

MRS. HUEBNER: Well, now I am offended. Right here in my hometown too. I'm the Official Witch.

PROFESSOR KOSSIS: Oh?

Perhaps we had gotten off to a bad start. Since we were now well off the track of the interview — attempting an easy manner — I inquired as to the national origin of his name.

"*American!*" he snarled, with the first show of energy since we had started.

"Oh — but back, Professor — your heritage: is the name of Turkish origin?"

"*American!*"

I then decided to get quickly to the point.

Astrologers, numerologists, palmists, card-readers, and psychics in general often can take a series of coincidences that seem always to exist in particular happenings and from them predict future happenings accurately. Why should this be so? Is there any way at all for mathematics to answer how this is accomplished?

The professor said there was of course a way. Predictions coming true are a probability. He said they only seem mysterious because everyone isn't looking at the entire picture.

What picture?

Well, he told me to take a look at the freeways. He said you are in a slow lane and decide to change to another that is moving freely, and just as you do, your old lane speeds up and the second choice slows down. It had to happen. It was probable.

The freeways didn't enlighten me. Why, at the precise moment I switch over, does that happen? The professor told me it always happened. Then he went on to explain a gambler and a lucky streak.

He told me you could mathematically calculate how long a lucky streak would continue, and how long, when it came to an end, the unlucky period would last.

"Probabilities! It's all probabilities."

What would you take into consideration?

"All the evidence."

What evidence?

He told me you would consider how long the luck was in effect, when the gambler was last lucky, and the length of time his previous luck lasted. Also, how many other people gambled in that location, their wins, and the duration of their lucky periods. In other words you looked at everything — all the past facts — added it all up, and came out with the probability of a happening. But, surely, this was not an accurate method? The professor assured me. It worked!

But doesn't that imply that there is some order to everything?

He said there was indeed. And he went on to list everything in the universe that is balanced, including cell structures. It was impressive.

In the moment's silence I took to contemplate the magnitude of his statements, he asked; "Lana, whatever became of Lana?"

She never had interested me too much. I hadn't kept in touch with her, and I told him so. But since he brought her up again, I asked him what he thought of our present experience. How could you attempt to calculate the odds in our coincidence? How many witches telephone strange professors of probability, only to discover the professor once knew her husband's ex-wife? Surely, that coincidence was not probable?

He said it was all very probable and the coincidence certainly had no significance. The fact that three million people live in our area added *nothing* to our coincidence.

We went back to more certain probabilities. How could every unusual happening be attributed to coincidence. Surely not all coincidences are results of probabilities? He said they were.

"There is simple order everywhere! Paterns. Just coincidences."

Granted, but what of man-made chaos? Surely, there is no real set pattern to human accident?

"Mrs. Huebner, there is a pattern. People just don't see the entire picture. If they did, they would know that chaos can be enclosed within a definite pattern."

"Professor, may I quote you? It's an interesting thought."

"*No!* I don't want to be quoted. I'm not thinking clearly today and I may not be saying it right. But it's something like that. It's close."

"O.K. But, Professor, why, why should there be any order to an accident? How can that be? How can there be order to freeway lanes taking turns in loosening up, just at random moments? Or lines in the banks or the post offices? Or at the checkout counters? Shouldn't that just be wild chance?"

"No, They are probabilities and can be calculated. There is order to all things."

"Professor, could you explain this again."

"She got fat you know. I ran into her in San Francisco once . . . and she was fat."

"Professor, could you explain why you think strong coincidences exist?

"They just do that's all!"

Well, if they do exist, and we know they exist, couldn't they be added up and couldn't prediction of "probabilities" be based upon them? The professor said *NO*. He said fortune-tellers attribute too much significance to the coincidences. They were nothing, just coincidences, and only existed in co-relationships—casual relationships. They meant nothing. It was merely probable for coincidences to occur coincidentally.

"But, Professor, if they occur, and even if they mean nothing, but they are always in evidence during specific moments, couldn't they be used as a basis to calculate future probable occurrances?"

"No, they cannot, Mrs. Huebner."

"Why not?"

"Because, Mrs. Huebner, there are no probabilities in probabilities."

I was glad Lana had met him first.

Unmindful of Professor Kossis's suggestion that only mathematicians be free to calculate the probabilities, Dale Richardson, researcher and writer for national astrology magazines, specializes in investment charts, with great success, and has a steady and influential clientel. What is it he does?

"Astrology cannot be an exact science as it cannot be limited to that which can only be weighed and measured. I had a client once who got all his accounting from his business manager and board of directors who told him that he was going bankrupt. My astrological indications showed that this was not the case, and I was the only one that said he was not going bankrupt. And that he would in five years achieve a new pinnacle. There was a storm, but it passed, and he has since gone on to better and better times.

"If the astrologer's analysis of past situations and present situations is accurate, then we can place a certain degree of reliability on the astrologers' projection of the future. If the past has been reliable, and the present is reliable, then the future may also be expected to be reliable. We're simply playing the odds."

The Five's Have It

Mayne Kenny is a researcher, writer, teacher and astrologer. She is President of Educational Astrology, one of the largest and oldest astrology groups in Southern California. She pays close attention to coincidence.

On November 7, 1967, Mayne had a serious operation. Everybody knows that that date adds up to *number five*. $1+1+7+1+9+6+7=32=3+2=5$. And astrologers know *number five* is a *Mercury number*, and rules the sign of Virgo. And Mayne knew Virgo ruled her House of Health. A minor coincidence? Right?

Mayne's doctor, Dr. Arthur Tobin, has his office on 3731 Stocker, and that also adds up to *number five*. He is in Suite 203. *Five* again. Dr. Tobin is Mayne's family doctor and he sent her to a surgeon, Dr. James Locke Meler. And his suite number is 203. Also adding up to *number five*. The surgeon sent Mayne to the Crenshaw Center Hospital, and there her bed number was *five*. Later she was sent for treatments to a Dr. Craig. His suite number? 203. *Five!* At the time of her illness, Mayne lived in apartment 203. *Five.*

During the year of her illness she was sick with it five times, and visited the hospital five times.

Wistfully, Mayne notes that there are five letters in each of the names involved. Dr. Arthur Tobin, Dr. James Locke Meler, Dr. Craig, and a nurse Doris Adams, was especially assigned to her — certainly a potent array of coincidences.

Mayne says she doesn't know why these coincidences took place. She only knows they did. She said you couldn't calculate them, but you would have to be "an idiot to ignore them."

Mayne didn't ignore them.

Of course, the series of coincidences were probably quite probable and nothing at all to get excited about. The same experiences must occur repeatedly to all people all the time.

Mayne has had other Professor-Kossis-defying experiences. One of them is quite remarkable.

One afternoon, Mayne was seated at a bus stop at Crenshaw and Venice, waiting for the Crenshaw bus, when the Venice bus stopped and an old woman carrying flowers, got off, approached her, and asked if the Crenshaw bus stopped at Manchester, Mayne replied, "Yes, but if you are going to the cemetery you can get off at Florence."

The old woman said she was visiting the cemetery. And when the bus arrived, they both got on it and decided to sit together.

Neither one told the other her name, but the old woman did tell Mayne about a problem. Last year she and her husband had purchased lots in an undeveloped land area at the Inglewood Park cemetery. They were told that if either passed away before the land was developed, they could be placed in a mausoleum temporarily. Just a few weeks ago though, her husband had died. The land was as yet undeveloped, and the cemetery for awhile placed the husband in the mausoleum as promised. However, they soon told her he had to be moved, and suggested that she buy lots over in the older, developed section. She agreed. And at the same time ordered a double tombstone. Now, for the first time, she was about to visit the cemetery, to check out the stones, the lots, and his move.

By the time she finished her story the bus reached Mayne's stop at 67th Street, and Mayne said goodbye to the old woman and got off.

Later when Mayne's husband, Robert, arrived home from work, she related the incident to him, and suggested they drive over to the cemetery to check out their own lots. They too, had purchased lots in the new undeveloped portion.

When they did get there, they were reasurred, as their lots were in an area that had just recently been developed. As they were driving away, Mayne asked Robert to stop the car. They were now near the old section. She got out, and with a breathless "Wait here," dashed off. She ran across the park in a diagonal and headed past a couple of hundred graves, straight toward *one*. She stopped at a grave with a double tombstone. One side was marked Walter C. Manlove, the other was marked for Antoinette. Mayne thought Mrs. Manlove would approve of the stone, and went back to her car.

She said, "I think Mrs. Manlove will be pleased with the stone." Yet she couldn't explain how she had "known" where Mr. Manlove's grave was located. They had a difficult time finding their own!

After they arrived home, still disturbed by her "knowledge," Mayne called a friend living in Venice and asked if a Walter C. Manlove was listed in the telephone directory. He was. Mayne called the number. "Antoinette, remember me? I'm the lady you met at the bus stop this morning. I just called to tell you my husband and I visited your husband's grave, and we think the tombstone is very nice."

"Oh, how sweet of you to call, dear. Yes, I did like it too."

Mrs. Manlove never thought the happening was unusual. I guess she is a follower of Professor Kossis. And after all there's nothing to get excited about. Just a probability! It happens all the time.

There have been many times in my life when I have had experiences that would have been impossible to calculate as probable coincidences. One night I dreamed I was on a street corner in Paris, waiting for the light to change. Across the street, my husband was talking to a woman. He stood in the sunlight, she was in the shadows, though I couldn't see him clearly, I could make out her hair color and build.

He motioned me to hurry over to meet her. "Hurry," he said, "Last time we were in Paris, you didn't meet her." There were crowds of people milling about. The traffic flow was endless, and the light didn't change. Just as it finally changed, the crowd made it impossible for me to move quickly, and when I did, a bus pulled up to the other street corner and the woman got on, and I got there just as it pulled away. When I got to the other side of the street my husband said, "Oh, too bad. You would have liked her. She was nice."

In the morning over coffee I related my dream. "Ah hah. *Who* was the blond?"

At about three-thirty that afternoon, my husband "happened," "coincidentally," to stop at a huge discount store to purchase a very little needed, "on sale for just that day only" waste paper basket. Surrounded by crowds of people, he stood waiting at the checkout counter. Someone tapped him on the shoulder. A woman. Her description, the same as the one I had given him at breakfast that morning.

"Hi, remember me? I was the teller in the bank in Paris!"

For a few moments, they went through the usual "Isn't it a funny coincidence" routine. Just a few months ago she married an American. It was her first visit to that particular discount shop. My husband's first in two years. They had not met in six years. Her last words were, "Bye. Have to catch a bus!"

That's all there was to it. Nothing earth-shaking. In the split dimensions of psychic phenomena, I guess I just didn't cross the street in time. I wonder how Professor Kossis would calculate the probabilities of *that* coincidence?

But I'm not going to get excited.

A GAMBLER

Howard Scheinfeld III

"*If I feel it, I bet. If I don't feel it, I sit.* Because based on the probabilities you can't win. You can't beat the odds. You don't have a chance unless you are riding a lucky streak. Normal betting, normal conditions, it's impossible to win. Even winning you lose in theory. The house has a 7/10 percent edge in their favor. If you bet a dollar and you win, you win back 98.6 percent of the dollar. If a gambler made the same bet in the same spot at the same time every day, he would lose. But he couldn't be bankrupt completely. He would always have to end up with at least $0.0000000001. If you come up with four on the first roll, you have a chance of 165 rolls out of 1980 rolls that you will make four again. Or 3 out of 36. With 55 wins to the 110 losses possible. How can you win? There are only 36 different ways dice can turn up."

Number 2	1 and 1
(one way)	
Number 3	1 and 2
(two ways)	2 and 1
Number 4	1 and 3
(three ways)	3 and 1
	2 and 2
Number 5	3 and 2
(four ways)	2 and 3
	4 and 1
	1 and 4
Number 6	3 and 3
(five ways)	1 and 5
	5 and 1
	4 and 2
	2 and 4
Number 7	6 and 1
(six ways)	1 and 6
	5 and 2
	2 and 5
	4 and 3
	3 and 4
Number 8	4 and 4
(five ways)	2 and 6
	6 and 2
	3 and 5
	5 and 3
Number 9	5 and 4
(four ways)	4 and 5
	6 and 3
	3 and 6
Number 10	4 and 6
(three ways)	6 and 4
	5 and 5

Number 11   6 and 5
(two ways)   5 and 6
Number 12   6 and 6
(one way)

EXAMPLE:

"Number Five comes out 220 times in 1980 rolls. With 88 wins probable and 132 losses probable. The 3 out of 5 ratio insures losses for more than half of the bets.

"To all intents and purposes a person would have to roll the dice an infinite number of times in order to show the correct odds. But for percentage purposes pretend the dice behave the same as they would for 10 million —. Number 2, 3, and 12 lose on the first roll. Numbers 11 and 7 win on the first roll."

Out of 1980 Rolls

	Wins	*Losses*
2		55
3		110
11	110	
12	standoff	55
7	330	
4	55	110
10	55	110
5	88	132
9	88	132
6	125	150
8	125	150
Total 976		1004

"Divide 976 possible wins into 1980 rolls and you get a percentage of 49.3."

"Divide 1004 possible losses into 1980 rolls and you get a percentage of 50.7. This appears to give the house an edge of 1.4 percent.

"However, allowing for Number 12 being a standoff and eliminating its 55 rolls, you in reality are dealing with 1935 rolls. This brings the house edge to only 7/10 of one percent. And that is what a gambler bases his chance upon.

"Something — affecting that 7/10 of one percent."

And there are all sorts of things that affect that 7/10 of one percent edge! The odds are based upon all things remaining the same: same gambler, same amount of bet, same time, same place.

Mr. Scheinfeld assured me that all was not hopeless! One could occasionally beat the odds. Varying your method of betting is one way. Then there is also the unexplainable "lucky streak." Professor Kossis said you could calculate the run of a lucky streak, but you really can't — because we're not robots. We are unique. We get . . . "funny feelings" . . . indigestion; we vary our bets, we are happy, sad, and fabulously creative. And who is to swear that 1980 rolls do in fact behave the same as 10 billion rolls. And who knows if your first twenty rolls in Vegas in fact make the 85 millionth in that particular spot?

The mathematicans say now that there is some variance in number sequence in higher levels. Maybe your moment is the moment that happens!

Maybe *you* can beat the odds because thc odds haven't accounted for you. Maybe *you* are the variant.

Mr. Scheinfeld's combinations and philosophical 7/10 of 1 percent edge in favor of the house are thought-provoking, but they don't leave a big enough margin for the irregular unpredictability of man and his relationship to the fifth dimension.

Christmas of 1944 found Howard Scheinfeld (Technical Sergeant) with heavy-spirited buddies. The morale of his battalion was extremely low. The men had never been more discouraged.

Scheinfeld wrote a "buck up" letter and tacked it up on the bulletin board. That letter proved that Mr. Scheinfeld believes in his odds about as much as I do. Because that letter gives the lie to the laws governing chance. That letter showed how he really felt about shooting craps. For in it he told the fellows not to worry, they would definitely go back to the States *on* July 21, 1945. They did!

He said the war in Europe would end April 28, 1945. It ended May 8, 1945. He said the war with Japan would be over on September 3, 1945. On September 3, 1945 on the battleship Missouri the peace treaty was signed with Japan!

He was only ten days short of being correct about the overprediction. He was 100 percent correct about two! *Exactly to the date*.

Maybe Professor Kossis could have done as well based on the mere probabilities. But I doubt it!

Maybe the house does have a 7/10 of 1 percent edge in its favor, but there will always be a Howard Scheinfeld, somewhere, beating the odds. *(If you use a method of progressive betting, you have greater odds in your favor. Varying the bets gradually, building slowly from smaller to larger amounts, and then decreasing slowly from the larger to the smaller amounts, but always with irregularity, never repeating a pattern, and at the same time vary your bets to favor the successive rolls either coming up with the duplications of the first roll or not, you can upset the odds! The same rule would apply to life happenings. Playing it loose, cool and creative can lead to success. Getting out of ruts . . . breaking rules . . . acting in a surprising manner . . . makes it impossible for the laws of chance and probability to control your life.)

What do they have that affects that 7/10 of 1 percent edge? Spirit!

And *that* is the real edge!

17

The Zodiac Killer

"The fault dear Brutus, is not in our stars, but in ourselves, that we are underlings . . . ."

— Shakespeare

In the San Francisco area, a madman who feels he is marked by destiny to become internationally recognized, uses astrology to insure his dream.

No careless psychotic compulsively striking whenever the "need" becomes irresistible, this is a cool, plodding, methodical, calculating, diabolical mentality, that seeks to perpetuate itself both here in the now, and later in the much-longed-for afterlife.

It is not the first time a deranged mind looked to astrology for answers. Remember Hitler? During World War II the Allies were forced to use the services of professional astrologers in order to second-guess his moves. Their insight into his beliefs worked! And up to a time the Allies knew as much about when Hitler would be guided to act as even he did. It was only when Hitler tired of the advice of his personal astrologers . . . and became suspicious of them, and began making moves not connected with the stars . . . that the Allies saw the end and failure of astrology. Hitler distrusted his astrologers and was unable to sustain a belief in their calculations.

But now, in San Francisco, there is another madman, and this time there is no chance he will lose confidence in his Guru. This time the madman seems to be an astrologer himself.

Since December 20, 1968, the killer who chooses to call himself "Zodiac," has outwitted San Francisco police, and has continued to avoid detection. Evidently only when he feels the "stars" are right will he allow them to discover him. Only when he calculates that the planetary patterns offer him the best opportunity for total noteriety, will he assist them and present himself as a gift. His will not have been overnight success. He will have been striving to reach his destination for a long time. Most of his life would have been directed toward this one ultimate conclusion.

The Zodiac Killer, has shown a way above average interest and knowledge of the occult, including astrology, and mythology. He is no Forecast-in-the-Daily-Newspaper-Variety-astrologer. He knows more than merely the Sun sign he was born under.

What he knows had to be derived from books, and over a period of some time. It appears he is able to calculate horoscopes for any given amount of time. To obtain this specialized information he would have to purchase books of instruction either through the mail order or from major book shops in the area. He may read books about the occult, astrology, and mythology that are not the usual common everyday fare for the average citizen residing in his part of the country.

In order to supplement his knowledge of the stars, he may have also requested special books from public libraries.

The Zodiac Killer may have at some time displayed a keen desire to meet with others interested in his favorite subject (astrology). Napa County, where most of the murders took place, can't possibly shelter too many individuals who are turned on by the stars. At least, not those turned on enough to have joined clubs, social gatherings, coffee clutches, or dinner meetings with lectures . . . all for the purpose of forwarding an interest in astrology. Clubs, social groups, astrology foundations, societies keep records of membership.

At some point the Zodiac Killer may have, as many do who study astrology, contacted an astrologer (professional) for a horoscope. An astrologer would have records and would know if a client came from a given county or area. An astrologer would know the name, the address, and the complete birthdate of anyone in the Napa County area who ever ordered a chart.

The Zodiac Killer seems to be power-motivated and looking for glory. And he is apparently close to reaching it. He has carefully charted a planned course of action in order to insure success in his project. To reach the dreamed-of level in the afterworld he has followed a course he believes has been ordained by the stars.

The killer repeatedly contacts the police and gives them coded clues as to his identity. But one clue he has not furnished and did not foresee that they would uncover is the clue of his exact planetary pattern of operations. He overlooked one tremendous possibility. The police might not believe in astrology, but if they suspect he does, then all they would need to do is contact an astrologer to assist them in calculating the Zodiac's next star-planned moves.

If the Zodiac Killer is making moves at specified times, he does so because he feels that they are astrologically important times for him. There would be an underlying similarity or connection hidden between all these seemingly unrelated moments. There would be a "theme" running throughout.

I was curious as to why he called himself the Zodiac, suspecting that he probably had an interest in astrology, I set up a mathematical pattern of the planetary positions for each of times and locations of all the known killings associated with the Zodiac. My next step was to explore all the probable astrological reasons these times may have been chosen. If I believed the choice deliberate, my third step was to wonder *why* these times were considered important to the killer. Once a clear-cut pattern was uncovered, it became a tedious but not impossible task to track down a probable birthdate that would fit this pattern. And once the pattern was discovered (suspecting the pattern would be repeated in the future) I could then attempt to predict his future activities.

The Zodiac Killer has shown a very strong interest in astrology. And each time Zodiac has struck there was a very significant clue. The clue was overlooked by the homicide department . . . and ignored by reporters. Yet even a small, school child could have noted the obvious and universal character of the day. And surely young lovers everywhere could have at least once, looked up and seen it.

THE MOON!

With the exception of July 5, 1969, which ties in to charts for other reasons, Zodiac has made a habit of killing, or seeking public notice during the times of the new and full moons. Without fail!

December 20, 1968 — One day after the new moon (killed)
July 31, 1969 — Three days after the full moon (commanded front-page coverage)
September 27, 1969 — Two days after a full moon (killed)
October 11, 1969 — One day after a new moon (killed)

The new and the full moon clue could have been determined by anyone anywhere in the world. With or without any training in astrology. It is the obvious signature of one who is motivated by a star patern, and who feels destined, fated and at one with the cosmos. For centuries the mystical man has been governed by the passages of the moon and has attempted to chart his life's course by its movements.

There are other more detailed coincidences, other more specific astrological clues. It is obvious when one studies these clues that Zodiac follows more of a complicated chart than an ordinary calendar could possibly offer.

At a glance into an ephemeris, an astrologer or astronomer could tell the position of the planets, sun, and moon for any day of the year. The book is available at most public libraries. And with just a quick educated look, an astrologer could note that upon several occasions Zodiac killed or sought public acclaim when the moon was in the sign of Aries.

The killing of July 5, 1969: Moon in Aries.
Front page coverage August 1, 1969: Moon in Aries.
September 27, 1969 killing: Moon in Aries.

When an astrologer "plans" a life course, certain times are sought that will add a favorable impetus to the birth pattern. Moments that will supplement the personal horoscope's energies. And moments when only certain degrees of the horoscope will be highlighted.

I discovered that for each one of the killings a particular degree of the zodiac was prominent. Even though the killings occurred on different days, during different hours, and in different locations. This was a very mysterious coincidence — beyond the laws of chance and ordinary possibility. Could it be a deliberate, planned action inspired by the disturbed hope that planetary patterns will assist in leading Zodiac on toward ultimate recognition and success?

On December 20, 1968, the angles of the horoscope for the killings held the signs Virgo and Pisces. On July 5, 1969, the angles of the horoscopes once again held the signs Virgo and Pisces. On September 27, 1969 the angles of the horoscopes held the signs Virgo and Pisces. On October 11, 1969 the angles once again were prominently held by the signs of Virgo and Pisces.

The charts for the time of the killings show three dozen or more "coincidences" which lead to a strong belief in the "deliberate."

In his messages to the police and newspaper Zodiac spoke of his victims becoming his slaves in the afterlife. This is a belief that coincides with the worship of the ancient god of the underworld, Pluto. Pluto, mythological god of the dark regions of the heavens and earth, has long been the favorite of the fanatical cultists who believe all things dangerous, deep, tormented, and sexual are done in honor of him. There is a strong link between this belief and homosexual activities connected with the occult. Throughout the United States there are those who psychotically believe they are intended to return time after time to cleanse the world, and attempt to praise Pluto by perverted actions.

In his messages to the press and police there were references made connected with the "afterlife" of victims and their conversion into slavery for his benefit. A student of mythology could associate the remarks with the killer's probable interest in Pluto. Following this train of reasoning, an astrologer would look to find a pinpoint of focusing of aspects within the utilized planetary pattern in order to see if the planet Pluto was being spotlighted anywhere in the horoscopes.

Since the planet Pluto, due to its uneven elliptical orbit of the Sun, travels sometimes 360 years in circling it, this could cause the planet to linger one year on only one or two degrees of the Heaven's Zodiac. It is possible to trace any year by the degree the planet may have held.

Zodiac has favored only certain degrees in the horoscopes connected with the killings. One special area has been around the nineteeth to the twenty-first degree of the sign Cancer. During the 1930's the planet Pluto traveled over these degrees. The birthdate of the killer could be found then somewhere during the years when the planet Pluto was on one of those degrees. This of course considers only one small facet of the pattern he uses.

The mad astrologer has indicated a preference for specific degrees within the signs of Pisces and Virgo. And he has also shown that he is partial to the Moon in Aries. Could he perhaps be attempting to establish a pattern that would give the position of the Sun in his birth horoscope a prominent position within the horoscopes for the moment of the killings? Prominent positions believed by astrologers to "insure" fame?

Zodiac also stresses the new and full moons. He has used the Moon in Aries beyond the point of coincidence. Could it be the killer was born after a new or full moon . . . and when the Moon was located in Aries . . . and therefore is attempting a duplication of a mood?

If there is a pattern, and it can be discerned, could we then from past actions, project into the future? Maybe! If the Zodiac Killer is using astrology, as it appears he is, then all the full and new moons until he is captured will be significant. If he is using astrology in order to determine the correct *times*, then the hours when Virgo and Pisces hold angles in the horoscopes of the day will most decidedly be IT!

If he has chosen a preference in the past for the Moon being located in the sign of Aries, then the days when this occurs should be very important. The pattern seems obvious, and no doubt one he will continue to use until he is discovered. Astrology points out his road clearly. Even if he is not deliberately acting at special times, with such an obvious pattern in operation, couldn't we still be pretty well ahead?

By using a projection of a planetary pattern thought to be favored by the Zodiac Killer, Louise was able to predict on KABC-T.V. Eye Witness News the exact date the killer, seeking help, contacted San Francisco attorney Melvin Belli.

☾

18

The Tate Murders

The House in Benidict Canyon

"I suppose I've passed it a hundred times, but I always stop a minute, and look at the house, the tragic house, the house with nobody in it."   — Joyce Kilmer

He had come from the East for the sun and the rest.

Wiry, well-built, quick, tanned, slightly uneasy in white jeans and sneakers, eager not to offend, he was willing to go native and attempt to act like the Romans, but only his hairdo made it. It was soon apparent he had never experienced a bacchanal at Nero's court, and it was a certainty he would never want to.

The sun was great, he admitted, but there was one problem . . . the flies. A mother cat had come down from the brush, hungry, leading a litter of colorful tributes to her earlier more carefree days. She dominated the front step. Who could turn

287

her away? It was difficult getting in and out of the door so we decided to visit in the middle of the road.

The sun was hot. Our conversation ran its course through astrology, television, radio talk shows, women's magazines (that was his business), birthdays, the sun god and back again to birthdays.

He was born under the sign of Libra. Astrology says Libra is the sign of the lover. Those born under the sign are supposed to be lighthearted, breezy, intellectual, witty and charming. He was. They are said to do well if they marry either Gemini or Aquarius. This Libra had done well. His wife is Gemini. Gemini is considered a verbal sign and tends toward nervousness. She was and is! Twice she said, "Shut the door, you're letting in the flies."

It was very hot.

Libra seemed to be an authority on the sun god, so naturally that discussion began again. Libra said the sun god concept was the genius of an ancient king who was depicted as having been, happily married to a beautiful woman, but in reality, it was known that he had been a homosexual. I wondered how accurate this rumor could be. Time and fancy have been known to distort. Libra said the sun god theory was the belief that eventually led to Judaism and then Christianity — the belief in one Supreme Power.

That was interesting.

The road was becoming noisy. The sightseers double-parked, shouted, shrieked, called out, laughed, posed for pictures, left refuse, and roared away. The sun god was working overtime, and we moved toward the shade.

Libra didn't think he would leave until the lease was up. He and Gemini intended to stay out the full month. He supposed though, if they wanted to, they could break the lease. His main worry seemed to be the cats. What would happen to the cats? Besides the wild matron and her entourage he informed me that there was also available an exotic adult male, fixed, former-darling of a famous singer, who would prove loyal if given a decent chance. He shed. But he was beautiful.

What would happen to the cats?

The fate of the felines took up most of our conversation. Silently musing for a while, we went on.

Would Libra come back next year? He didn't know. He liked the neighborhood. It was a restful spot above the smog. The neighbors were nice: sweet kids, always a smile, quiet.

Another neighbor, solid build, shaggy-maned, clad in pajamas and robe, curious about our meeting, and feeling ignored, wandered about his driveway banging the lids on his garbage cans to attract our attention. He did, smiled tentatively, and then decided to saunter over and join us. We all nodded.

Everyone looked at a file of ants who were busy making their way to the Kitty Litter box.

Shaggy Neighbor cleared his throat. Libra said, "They are with a newspaper." Shaggy smiled. We looked up at the telephone pole. The wires the murderers had cut were all nearly back up and in place. The sky was bright blue. It was hot. I told Libra not to worry I would take the cats.

The Scoop

Someday I'll pass by the Great Gates of Gold,
And see a man pass through unquestioned and bold.
"A Saint?" I'll ask, and old Peter'll reply:
"No, he carries a pass — he's a newspaper guy."

— The Newspaper Guy
— *Benjamin Scoville*

When most of your life you exhibit some obvious amount of psychic ability, you are immediately lumped with all others who have shown similar traits. It's the worst sort of prejudice imaginable. It is assumed that because you are psychic you can bring back the dead, prevent natural disasters, and mastermind criminal investigations. Then there is the other view, the one that believes you are nuts. And let's face it, most psychics eventually are! With either opinion you are put into an uncomfortable position.

Ed DeVere from the *Evening Outlook* invited me to visit the Tate house with him to see what I could "pick up," about the killers. I explained to Ed that I wasn't that kind of psychic. Tuning in killings, rapes, kidnappings, plane crashes and bank robberies were not my "thing." I have always believed my own so-called ability was an extreme sensitivity to another live-being's emotional temperament in any one given moment. And I believe the only way you can tune in to the dead is by tuning in to the *living's* concept of them. And, since I never imagined myself to be God's gift to the Police Department, I preferred to leave the psychic detective work to Lotte Von Strohl and Peter Hurkos. I just didn't want to be thought of as a nutty psychic and besides violence turns me off.

But Ed insisted, and I am nosey as hell, so I went with him, and I wondered about what I might feel. I was afraid I would brood about what I did feel . . . for days. And I was right. I did.

Marcia Dickenson, who is a field representative for the city of Los Angeles, and I have been friends for many years and have a telepathic tie.

Too many times to be considered just a normal coincidence, she and I have 'known' what the other one felt. Sometimes we knew in advance of a mood. Sometimes we would know at the moment it occurred. Marcia has had some success in reading the Tarot and since she is very interested in any phenomena connected with the psyche, I invited her to go along with us.

We never for a moment considered the possibility of our "tuning in" to who the killers might be. That was not my objective or Marcia's, though I am certain Ed hoped we might. It would have been a scoop for the *Outlook*.

The whole idea embarrassed me. I was raised in an atmosphere of psychic phenomena. It's difficult for me to explain, but whenever I read one or another of the world's psychics volunteering to aid the police, I feel creepy-crawly.

I guess it's the same sort of emotional reaction third-generation Americans must have about generalized accusations that indiscriminately attribute fatness to Italians, garlic breath to Greeks, and drunkenness to the Irish.

While we were there the KABC television crew from Eye Witness News, friends of mine, pulled up, cruising for a story and were told confidently by Ed that "Louise will find the killers."

I thought I would die!

I happen to have personal and unidentified subconscious reactions, and am uncomfortable and uneasy about psychics who delight in "helping the police."

It's obvious that a good way to get publicity if you are psychic and *don't do much else* is to be associated in some way with a front page crime. Reporters tell me that most psychic detectives are never called in by the police, but rather the psychics turned themselves in as volunteers.

Headlines always state: "Police Call in Famous Psychic Roger Vandershmeer to Help Find Killers"; however, it's just not true.

I never want to tune in to a killer's mentality. To form a rapport (little understood, yet seemingly emotional) with unpleasantness, disturbs me. And it is also painful for me to consider an association with the type of personalities who might not object, and who in fact delight, in that sort of pastime. Some of my best friends . . . are *not* psychic detectives.

Being psychic means I am more aware of my own surroundings — more open to the needs of my friends. I sense meanings accurately, and understand others because of it. I get along. To me psychic means being tuned in and aware — sensitive, and operating on an emotional-response level.

My friends who are psychic are artists, actors, reporters, writers, musicians, doctors, lawyers, politicians, and producers. They are in all fields. And they use what they are to do what they do — well!

One thing they don't do is race about offering themselves to the police as psychic aids. And being sensitive, one other thing they never do is try to capture killers. Maybe I'm a snob. At any rate I can't see how my emotional reactions to any criminal situation could be utilized by the police department.

However I *did* feel something. Just as we reached the crossroads and were about to turn up Cielo Drive, I panicked. A wild, primitive fear grabbed me. It wasn't a panic connected with going up to the house. And I only felt it at the crossroads — in fact just near the house that stands at the corner. Marcia felt it too. When we left to go back down the hill and once again passed the corner, it hit again.

To stretch a point and credit with greater value our Extra Sensory Perception, I later found out from reporters, that was the spot where the killers had parked their car before walking back up to the house. Outside of the wild, cold, chill of fear that hit us twice, and each time only at the corner, we felt nothing. Marcia, not being in an area of psychic work, I guess can be forgiven. To defend myself though I must add that I wasn't completely without sensitivity.

I did feel a variety of specific sensations, but I doubt the police would care.

The sightseers turned me off. I felt a horror toward their

almost carnival spirit. Then I remembered that in a way we were also not on home ground. Only I guess since we were with the newspaper and not eating ice pops it did make a difference.

I did "tune in" to the neighbor. I could sense his over-controlled reactions and orderly shock. I could also sense he wasn't quite making it with his wife. But I don't believe Ed brought me up to the house to gain that insight! I even felt an empathy for the-trashcan-lid-banger who sought attention in another experience. He might have been a very nice guy. He was cute and looked like Walter Mathau.

Nevertheless, I *never* did pick up one vibration about the killers:

No initials, no hair coloring, no generalized descriptions of probable personalities!

I couldn't bring myself to say the killers were disturbed types. After all, that was obvious. As a psychic aid to the police I guess I was a failure. And as a psychic reporter for the *Evening Outlook* I guess I also failed.

But as a disappointment to my pal Ed DeVere I know I was without doubt — *The Greatest!*

Sharon Tate and Roman Polansky: Victims of the Stars

> "Do planets have hearts, I wonder
> Or do they just sail in gentle breeze,
> Or what happens when they touch each other.
> Without measuring the degrees.

Do planets cry, I think they do
But can they shed tears?
I think, I know, for I have heard them sob
— When no one hears."

— Bernard

Marked by the cosmos, Sharon Tate and Roman Polansky were predestined to meet and marry. Sharon born three days after an eclipse of the moon, and Roman Polansky, born three days prior to an eclipse of the sun, could not escape the star patterns that demanded she be the only woman able to fulfill his tragic destiny.

A total eclipse of the sun or moon is rare, and that two people should become involved who have an eclipse pattern operating within their individual horoscopes is even more than a bit unusual — particularly when the eclipse patterns in both horoscopes show similarities. It is most remarkable that two people should have eclipses in their horoscopes on the same degrees and in identical astrological signs, especially since the facts of their birthdates (day, month, year, and time), along with the locations of their birthplaces, are so varied.

Yet this is the case of the planetary patterns in the Tate and Polansky birth charts.

Eclipses can occur only during the times of the new and full moons. For an eclipse to exist at all, the sun, the earth and the moon must be in proper alignment. The eclipse patterns follow a definite and regularly timed pattern. And for an eclipse to repeat itself on an exact degree of the zodiac takes over nineteen years.

Sharon's birthdate was in January 1943, just three days after a *full moon eclipse*. At the time of the eclipse, the sun appeared in the sign of Aquarius and the moon passed through Leo. The mathematical points triggering the eclipse involved the twenty-sixth degrees of those two signs.

Roman Polansky was born in August 1933, just three days

before a *solar eclipse* (due to a new moon). At the time of the eclipse, the sun and the moon and the mathematical points triggering the eclipse, were located on the twenty-sixth degree of the sign Leo.

The probabilities against this being a mere "coincidence" are overwhelming, and are too numerous to contemplate as a consideration. Of course we must continue to think of the phenomena as a coincidence until explored evidence proves otherwise. We can only believe that the similarities within the two birthday horoscopes are accidental, co-timed happenings. But, there is always the secret thought of predestination.

Horoscopes are said to indicate personal tensions and the attitudes used in order to express these tensions in relation to others. Perhaps living an isolated life on a far-off desert island one would not fulfill one's star destiny. But the environmental conditions surrounding Sharon and Roman made their life paths inevitable.

Jay Sebring, born October 1933, added just enough of the planetary patterns needed to complete the tension. While the Tate-Polansky planetary patterns were loaded and ready, it was necessary for the Sebring chart to act as a catalyst and "aim" the power. The scene was set . . . waiting for the stars to pull the trigger.

The list of coincidences is impressive: both Polansky and Sebring were born when the moon was in the sign of Cancer — an indication of similar tastes in women, and in parallel emotional outlets. On August 8, 1969, the night of the atrocities, the moon had just entered the sign of Cancer, spotlighting the potential held in their charts. At Sharon's birth the planet Jupiter was closely conjunct the degrees of the Polansky/Sebring moon positions, indicating that her personality had an exaggerated impact upon both their male concepts of feminity. The full moon eclipse potential in Aquarius and Leo that existed in her birth chart duplicated the influence of the new moon solar eclipse that existed in Polansky's chart and would reach fruition in 1969.

The emphasis of the full moon eclipse in Sharon's chart during 1969 was established at zero degrees of the signs Pisces and Virgo creating a ninety degree angle to the position of the planet Uranus (in Gemini) in her 1969 horoscope. This was intensified by Sebring's 1969 position for the planet Mercury at Zero degrees in the sign of Sagittarius (within his chart).

Astrological research done by Dr. Rudolf Tomaschek supports the theory that an influential location of the planet Uranus is frequently coincidental to earthquakes. And in fact he correlated 134 tremors with this planet's location.

Could man also be subject to similar influences? The environmental factors that invited release of the potent interrelated astrological aspects were made certain when, during 1969, the planet Venus in Sharon's horoscope formed a 120 degree angle to the planet Venus in Jay's horoscope and a 180 degree angle to the planet Venus in her husband's chart.

The Planet Venus in Jay Sebring's chart picked up the eclipse patterns within the Polanskys' charts by forming an exact 90 degree angle to them and aspecting at the same time the planet Venus in Roman Polansky's chart. A planet Venus, in the sign of Virgo, many Astrologers insist, is frequently evident in the horoscopes of widows.

During 1969 the planet Mars in Sebring's chart reached the exact position of where the planet Mars had been located at the time of Tate's birth. Astrologers insist the planet Mars governs violence, and that the planet, if found in two different horoscopes on the exact degree, would have to intensify its potential.

There are many thousands of complicating factors that support a theory of predestination and planetary influence over men's lives, but there will always remain strong evidence to support mere coincidence. But it is strange, for on that fatal day in August, when the planet Neptune (which takes over 140 years to orbit the Sun) was conjunct with the location of the planet Venus in Sebring's chart (triggering the dangerous eclipse patterns) at the same time it made contact with the location of the planet Venus in both Sharon's and Roman's horoscopes.

Also offering powerful support in favor of man's helplessness, the planet Pluto, an astrological indicator of mobs, violence, and sexual degeneration, while on its three-hundred-odd-year journey around the sun, easily sailed over the sensitive point in Polansky's horoscope that had at the time of his birth held the planet Venus. Only once in many lifetimes, while on one of its distant, cold, and eerie journeys, could Pluto pass over that particular degree of the zodiac. Only once in many lifetimes could the Polansky Venus, pressured from all sides, feel the impact of the influence of this cruel planet, an influence that took its time, but made certain of Roman Polansky's widowerhood!

Could Astrology have predicted the exact happenings in advance?

NO!

19

Crystal Balls at City Hall

Crystal balls
Cards
Stars
And such other ways in which to see one's future joys
Are fine!

But not for me.

— Louise Huebner

"I don't really believe in this stuff, but occasionally something happens that makes you feel, well, maybe there is something in it after all.

"I know that when I first ran for office in 1967 Louise did my horoscope, and a horoscope for the election, and told me that the election would be a very close one, and it would be a three-week-long crisis. But, I would win in the primary election.

"She told me there would be a crisis on election day of course, but it would be resolved in my favor. And then she said another crisis would follow a week later, which would also be resolved in my favor. And then a third crisis would follow a week after that, which would once again be resolved in my favor. And finally — the third crisis would be the end of it.

"Well of course anybody can tell you that there is to be a crisis on election day. And most bets were going that I would at least end up as the top candidate. I had eight opponents. If I won in the primary there would be no run off election six weeks later.

"Well on election day sure enough I did end up as a top candidate, but only by 38 votes. So this was still pretty inconclusive when you consider a lot of absentee ballots were out. One week later when they counted the absentee ballots, at that point I picked up another 100 votes.

"And then I suppose you could say Louise figured out there was going to be an absentee ballot count, and that the time was set for it in advance. But, I didn't believe Louise could know that. It's a technicality. And not too many people are aware of it. I didn't have any idea Louise might know about it.

"But — there is one thing that she couldn't have figured out — and that was the crisis that came a week after. The third crisis. One of the candidates asked for a recount of the ballots.

"They always set the date for the recount at the *convenience* of the City Clerk's office. And it just happened to be set for a day one week later. Louise had predicted the date *in advance*. When they finished the recount I picked up one more vote and that was finally the end of the election.

"You could say it's all coincidence. But it's difficult to ignore the fact that it would be pretty hard for anyone to pick dates in that way — and then have them come true in the way that they did. And Louise did do just that — so maybe — there is something to it."

— *Councilman Arthur Kress Snyder*
Los Angeles, California

$\mathcal{H}$

There are, however a few politicians, who do actively believe in the "stuff." All through history leaders have sought comforting confirmation, through a peek at the stars, and through the insights of some intuitive mind. And except for only an occasional accurate zeroing in on specifics, most predictions have been as vague as Spurinna's "Beware the Ides of March" warning to Caesar. How and where was poor Caesar to beware them? It's not practical to expect one's client to stay in bed all day, and especially not if he is a busy-leader type.

Yet, despite lack of any real clarity in the majority of the readings, royalty, dictators, and elected officials still willingly keep the mystics occupied.

It's a tricky business being a Happy Medium for a politician. First of all, there isn't ever going to be a breed of politician who will want to hear that he may lose an election! A psychic is better off to plead insanity and lay low until after the moment of truth. You could, though, bravely inform the guy of "better" days ahead. But if *your* better days don't coincide with his financial backing, and the pressures of his party to "GO!" there isn't too much likelihood that he will listen to you. He certainly will not appreciate your warning. He most certainly will not be able to hold any real affection for you after you have once "let him down."

Most politicians don't want you to tell them what is about to happen; they want you to make it happen, and make it happen right! Who was the ancient pharaoh who, upon receiving a not so jolly message from a poor intermediary, ordered: "Chop off his head!"?

And, if a psychic does manage to sustain a delicately balanced relationship with a politician, it would be a rare politician who would ever admit its existence. The steps of city halls all over the world are littered with the debris of discarded fortune-tellers, unpleasant prognostications, and crystal balls.

The late Goodwyn Knight, when he was Governor of California, was believed to be very involved with astrology. It is said he visited many astrologers for "clues" even though it is also believed he had studied astrology and could accurately calculate and interpret charts for his office staff. A bookstore in Los Angeles that specializes in astrology books boasts having sold to him throughout the years many advanced books on the subject.

It is certainly not the only time an elected official pursued this interest. The late Prime Minister of Canada — Mac-Kenzie — was openly engaged in similar activities. But it isn't only the politicians who are interested in political horoscopes; television newsmen are also curious.

When Governor Ronald Reagan of California was seeking election the first time, a network television news program called me. At that time it had been rumored that Reagan was using astrological information of planetary patterns in order to run his campaign. They asked me to help discover if this was true. I was to be an astro-spy! It was great fun. The news program followed the same technique used by the Allies during the Second World War, when it was strongly believed that Adolf Hitler sought astrological advice. The allies hired astrologers to tell them — whatever it might be the German Astrologers were telling Hitler. In that way the Allies hoped to anticipate his moves. It didn't matter whether or not the Allies "believed" in Astrology. An important factor was that German, English, American, French, or Hindustani astrologers could base interpretations on the same specific aspects. If a German astrologer bases a bit of advice on the planet Pluto being in a ninety-degree angle from the planet Uranus, rest assured that astrologers all over the world will see the same aspect. Aspects are identical throughout the world. And though some minor interpretations might vary, the Allies could at least be certain of Hitler's astrological action plan.

The newsmen wanted to know if I could do Reagan's chart, and, from that, make a series of predictions as to when I felt certain planetary patterns would be strong enough for Reagan's astrologer to advise him to take "action." *Provided of course Reagan even had an astrologer to advise him.*

I was fascinated, so I agreed. Dropping everything, I threw myself body and soul into preparing Reagan's chart. It was next to impossible to find Reagan's exact moment of birth. I called his campaign headquarters, and they informed me that his birth hour was top secret. I thought this unusual. If astrology doesn't work, and if Reagan wasn't using astrology, and if no one cared anyway, why would it matter if I calculated his chart? Reagan's office was not aware I was on the job for any reason other than to satisfy my curiosity or to prepare a fun horoscope for KLAC radio. There was no reason to hide the hour from me.

It took me a bit longer without their cooperation, but the press must never be underestimated. I got the facts I needed, and did the chart. When the newsmen came to me, Reagan and his campaign had been strangely silent for some time. They told me that he seemed to have a pattern of behavior that they felt to be beyond coincidence. They asked me to determine in advance when he would activate his campaign again. This they said would convince them and prove to them absolutely that Reagan followed the stars.

I did find significant coincidence between planetary patterns in Reagan's chart and his activities. But so what. After many weeks of hard work, what had I really determined? Was Reagan making moves deliberately to fit powerful planetary aspects . . . or were powerful planetary aspects making Reagan move?

I told the newsmen I certainly would not make any statement to support their suspicions. It was impossible to know with any certainty if what I had discovered could be credited *only* to Reagan's interest in astrology.

My specialty has always been political horoscopes. In every horoscope I discover patterns coinciding with events. In the majority of cases the men don't know anything about astrology beyond the fact of the sign they were born under. This same could also have been true of Reagan. However, later, when Reagan was sworn into office at a peculiar hour of slightly past midnight (which really was a lot of coincidence to swallow — without choking), the local news contacted me for a statement. I had to admit, that the chance against that moment and his horoscope, coincidentally showing similar patterns and powerful links, would have to run eighteen billion to one!

The next day Reagan's man Bataglia appeared on every news program in California stating emphatically "Governor Reagan does not follow the stars."

The hour of birth is a primary factor in astrology. It is the only means to an accurate horoscope. The entire basis of the interpretation of any planetary pattern should be, of course, the moment it occurs. Without the exact hour, all births taking place during a twenty-four hour period would be given the same forecast. During the governor's race in 1966, I was working for KLAC Radio in Los Angeles, California. The week prior to the election I broadcast one candidate's horoscope for each day.

Governor Edmund G. Brown, who made a deliberate effort to inform the press that he did not "believe" in astrology, was called a "sure winner" by every psychic and astrologer in the country.

When I researched his chart for KLAC Radio his office was most cooperative, and his field representative in Los Angeles managed to get the exact hour for me from his grandmother's family Bible that was stored in a trunk.

I thought that was very nice; even so, I predicted flatly that he could not beat the Reagan horoscope, and on KTTV-T.V. I clearly stated Brown could not win. . . . I was right!

The difference that made my prediction right and the other astrologers' predictions wrong was that I had the exact hour of birth. I did a horoscope for his moment of birth; the others did one for the day of his birth. Astrologers contradict themselves when they support planetary pattern influences and then base predictions on patterns that may not be connected with the moments in question. It's sloppy.

Just for the Reagan horoscope alone I spent over a week making phone calls trying to get accurate information. And whenever I go to a lot of trouble to research facts, I guard them possessively.

In the fall of 1969 I received a phone call from a television producer who was active in politics, and he suggested I "predict" that Allioto would win the nomination and go on to become governor of California. The producer felt I would get "tremendous" publicity, and that would help both me and Allioto. I was absolutely amazed!

The producer then gave me the name of a well-known newsman who was working for Allioto in his campaign. He told me to think it over, and then call the newsman. He said they all thought it was a "cute" idea, and that the psychology of it would work.

A short time later I received another phone call. This time it was from Tom Allioto. He said he understood I was doing his father's horoscope, and that he too studied astrology, and would anxiously await my "findings."

He asked me to give him Reagan's horoscope so that he could study it and gain some insight that might benefit his father, San Francisco's Mayor Joseph Allioto. I said No! He was quite perturbed and said I was not terribly enlightened. I said if what he called enlightenment was indeed enlightenment, then I had to agree, I wasn't!

The pressures of a campaign are great, so it's no wonder more people from the political field than from any other look to everything and anything for moral support and insight.

One female campaign manager for a candidate seeking the governor's office in California, at the time of the campaign, made weekly visits to a spiritualist. She was very excited about his ability, and invited me to attend one session because, as she said, "Louise, you will love him! He's terrific!" We went. His meetings took place in a private home off Wilshire Boulevard. When you entered the foyer, you were met by a basket with a sign that invited "$1.00 a question." A few feet further in and you were handed an index card — lined — an envelope, and a pen. It was very simple. You wrote your question on the lined card, placed it in the envelope, sealed the envelope, and placed the envelope in a basket up at the podium, in full view of the audience. No one could interfere with the questions inside of the sealed envelopes.

She was right, the fellow was terrific. And I must give him credit for three things. His two good eyes and his guts. I wrote neatly, "Will Mentor soon go to Europe on a movie?" And he answered neatly, "Yes, Mentor will soon go to Europe on a movie."

Some people in the back of the room got the usual mundane readings connected with car sales, raises, operations, etc., and I guess that's what they asked about. There was a lot of gasping. Word-for-word questions were answered as asked. Not once was a word misplaced or substituted for another. He wasn't very original. The audience was convinced the man was a mind-reader or had psychic contact with the spirit world.

The guy had missed his calling. He should have been a campaign manager, because, although he convinced everyone including my friend that he was psychic, my friend wasn't able to convince California that they needed her candidate! Maybe it's just as well.

Once a delightful lady, very involved in the political arena and respected within her community, had a long, lively discussion with me on Extra Sensory Perception. We got together frequently for lunch. She impressed me with her keen intuitive qualities and rational approach. She said not a day passed that she was not benefitted in some way by her extra insight.

Since she agreed with me that E.S.P. was no doubt a result of chemical, glandular, electrical activity in one's body, and would seem to be a supernormal and not a supernatural function of the physical senses, I believed she would be an excellent guest on radio. I invited her to join me on the two-way radio, listener-call-in program.

All went well — until the first commercial. Months of pleasant, sane lunches together had in no way prepared me for the "evil forces," "good forces," "demons," "spirits," "after-life," "other world," and "visitations" that had evidently pain-fully plagued her since childhood. The audience was thrilled! She attacked me, stating I was headed in the wrong direction and would someday see the truth . . . and be sorry.

I was already sorry.

Once I prepared a chart for a very powerful politician. In my analysis I believed he would, in two years time, run into a small scandal, a divorce, and a re-marriage. His horoscope indicated that his marriage was not too happy, and had not been for many years.

I stupidly told him so. He got uptight. I guess it was only natural. I was working at KLAC, and he thought I might publicize the reading. I assured him that that was *not* my intention, nor was it the sort of feature I did or that the program director would allow. But he continued to vehe-mently assure me that his marriage had endured for twenty-five years . . . and would for at least another twenty-five.

After that, whenever I ran into him, he snubbed me, and pretended we had never met. Hardly the way to keep someone friendly if you are worried about them. I didn't think he was showing good political sense.

Well, the two years passed. The small scandal hit. Then the divorce. And then the really happy re-marriage. Afterwards at a party, when he seemed relaxed and appeared to have forgiven me for my admittedly stupid and tactless "insight," I whispered into his ear, "Hey, remember what I said. Was I right?" In return for my naiveté I got a cold-fish stare, and a shoulder of equal warmth.

Although reports are always looking for "political predictions," there are many that, once made, never make it to the public.

In 1968 I was asked to make predictions for a television news program about world figures for the New Year that was coming up — 1969. I was given a list of select names, and later I submitted my impressions for the New Year's Eve news program.

I predicted a nationally prominent political figure had an unfortunate horoscope that was developing some very bad patterns. I was sure all was not as it seemed to be in his home life. My guess was he would be involved in some sort of deep emotional trouble, and his life would never again be the same . . . come July. The newsman in charge said, "Unh, unh!" But the prediction came true — despite him.

John F. Kennedy's assassination was predicted by astrologers and psychics all over the world. They had been predicting it would happen since before Roosevelt died in office. Beginning with Abraham Lincoln the United States has been involved in an almost unbelievable cycle. Astrologers insist the phenomena is in some way connected with the apparent conjunction of two planets, Jupiter and Saturn. Jupiter orbits the Sun in about every twelve years and Saturn in about twenty-eight, and they meet every twenty years on the same degree of the zodiac.

Theory has it that whenever a President is elected to office under the Jupiter/Saturn conjunction, he will die in office. And one hundred years of American history heavily supports this theory.

Due to my knowledge of this empirical evidence, I ran into quite a problem. In 1960 I wrote for a shopping center throw-away newspaper. My column "You Are Unique" was on astrology. Along with writing the column I also made many appearances as a promotion for the center. The readers were constantly asking about the election. It is absolutely next to impossible to be an astrologer, write about astrology, and get away with not making predictions. You must! It's expected. If you don't everyone thinks it's a cop-out.

I studied the horoscopes of the candidates. My impression was that Richard Nixon's horoscope was superior to John F. Kennedy's. Since there has been no real scientific research in Astrology, and what has been done is so outdated it cannot be applied properly, astrologers are unable to exactly pinpoint meaning. There are continuous disagreements.

In my own horoscope I had what is known as a progressed solar eclipse during the summer of 1968. There are two theories governing the interpretation of this aspect. What little research that has been compiled would lead one to believe that a progressed solar eclipse would be evident when:

(1) you led an army into battle for your Caesar; or, (2) you dropped dead! At the time of my eclipse I was designated Official Witch for Los Angeles County. And a supervisor almost dropped dead.

Believing Richard Nixon's horoscope showed the most powerful aspects, I could not analyze its meaning to my own satisfaction. My prediction? I said his chart was the most dynamic, so he would be elected President, or John F. Kennedy would be elected President and Nixon would live.

I couldn't figure out if the dynamic stood for victory or survival! Later, when Kennedy was elected, I was certain Nixon's chart meant he would eventually be President, and I said so. I predicted his eventual victory before his party chose him this last time around. When I checked his chart, I saw that he had an aspect due exactly on election day; so, on KNBC-T.V. I predicted his victory.

PRESIDENTS WHO DIED IN OFFICE

1. Abraham Lincoln	1861-1865	R
2. James A. Garfield	1881-1881	R
3. William McKinley	1897-1901	R
4. Warren G. Harding	1921-1922	R
5. Franklin D. Roosevelt	1933-1945	D
6. John F. Kennedy	1960-1963	D

Astrologer Carl Payne Tobey predicted the arrest and subsequent liquidation of Lavrenti Beria, Russian chief of the secret police. After studying the horoscope of Georgi Malenkov in April of 1953, he stated that in July of 1953 an event of major importance would take place in the Kremlin. However, I am certain that if he had Lavrenti Beria's own horoscope he might have been more specific.

For KABC-Television news I prepared the New Year's Eve predictions, and based Jacqueline Kennedy's marriage the following year upon certain indications I noted forming within her horoscope. Later, though, while studying another chart I had prepared for the time of the assassination in Dallas, I interpreted the then current aspects, and reported in *Tempo* (a black paper in Watts) that "Much attention will surround a Kennedy woman," and the time I predicted later turned out to be the exact week of Jacqueline's re-marriage. Being the dummy that I am, I never bothered to coincide my two predictions. My information stemmed from two separate charts — I never tied them together! Very sloppy.

On KABC-Television May 4, 1964, I predicted that riots in the Los Angeles area would occur between April and October of 1965. The Watts riots happened in August 1965. Considering that there had been· no previous riots, that was pretty close. This will sound like a cop-out, but I am certain a specific prediction could have been made if horoscopes of every community in Los Angeles had been studied. But who has the time? I'm just not that dedicated to the cause.

Once while working with newsman Roger Aldi on KHJ Radio in Los Angeles, I was giving capsule "readings" for all of the Los Angeles Council. It was to be all in fun. We were keeping it light. Yet when I got to Thomas Sheppard's horoscope, I impulsively said he was headed for big trouble. He was involved in shady deals, would be caught, and in eighteen months his life pattern would be completely changed. The words just popped out of my mouth. Roger and I hoped no one from the council heard the program.

Eighteen months later Sheppard's trouble began. He was convicted and sent to prison.

On May 6, 1968, I told a listener who called in to the radio program that a shocking event would occur in the early morning hours following the June election. I said Los Angeles would be spotlighted and our United States history would be changed, and the entire world would be affected. I'm not sure if this counts as a bona-fide prediction or not, but it certainly coincides with Robert Kennedy's assassination.

One year before Lyndon Johnson decided not to run for re-election, I predicted his decision. The prediction was made in the *Alhambra Post Advocate,* on KFOX Radio in Long Beach, at the Highland Park Monday Morning Senior Citizens Meeting in Los Angeles, and at a great many women's group luncheons.

Because of this prediction I decided to study Hubert Humphrey's chart, and later predicted on KABC-Television, before Johnson retired, that Humphrey would hit a peak of popularity, but that it wouldn't do him any good.

It didn't!

Predicting Sam Yorty's victory was a very big thrill for me. The odds were really stacked against him . . . and against my being right.

Sam Yorty had been mayor of Los Angeles for two terms (eight years) when he was defeated in a primary election by a black opponent on April 1, 1969. In Los Angeles, whenever an incumbent has been defeated in the primary election, he has had it.

Around the United States unimaginative pollsters took every conceivable factor into consideration: the black vote, the white vote, the conservative vote, the liberal vote, the young vote, the old vote, the middle-aged vote, Viet Nam, the harbor scandal, hay fever, and a Midwestern twang. Everything was studied. Everything was analyzed. And everything added up against Yorty. One major support was ignored . . . his horoscope.

The mayor's horoscope had more than fifteen strong aspects forming — they had appeared before, during his other more successful moments. When you multiply these fifteen aspects with the eighteen-billion-to-one concept, it becomes difficult to ignore them.

At birth (October 1, 1909), Yorty's horoscope has the planet Jupiter placed in the sign of Virgo. As the years progressed the planet has held an increasingly prominent position within his chart. Each time he was elected to a public office he had what is known in astrological jargon as a

"Jupiter aspect." When Councilwoman Roseland Wynman left the arena, Yorty had a "good Jupiter aspect." When Yorty won a mayorality election in 1965 with a sweeping victory, he had a *"magnificent* Jupiter aspect."

In 1969, however, that good old Jupiter aspect would not take place until *after* the primary election in April. But it was there, and it was building toward a climax, and I believed it would pay off.

I had no intention of making a prediction. It happened quite accidently. On May 7, 1969 I was driving to Universal Studios, where I was to entertain at a luncheon for the California Anti-Litter League, in connection with Governor's Reagan's Conservationist Board. When I turned on the car radio, the song "Aquarius" from the musical *Hair* ("When the Moon is in the Seventh House, and Jupiter aligns with Mars") reminded me of Yorty's horoscope. Those are his aspects exactly. It caused me to think about his horoscope again.

And so, just before the luncheon, when a reporter from KGIL Radio asked, "Hey Louise, what do you think will happen in the May 27 run-off election?", I blurted out my prediction. I said that his chart showed increased power during the last week before the May 27 run off, and he would go sailing through the election. Astrologically, he had to win!

The next I knew all the other stations picked it up, and May 7, 8, 9, and 10 of 1969, I spent cringing, as every radio and television news program and every paper in L.A. except the *Los Angeles Times,* carried my prediction. Everyone I knew said I was an idiot.

The coincidences I calculated in arriving at my probabilities were *not* those used by the mathematicians. I didn't use weight, color, sex, or religion. I used the *stars*.

Sam Yorty was re-elected mayor of Los Angeles for a third four-year term. And he was the *first* incumbent in the city's

FIGURE XIX   *A MAYOR AND A WITCH*

history to suffer a shattering defeat in a primary election and later come through with a resounding victory in the run off.

It had never happened before, but after all, "When the Moon is in the Seventh House, and Jupiter aligns with Mars" what else can you expect?

20

Jupiter-How to Get the Hang of It

JUPITER IN SCORPIO

August 15, 1970 to January 15, 1971
June 5, 1971 to September 12, 1971
November 1, 1981 to December 30, 1982
November 1, 1993 to December 31, 1994
And during the years: 2006 A.D.
2018 A.D.
2030 A.D.
2042 A.D.
2054 A.D.
2066 A.D.
2078 A.D.
2090 A.D.
3002 A.D.

317

If you be Jupiter
Oh pray let me be Mars
Let me be Heaven
To display your brilliant stars.
Let me be sleep
So you may be my dream.
And I would even turn to darkness
To give your Moon full beam!
                              — *Louise Huebner*

♃ ♏

"Did not Jupiter transform himself into the shape of Amphitrio to embrace Alcamaena; into a Bull to beguile Io; into a shower of gold to win Dianae?"

Jupiter in Scorpio

November 26, 1898 — to December 25, 1899
November 11, 1910 — to December 9, 1911
October 26, 1922 — to November 24, 1923
October 11, 1934 — to November 9, 1935
September 25, 1946 — to October 24, 1947
January 13, 1958 — to March 20, 1958
September 7, 1958 — to February 10, 1959
April 24, 1959   — to October 5, 1959
December 16, 1969 — to April 30, 1970
August 15, 1970   — to January 1971

Jupiter, the largest, most massive of the planets within our solar system, is named in honor of an ancient pagan god who is considered to be a creative force of major proportions.

Astrologers believe that where the planet Jupiter is located in a horoscope, expansive, exaggerated conditions invariably exist. Usually its location marks areas of easy expression. Since Scorpio is the section of the zodiac related to sexual activities, Jupiter found in that sign can create quite a potent impact. Primarily, the sexual organs will be affected. In female horoscopes, large and full breasts will be an obvious result. In male horoscopes, Jupiter in Scorpio insures spectacular development.

All males and females with this planet placement will exhibit phenomenal interest in sexual involvements. Reactions to love partners and romantic stimulations will be impressive.

The position of the Sun in relation to the planet's position in Scorpio, will, of course, vary the character of the influence. *All,* will be sexually motivated. *All* males will be significantly proportioned.

However, if you are *Scorpio,* born with the planet Jupiter conjunct the Sun, you will be helplessly victimized by your own flaming desires. Despite surface appearance, you will project an irresistible magnetism. Expression of sexual and emotional drives will involve most of your daily thoughts. You are emotionally powerful. You may get heavy.

A *Sagittarius* Sun sign with the Jupiter/Scorpio syndrome semi-sextile will stimulate the subconscious. Your needs, well hidden from the world, nevertheless will act as a generator and send you forth to conquer. Strange ideas about sex will embarrass you. Partners will be crazy about you. You could love someone in show business.

The combustible combination sextiles the *Capricorn* Sun and makes it easy to cope. You will be extremely popular, with no hangups. You will be discriminate and have sexual alliances only with those who are famous or in power. You will gain much money from lovers.

Aquarius feels the aspect most forcibly. It creates awkward tensions. The ninety-degree angle makes the gift a real problem. You will vacillate between extremes of passion and aloofness. Periods of coldness will coincide with great material success. The inner turmoil adds to magnetism.

The *Pisces* Sun forms a favorable 120-degree angle to the Scorpio/Jupiter influence. Sexual involvements with government workers, politicians, spiritual leaders, and foreigners, will be an impetus to fame. Your easy manner will transform scandal into beneficial outlets. You're a cool baby! where it counts.

The *Aries* Sun in conjunct with the potent influence insures tremendous sexual drive and unbelievable stamina, along with great emotional depths. Partners will swirl about, needing you more than you need them. There will be periods of drought, balanced by periods of fantastic creativity. With a compatible sex partner you could conquer the world.

The sign *Taurus* has the Sun in exact opposition to the Jupiter in Scorpio vortex. Preoccupied with emotional problems, material interests may be ignored. However, partners are usually loaded, so there is no worry here. This aspect creates a sensual and voluptuous nature. The world . . . ? Well lost for love. And love always leads to security — an aspect of success.

Gemini has the Sun in a 150-degree difficult angle to Jupiter in Scorpio. Health will be affected by excessive physical demands from partner. Dreams of an intellectual and spiritual rapport will be thwarted by continuous involvements with sex fiends. Eventually though, you grow to like it.

Cancer, with the Sun forming a cozy trine to the Jupiter/-Scorpio, indicates promiscuous behavior, and will not be in conflict. There will be persistent joyful unions, delightfully indecent. A powerhouse of sex energy, there can be no fidelity. The conscience is nonexistent. You seduce through vulnerability. Indiscriminate lovers, but never get caught!

Leo is the sign most upset by the uncomfortable yearnings of Jupiter in Scorpio. The ninety-degree angle causes too many romances, and is a danger to the domestic environment. Vain, with a flair for the dramatic and a taste for the exotic, they always get caught, never settle down. They are not good marriage risks, but make a lot of money in real estate.

The *Virgo* Sun sign makes an easy sextile to the Scorpio/-Jupiter configuration. Relatives and neighbors will offer casual sexual outlets. Careless attitude concerning reputation will rapidly insure lack of one. The aspect creates dirty old men and women.

The Sun position for the sign *Libra* causes a cool approach to the dynamic potential offered by Jupiter in Scorpio. A tendency to get the most out of any situation will lead to continuous romantic transactions. Desire is strong, but controlled — and always, "First, a gift from the sponsor!"

Another important facet shared by all the Jupiter in Scorpio personalities is adaptibility. Alert to spot a partner's real needs, they are able to couple magnificent physical attributes with a cooperative intent to please.

The men, though, well hung by birth, and since birth, are quick to get the hang of it!

Note:

Each time Jupiter enters the sign of Scorpio, the Sun signs may expect the character of that year to be influenced and to affect them accordingly. Check local observatory for planetary information. Jupiter orbits the Sun in approximately twelve years.

♃

In a dark place coiled and ready
Waiting softly lay my love.

Then the moment of its being fell upon it.
Blind, unseeing.

In the darkness sprang its power
Glittering, gleaming for its hour.

Strangely silent was the struggle
As the jaws in pain complied

Opened wider
Fed its hunger
Love grew fatter
Loved one died

— *Louise Huebner*

21

A Way Out

☽ ♆

The Oriental New Year always falls on the day of the first new moon in the sign of Aquarius. And this always comes each year sometime between January 20 and February 19. According to the Chinese astrologers, the 1970s began on February 6, 1970, with the Year of the Dog. The Eastern method of divining the future is marked with a variety of vague and nondescript generalizations. Always the good is equally balanced with evil so as to contradict any and all predictions and to insure satisfaction for all. No one can complain about what is coming, for everyone is always sure to get only enough bitter to balance the sweet. Mainly they claim the year 1970 sets the pace for the remaining nine years. The decade will allow for attitudes of unselfishness with strong leanings toward duty, loyalty, justice, last minute help in financial difficulties added to some small deceits, sarcasm, and blind aggression just to even it all out.

The Chinese seers predict that 1970 ushered in a decade

that should inspire confidence in us all. Labor groups will prosper, creative activities wil be rewarded, investments of a spectacular nature will be successful, medical discoveries profound, and increased love, merriment and good cheer will bless the deserving.

But: the subtle Chinese offer a word of caution. Ox and Cock people beware! (See chart.) The year ahead is a tricky one. If your birthday was in the year of the Cock or the year of the Ox, be keenly alert concerning your emotional alliances. Marriages will suddenly switch course. Partners will prove unfaithful. Business contracts will have complicated translations and hidden clauses. Old loves will shatter. The entire emotional and security pattern of your existence will have to be re-established. Nothing will remain the same. Nothing will stay as it appears. The truth will out and the spots won't! Hole up and wait it out. Make moves only after much weighing of facts. Keep steady.

However, the Tiger, Hare, and Horse people should find themselves way out in front of the crowd with fabulous success and tremendous gain in all activities. The past years of effort will now bear fruit. Whatever was begun in 1965 (the Year of the Snake), is now ready to pay off: Experiences thought to be unnecessary will now lead to solid financial security. New love affairs are not impossible during this exciting period. These may be complicated unions sporting incredible age differences, or some other seemingly uncomfortable symptom, but they will be handled cleverly. Magnetism will reach fantastic peaks. Magnificent attractions will create ecstatic involvements.

The Dragon and Sheep will make fools of themselves. No amount of caution will help. The 70s, particularly the first four years, will be needed in order to develop some sadly missing ingredient in the Dragon/Sheep characters. Much will happen that will appear to be of value. However, situations will not be boring. There will be no real danger, only elaborately gauche reactions.

As for the Rat, Snake, Monkey and Pig people, the decade ahead is merely not disastrous.

The Dog people will have a decade full of promise. Whenever the first year of the decade ahead and the year of one's birth are symbolized by the same animal, the decade ahead is one of getting what you deserve, despite all existing odds. This is also true when a current year is symbolized by the same animal as the year of your birth. That is when you are the luckiest. This was true in the case of Mayor Sam Yorty (Cock), at the time of his successful third-term re-election in 1969 (the Year of the Cock).

Eastern astrology and Western astrology have both been around for several thousand years, and both have cultivated dedicated followers that number into the millions. Both have at times managed to produce valid examples to the credit of their own special forms of fathoming the hidden.

Due to language differences, sometimes something subtle is lost in the translation of the Eastern philosophy, and we are left with inept and frequently mediocre prognostications. Not so, however, in the case for the Western method of interpreting the star patterns. If we follow the teachings left to us by our ancient friends the Babylonians, we happily are led to a more exciting and encouraging viewpoint of the next decade's potential.

If the old laws prevail, the years ahead will pulsate with urgent pagan rhythms, irresistible primeval beats and lush tropical awareness. The Earth's atmosphere will be charged with high-keyed emotionalism. The accent will be upon glamorous and complicated entanglements. A wildness will tremble through the souls of even the steadiest. Primitive longings will demand recognition. Emotional extravagances and impulsive and heated unions will be common. No one will be able to escape destiny as the planets vibrate to the calls of romantic and passionate adventures. Caught in the eye of the planetary hurricane, the next decade will demand fated, longterm, powerful, and intensely sensual alliances.

Western astrology says the Fire Signs of Aries, Leo and Sagittarius will be inspired to even greater achievements than they had ever dreamed possible. Taurus, Virgo, and Capricorn (the Earth Signs) will accumulate fantastic properties and will establish strong secure roots. The Air Signs of Gemini, Libra, and Aquarius will do much travel. Their lives will take on much of the unexpected. And Cancer, Scorpio, and Pisces, the Water Signs are about to become even more emotional. Luck finds them ready!

Can we though, accept the competency of the astrologers along with the validity of their interpretations of what is to come? The Orientals had based their "end of the world" prediction upon what seemed to them solid solar evidence. On February 5, 1962, in the Year of the Tiger, their astrologers noted a heavy emphasis in the sign of Aquarius (symbol of explosions, also bright thoughts, warm brotherly love and idealism). At the time of their New Year, at dawn, the positions of the sun, moon and the planets Saturn, Jupiter, Mars and Mercury were conjunct. Later when it became obvious that nothing much was happening, the alternate was chosen and the prediction was uniformly switched to be indicative of a new era in man's development. The Age of Aquarius was loudly proclaimed to have been born! Due to the varying rates of speed with which the planets orbit through space. the planetary pattern that exists during any one moment of time cannot be duplicated for over twenty-five thousand years.

If this pattern may be thought to coincide in any way with human personality and destiny, the character of the man and the nature of the events experienced should be as complicated as the design.

With the knowledge that exists today it is possible to calculate an alternating pattern once each and every four minutes of every day, in any particular latitude and longitude of the world. This gives the planet Earth 360 horoscopes every day of every year in every location.

It is a false premise that astrology divides humanity into only twelve personality types, when actually according to astrology there are not merely twelve types born in eternity, but over 131,400 types born *each year* in every *single small section* of the world every 25,000 years.

Fantastic!

In order for the Sun Signs, descriptions, and predictions to be accurate, one would have to be a pure-born Aries, Taurus, Gemini, or Cancer.

To be 100 percent of any sign it would be necessary to have been born at sunrise on a day such as the day in February of 1962, when the sun, moon, Neptune, Pluto, Saturn, Jupiter, Uranus, Mars, Mercury and Venus were seen rising on the ascendant of the one sign. This would be quite a feat for you and for the universe! It happens rarely. The moon spins around the earth once each month, the earth orbits the sun each year. Venus and Mars make it in slightly less time. Mercury does it usually in under half a year. The planet Jupiter takes 12 years. Saturn 28. Uranus 84. Neptune 144 or so. Pluto sometimes takes 360 years to orbit the Sun. Of course, though, a phenomenon did occur to some extent in February of 1962, but while the heavens were busy precluding true Aquarianism to any child born at dawn, the kooks and quasi-religious mystical fanatics were busy hollering doom and damnation.

But the planets moved on. And the world didn't end. We all have to remain content with being only one small part of what we think we are. That anyone should seem at all like his astrological Sun Sign is a tribute to man's thirst for identity.

The planet Jupiter, orbiting the Sun in approximately twelve years, has a cycle that is closely allied with the cycles used in moon astrology. Moon astrology (or Chinese astrology) conincides with Western astrology's Jupiter pattern. On December 16, 1969, Jupiter, Western astrological symbol for robust creativity, flamboyant attitudes, zestful living, healthy animal drives and instincts, began its year-long visit into Scorpio. This sign is associated with violent passions, intrigues, daring acts, clandestine relationships, eroticism, and lust. To a trained observer of the stars it is clearly apparent what the heavens are *offering*. It is comforting to know that those who have habitually used sex as a crutch will not be forced to limp any longer.

But the moon-cycle believers won't let well enough alone. They insist that doom and damnation are once again upon us. On October 30, 1970 (the anniversary of the sinking of the continent of Atlantis), an awe-inspiring lineup of planets will exist in the sign of Scorpio. Once again for the first time since February of 1962, the lunatics turned on! They believed that the sun, moon, Neptune, Jupiter, Venus and Mercury lineup triggered ultimate disaster for the world. The massive groupings of the heavenly bodies were said to create a dynamic situation. Whirling through Scorpio, Jupiter, stimulating passions, intrigues, daring acts, clandestine relationships, sexual promiscuity, eroticism, and lust may indeed bring the world to an end!

But really now, if the world does end, *what a way to go!*

♃

When my time is up
And a smile won't get me more
And no strength of will can move
The Magnificent Unknown —
If nothing gives to my resistance
And no one echoes back my shout
As the explosion of my being is met with cool disdain
With the force of sheer emotion
I will tumble into space
And for all my damned commotion
Leave no trace

— Louise Huebner

22

Rare Medium Done

Believing a telepathic happening to be a condition of my mind and the probable result of a possible physiological combination — not an accidental benefit from the spirit world — and being attentive of it and recognizing its character, enables me to duplicate moods and sensations needed in order to trigger its happening leaving me better able to control and influence its repetition.

Helen Keller, blind and deaf since infancy, illustrates a mental process not dependent upon sight and sound. We are told she communicated by touch. Substantially, yes. But, abstractly? How was thinking accomplished? Could memory banks let loose wide visions never seen? Could recall take place with sounds never heard? Hardly. How then was information stored in this brilliant woman's mind? *Sensationally!*

Helen Keller "thought" in emotional sensations. Knowledge reached her through feeling. Utilizing the sixth sense, when the others failed, she achieved through expression of this sixth sense international recognition as a philosopher and poet. Perhaps no extreme need ever develops that demands exclusive use of this sense, but permitting its development can increase one's potentials. Use of it will offer new dimensions of experience. It's an exciting and adventuresome way to pass the time.

I was in a film directed by Henri Cartier-Bresson, and he told me that he understood what takes place in the psychic moment. He said he could relate to what a psychic calls "tuning in." He said he was able to do this with his camera.

Knowing me, and understanding me "intuitively," he could express his insight about me on film. Instead of verbalizing his knowledge about me, he could film it. For him, the psychic force and the creative force are one and the same. They are a means of coming to the truth of a matter — the heart.

My husband, Mentor, has fantastic insights about people. It is not always possible for him to create a verbal impression of their personality, but with oil paint he is able to capture their souls.

Isn't a composer able to convey truth through music? And isn't love a psychic contact? An awareness of the essence of the loved one? The moment when an invisible but powerful surge of emotion is transmitted from one to another is a psychic moment.

A psychic bond has always existed between lovers. A man and a woman in love can tune in to each other from great distances. Often, lovers are not aware of this special ability. It develops, in many cases, during the time of their greatest sexual involvement, when the life force, the creative force, is dynamically triggered.

There are some who have a greater capacity for this experience — for the psychic moment. But, when it hits, whomever it hits is placed in a moment free from doubt. Something is known, and known deeply. You are able to become one with the knowledge or insight. In instances where this exchange takes place with people — and not just with ideas — there is a fusion of personality. Once having felt the bond, there is no return to an indifferent state. Sometimes it is difficult, for the moment, to truly know where one personality leaves off and the other begins. When this happens with an idea you become passionately involved and dedicated to a cause. With either the idea or the person the "psychic" clarity must be expressed.

Whether you find an outlet for this expression through the use of words, a photograph, a painting, a dramatic production, a song, a poem, or lovemaking, the psychic rapport increases the value. And you are better off with it than without it.

When extra sensory perception allows you to "tune in" the moment is clear and brilliant with *sparkling truth*. The condition though, is vulnerable, and sometimes it is very difficult to determine whose truth!

In April of 1964 I calculated Pamela Mason's horoscope and read it on KABC television in a series of three syndicated programs. I began with the year of her birth and then offered a brief descriptive statement covering each year of her life up to the date of the taping of the shows. Pamela, enthusiastically nodded, and verbally agreed to each one of my statements about each of the past years of her life.

I was really turned on to my own daring, at being so specific on camera. A TV show is not the safest showcase to exhibit your calculated probabilities. If there is a goof-up it's quite noticeable. Giddy by nature, I am never too concerned about potential goof-ups, so I predicted into the next ten years of her life — up to around 1975. It's all on tape!

Every once in a while I play the shows back, and listen in amazement. I projected into her future starting with her

FIGURE XX   *PAMELA AND A GRINCH*

1965 birthday. It's in March. March 10. My birthday is March 22.

I told Pamela, that exactly on her birthday in 1965 her life pattern would alter, and a series of events would begin. I was specific about each year's probable trend. Even to the extent of mentioning important dates here and there, and birthdates of key people who were to be involved. It was all very stimulating. I remember vaguely thinking how marvelous it would be to have Pamela's future.

Well, except for an occasional intimate coincidence here and there — like her divorce — *nothing* I predicted for Pamela happened!

Once when I ran into Pamela at CBS where we were both doing a show, she called out from across the stage, "Louise, I'm still waiting!" It was embarrassing! I could never bring myself to tell her. We had such a good rapport that day on KABC. We felt warm and friendly. Evidently our wavelengths had crossed, or meshed. Pamela may have even acted the role of an innocent medium. For I *was* truly psychic that day — really turned on! I could feel it. She could feel it. The entire crew could feel it. The atmosphere was electric.

Truth was crystal bright.

And my predictions *did* come true. All of them! Only, since March of 1965, *everything* I predicted for Pamela happened instead to me.

I guess you might say I'm the psychic Grinch who stole aspects from Pamela's chart.

— 360° and out —